A JOURNEY AMONGST THE GOOD AND THE GREAT

A
JOURNEY
AMONGST
THE GOOD
AND
THE GREAT

by
Andy Kerr

NAVAL INSTITUTE PRESS
Annapolis, Maryland

Library of Congress Cataloging-in-Publication Data

Kerr, Andy, 1922–
    A journey amongst the good and the great.

    1. Kerr, Andy, 1922–   . 2. Naval biography—United
States.   3. United States. Navy Dept.—Biography. I. Title.
V63.K47A3   1987   353.7′092′4 [B]   87-1509
ISBN 0-87021-333-4

Printed in the United States of America

Contents

Preface

This book was written aboard our 43-foot sailing cutter *Andiamo* III at anchor in lovely Cook's Bay, Moorea, in French Polynesia. My wife Susan and I were waiting there for the end of the 1985 hurricane season before continuing with our planned circumnavigation of the world. Our cruise had commenced in England almost seven years before, and 40,000 miles of ocean had already passed under our keel.

I have never kept a journal, diary, or private file. This book, then, was written from memory. The only reference material aboard *Andiamo* other than a dictionary was the transcript of seven sessions in which I was interviewed a year earlier by Paul Stillwell of the U.S. Naval Institute in the course of the Institute's Oral History program. Indeed, it was at his urging and with his encouragement that this writing was undertaken.

Without access to newspaper and magazine files or to books dealing with the same period, there are doubtless some errors. I hope there are none of substance. Quoted conversations are, of course, approximations.

There are bound to be conflicts with other accounts of the same events. The reader can be sure of only one thing—I have presented these episodes in the way I believe them to have happened. I have engaged in no intentional fiction.

I dedicate this book to the memory of my deceased wife, Rusty, who provided love and the tranquil haven required as a respite from the tumult and tempests of the years of struggle; and to my present wife, Susan, who provides love and the tumult and tempests required as stimulating respites from the tranquil haven of retirement.

A JOURNEY AMONGST THE GOOD AND THE GREAT

I

Prologue

One day we got a letter from Lee Harvey Oswald. The name meant nothing to us then. The letter was long and hand-written and was mailed from Russia where Oswald was living with his wife, Marina. It was addressed to "The Honorable John Connally" who was then the secretary of the navy in the Kennedy Administration. It had been processed routinely in the secretary's mail room. Someone there decided that I, as special counsel to the secretary, should "staff" the letter. The decision was logical because the letter had legal overtones. Also, the mail room had a limited choice. The secretary's personal staff consisted of only four people: The naval aide was Captain Bill Anderson, who had been skipper of the nuclear submarine *Nautilus* on her historic voyage under the ice at the North Pole and was later to become a congressman from Tennessee. Colonel Ed Wheeler, later to become a lieutenant general and a hero of the Vietnam War, was the marine aide. Commander Jim Jenkins, the special assistant for public affairs, was my close friend from days of duty together in Naples, Italy. Jim was destined to become the secretary for Health, Education and Welfare for the state of California. Still later he was deputy counsellor to President Ronald Reagan, under Ed Meese.

I, as special counsel, was the fourth.

So it fell to me to decide what to do with the letter. It was essentially a complaint from Oswald about the character of his discharge from the Marine Corps, and a plea to Connally to use his authority as secretary of the navy to change the discharge to one more favorable.

Those unfamiliar with the U.S. military services should know at this point that the Marine Corps is part of the Navy Department. Even the secretary of the navy needed to remind himself of this fact from time to time to avoid oversights damaging to delicate Marine Corps sensibilities. Connally had a sign over the door leading out of his office that read, "Remember the Marines." It reminded him to call the Marine Corps commandant to apprise him of important decisions before they became public. The flamboyant commandant at that time, General David Shoup, could become particularly peevish if this were not done.

When Oswald left the Marine Corps and went to live in Russia, he was given an administrative discharge that was less than commendatory. As I recall, he was discharged as "undesirable." He thought that characterization unfair. Later events were to prove the epithet to have been exceptionally mild. The letter was an attention getter. You don't find many Marines defecting to the Soviet Union.

I sent to the Marine Corps Headquarters for Oswald's record, and studied the circumstances of his defection and subsequent discharge. There were no conflicts of fact between his letter and his record. A review of the statutes and regulations governing administrative discharges led to the conclusion that Oswald's discharge was in complete compliance with all legal requirements.

That, however, was not the end of it. The secretary can exercise clemency if he feels that there are strong extenuating circumstances. He may also intervene if an applicant's service was exceptionally meritorious.

Neither applied to Oswald. He had been a lousy Marine.

So I prepared the usual two papers that accompany all correspondence going into the secretary's "action" basket. The first was a brief, setting forth everything I thought the secretary needed to know in order to make an informed decision. It concluded with a recommendation for action. The second was a paper for the secretary to sign that would put the recommended action into effect.

In Oswald's case, my conclusions were that his complaint had no legal basis, his request was without merit, and that Connally should not involve himself in any way. I recommended that he refer the letter to the commandant of the Marine Corps for "appropriate action." This phrase meant, in clear officialese, that the secretary was washing his hands of the case. The commandant could do with it as he wished. No one could doubt what the result would be. It was a kiss-off.

A day or two later, Connally called me into his office. He had obviously read the entire file and was intrigued. We discussed the case for half an hour or so, and at the end he said, "I agree with you, Andy—this is the way we should handle it." He then signed that second piece of paper that sent Oswald's letter on its way, we thought, to oblivion.

But that's not exactly the way it turned out. On 22 November 1963, while riding beside President Kennedy in a motorcade in Dallas, John Connally, then governor of Texas, was shot through his arm and lung by Lee Harvey Oswald. President Kennedy was shot and killed in the same incident. The history books say it slightly differently—that Connally was wounded during Oswald's assassination of President Kennedy. The assumption is always that Oswald was shooting at Kennedy and that Connally was hit by accident or as a secondary target of opportunity. Could it not, however, have been the other way around? In spite of all of the investigations, including that of the Warren Commission, and the continuing fascination with and theories about the event, no one has yet come up with a credible motive for the shooting of Kennedy by Oswald. Against this, we know for a fact that Oswald once asked Connally for help in what may have been a *cri du coeur*. He was turned down flat. What greater motivation does a psychopath need?

Thus, by fortune I am able to provide a footnote to history. There were other instances, many of which I would have preferred to avoid. During the events I shall describe, I sometimes thought of myself as akin to a character in the Al Capp comic strip, "Li'l Abner,"—Joe Bfsptlk. This pathetic little fellow always appeared with a rain cloud over his head, amid scenes of calamity. Although only a bit-player on the stage, I found myself with eerie frequency involved in some of the most interesting and significant scenes of the times. My role, however, may have provided a perspective unavailable not only to the audience but to the major actors. Other episodes and observations, of no historic import whatsoever, make up the balance of the narrative.

2

An Australian Boy

I was born in Sydney, Australia, in 1922. My mother's grandfather Leary had been sent to Australia from Ireland in the early 1800s. Family tradition has it that he was transported as an innocent 12 year old. His family had been broken up and scattered by the British because of suspected activities against the Crown by one of his brothers.

The story might even be true. When I was growing up in Australia, however, there were values to be seen in a history of family respectability. It was thought a good thing not to have ancestors who were criminals. I understand that attitude has changed. Australians now boast of ancestors who were landed as convicts at Botany Bay, with as much pride as Americans who claim forebears among the passengers on the Mayflower.

My grandfather Leary married Mary Flanagan. She died as a young woman in the deserts of Western Australia during the Australian gold rush. Grandfather, unsuccessful in his quest for gold, returned to New South Wales, widowed, broke, and with three young children. He settled in Temora, a drought-ridden town in the outback, where he scratched out a living with a small sheep station. It was in Temora at grandfather's house that I spent part of my Australian childhood. My lasting memories are of heat, dust, poisonous snakes, and flying ants. There the belief was seared into my soul that water is precious and not a drop is ever to be wasted. The practice of the current "shower generation," among whom I number my own children, of taking daily showers of up to an hour's duration has, therefore, caused me considerable anguish.

That I know nothing of the history of the family of my maternal grandmother I now attribute to her early death. I have noticed a tendency of people to pass on stories of their own ancestors to the neglect of those of their in-laws.

My paternal grandparents were Scots. Grandfather Kerr was said to be poor but exceptionally graceful and handsome. He shocked his elders and gained the reputation of a ne'er-do-well when he danced for money in the local taverns. His bride, Janet Stuart, had lived in a nearby castle and was promptly disowned when they were married. Their marriage lasted 80 years. They were both nearly 100 years old when they died peacefully within days of each other.

They emigrated to Australia from Scotland and settled in Coledale in New South Wales, a mining town on the coast south of Sydney. Grandfather Kerr and my father's six brothers worked in the coal mine. Grandmother ran a miner's boarding house. In contrast to the heat and dust of Temora, my memory of Coledale is one of cool ocean breezes and the smell of the sea. I also remember the black faces of the miners as they washed up before dinner in wash tubs on the back porch of grandmother's boarding house.

My father escaped the pits by learning to play the violin. He was a professional violinist the rest of his life. At first he earned a living by playing in orchestras in the theaters where silent movies where shown. The majority of musicians in Australia were then so employed. When the "talkies" arrived, orchestras became superfluous. The musician's union reacted characteristically. It called a national musicians' strike in an effort to force the movie theaters to continue to employ orchestras. The futile strike lasted for years.

Unable to support his family as a musician in Australia, my father eventually found a job in an orchestra aboard a Canadian Pacific Steamship liner. It sailed regularly between Sydney and Vancouver. During the turn-around stays in British Columbia, father made several visits to Seattle. By this time he questioned whether he would ever be able to pursue his musical career in Australia. More importantly, he had come to the conclusion that educational opportunities for his children in the stratified Australian society of those days were extremely limited. A trade or vocational school was all that could be expected. The university, for one of our "class," was a practical impossibility. To the contrary, he had learned on his trips to the States that in that country, those who truly desired an education and were of average intelligence were limited only by their willingness to work hard. Finally, my father was nothing if not a family man. The seagoing life with its lengthy separations from home was not his cup of tea. Nor was it to my mother's liking. They decided to emigrate to the United States.

My recollection of these early times is far from coherent. I confess to feelings of inadequacy when I read autobiographical accounts of early childhood. Why is it that others who write of those times can remember with astonishing clarity all of the significant events of their earliest years? I am sure that much of it results from a recollection of what they have been later told by others. But there lingers the thought that in my case there may have been an element of simple heedlessness. I wonder if things might have been different if someone had said to me as a four or five year old, "Look here, young fellow! Pay attention to what is going on around you. Try to impress it on your memory, or one day you are going to feel like a dummy when you read other people's autobiographies or try to write your own!"

However, no one ever told me that, and my childhood memories are as spotty as anyone's. There is no real continuity until I was eight or nine. Some disconnected events, sounds, sights, and smells of earlier years come back with startling intensity. The taste, texture, and smell of a passion fruit or a fried black pudding are recalled vividly, as is the sight of a great tree burning night after night on a cliff high above Coledale. Some general impressions remain while the individual components that gave rise to them have vanished. From school I have the memory of strict discipline, much homework, and the relentless pounding into our heads of the basics of grammar and arithmetic. While the names and faces of classmates and teachers have gone completely, as have individual classroom incidents, I will never forget how to diagram a sentence. I coasted for years in later schooling in the United States on the strength of what had been drummed into me in those first few grades in Australian country schools.

My remembered self-image as a small boy was one of inferiority. The other boys all seemed to be bigger and tougher and stronger. Any successes I had at my studies I attributed to luck, extra preparation, or favoritism on the part of my teachers. They were inclined, I suppose, toward a serious little boy who did his schoolwork faithfully and caused no trouble. Thus, my unsought but oft-played role as teacher's pet did nothing for my self-esteem. Conversely, the resulting scorn of the other boys seemed all too justified. My response to this unhappy state of affairs was to study harder, which of course only made things worse! These childhood feelings of inadequacy, so intense at the time, have waxed and waned over the years but have never entirely disappeared.

One event of early childhood stands out above all others. In the mid-20s, when I was about six years old, the American Fleet visited Australia for the first time. It was a grand and historic occasion. Its impact can be appreciated only with the realization of the geographical and psychological isolation of Australia in those days. Mass air travel has tended to change all that. Then, however, there was a sense of separation from the rest of the world that was keenly felt by all Australians.

We were living in Sydney at the time, and I remember being caught up in the excitement. The people of Sydney had been asked by the city fathers to invite officers and men of the fleet to stay in their homes during the visit. It seemed that everyone in Sydney was responding to this appeal as my father and I stood in line to sign up.

Finally the day came. In majestic splendor, the fleet steamed through the Sydney Heads and dropped anchor in Sydney Harbor. It was a brilliant day. Flags whipped in the breeze as countless welcoming craft and ships' boats surrounded the great grey ships. What a sight! Even now, as I write this years later, the recollection brings a strong surge of emotion.

A yeoman from the battleship *New Mexico* stayed with us. I became his special charge and constant shadow. At night he was out on the town, but by day he took me out to the ships of the fleet. With senses dazzled by sunlit crests, salt spray, the smell of the sea, and the cry of gulls, I would ride out in the motor launches. The sailors wore their immaculate white uniforms, and the officers all looked to me like admirals. There were the shouts of the cox'ns, the shrill whistles of the bo's'n's pipes, the bugle calls, and formal ceremonies on the quarterdecks as dignitaries arrived and departed. It was all too splendid and exciting for words. And the food! I had never seen anything like it. Each meal in the crew's mess was a feast—great platters of meat and potatoes—fruit, pies, cakes—and above all, ice cream, all you could eat! I was in heaven.

I soon made up my mind and announced to my good new

friend that when I was old enough, I intended to join the U.S. Navy. He suggested that I should try to become an officer. He told me that being an enlisted man was okay and the life of a sailor was good, but that the life of an officer was better. I asked how I could go about that. He said that I would have to go to a school for officers called the Navy Academy at a place in the United States named Annapolis. I said, "All right, that's what I'll do." My friend didn't laugh.

Fifteen years later, as I was being sworn in as a midshipman in Bancroft Hall at the United States Naval Academy at Annapolis, I remembered those shining days in Sydney Harbor and the influence of an American sailor on one small Australian boy.

When we landed as immigrants in Seattle in the early thirties, the Great Depression had begun. Father, a quiet, gentle man, had his violin, ninety dollars, and boundless optimism. He also had a wife and three young children to support. I was the eldest, my brother Basil and sister Marjorie stair-steps behind. (Tom and Janet were to come later as natural-born Americans.) Thus, my father stood on the threshold of our adopted country with negligible material assets, heavy responsibilities, no job, no relatives, no friends, and a way of speaking English that Americans found odd. If there was such a thing as welfare assistance available, he would have scorned it as "the dole." If necessary, Father would have collected garbage. But we were fortunate. Within a day he got a job as a part-time elevator operator in the Smith Tower, then a proud landmark as the tallest building on the West Coast. Today it seems almost pathetic in downtown Seattle, dwarfed by its towering neighbors.

From then on, our family fought its own war against poverty. We didn't know, though, that that's what it was. We thought the process was normal. Father had his few violin students. There were never very many, for during the depression, music lessons were a dispensable luxury. At times he was able to find such supplementary work as night clerk in a hotel. We all worked, and our earnings went to the house.

Mother, who never met a stranger, ran the show. She believed, and managed to convince the rest of us, that we were a very special family with superior values that completely overshadowed our lowly economic position. Resolutely ignoring any evidence to the contrary, she led us to believe that we represented an oasis of refinement amid surrounding Philistines. It was a brilliant performance, particularly in light of her simple Australian background.

Only years later did I realize how profoundly I had been influenced by the Great Depression. I was too young to remember its start in 1929. Had I been a little older, I may still not have noticed the event, since we were already poor. The Depression simply perpetuated that condition. I therefore grew up with the conviction that struggle against poverty and insecurity was a permanent and universal human necessity. The extraordinary duration of the Depression was perhaps its most significant feature. It continued unabated into the forties. Ten million men in the United States were still unemployed when the Japanese attacked Pearl Harbor and Franklin Roosevelt was in his third term of office. World War II masked its continuation, but it was not until the late forties or early fifties that true recovery occurred, and at long last a period of prosperity began. Those of us who grew to maturity during that period tended to believe certain things to be immutable: milk was always ten cents a bottle, bread ten cents a loaf, and phone calls a nickel. A splendid house, one of the finest in town, could be bought for $10,000. An executive had arrived in the economic stratosphere when his salary reached $10,000 per year. That was how it was for years and years, and that was how it would always be!

I recall that on very special occasions we had bacon for breakfast. Each received his normal allotment—one rasher that had been cut in half. We learned that we could stretch the taste of this treat by making a bacon sandwich on toast out of each half slice. I do it to this day, and cannot bring myself to eat a piece of bacon plain. It is just too extravagant!

Milk was drunk by the single small jelly glass full only at meals. One day after school, in Salt Lake City, I went with my friends, the Halloran brothers, to their home. Their father owned a bank, the Halloran-Judge Trust Company. They went immediately to the refrigerator (we still had an ice box then) and to my astonishment poured for themselves huge glasses of milk. They each drank almost a quart! That was my first remembered exposure to the meaning of wealth in real life.

But far more important were the persistent basic attitudes that the period engendered: Only by diligent hard work could anything worthwhile be achieved: education was the key to salvation; security was the prize above all others. I believe that the rebellion of the youth of the sixties was a direct result of these attitudes, which characterized the children of the Depression. *Their* children, who knew only the subsequent period of affluence, found the views of their parents incomprehensible.

My own boyhood jobs included a magazine route (*Liberty, Saturday Evening Post,* and *Ladies Home Journal*), and a position as dishwasher in Doc Johnson's Car Barn Cafe on 5th South in Salt Lake City where we lived for a while. When we moved back to Seattle, I had a *Seattle Times* newspaper route in the Wallingford-Greenlake district, was a clerk in Cutter's Drug Store on University Way, then a bellhop and night clerk in the Eagle Hotel on Union Street. Finally, I was a doctor's helper in a Libby, McNeil and Libby salmon cannery in Alaska.

The job as doctor's helper may have speeded my growing up process. I had acquired the position because Libby's hiring agent had somehow got the impression that I was a pre-med student at the University of Washington.

I was, however, only 15 years old when my parents drove me to Seattle's Lake Union to board the ship that was to take me to Alaska. She was an ancient, rust-streaked coal-burning vessel with a pronounced list. I later found that the list was incurable. The ship was unstable at all angles within 10 degrees of the vertical. Her name was the *Gorgas*. She had previously flown the German flag and had the misfortune to be in Panama at the start of World War I. She was an old lady even then. Seized by the U.S. as a war prize, she was later acquired by Libby, McNeil and Libby to support its Alaska salmon-canning business. Her reciprocating steam engines, with their great pistons churning up and down, were of the type now seen only in maritime museums.

My mother found the scene at the dock appalling. It seemed that every whore in Seattle was there. As their drunken clients staggered aboard, the prostitutes screamed their farewells and endearments in vivid and explicit language. They promised their departing customers a splendid reception when they returned to Seattle in the fall with their season's earnings.

My mother said that I couldn't go. She could not allow her first-born son to be in such an unwholesome environment. My father, however, pointed out that I would be under the wing of a professional man, the doctor. Mother was still doubtful. We tried to find the doctor, so that Mother could personally entrust me to him. She wanted to get the doctor's promise that he would shield me from corrupting influences. It was fortunate that we failed to find him. He was drunk and had passed out somewhere aboard the ship. His intoxication, furthermore, was not the result of the departure festivities. It was, I soon found, his normal state. He was a confirmed alcoholic.

So without benefit of a direct change of custody from my parents to the doctor, I boarded the *Gorgas*. With three long blasts from her whistle and a cloud of sooty black smoke from her stack, she backed away from the dock. We were under way for the Bering Sea. There, in Bristol Bay, at the Aleut eskimo settlement of Ekuk on the Nushagak River was Libby's salmon cannery. We would be gone from Seattle for almost five months.

Until the mooring lines were finally cast off, my dominant emotion was anxiety that something would happen to prevent my departure. I feared that Libby would discover my inexperience, that my parents would have a change of heart, or the doctor would object to an assistant so unqualified. All that was now past, and I felt a moment of marvelous exhilaration. What a grand adventure! This feeling quickly faded, however, to be replaced by a growing sense of dread that now I would be found wanting. What indeed had I gotten myself into? Worse yet, would harm come to others because of my deficiencies? I suddenly felt myself to be the most presumptuous fool imaginable. But of course at that point there was no other course but to stick it out.

Prior to leaving for Alaska, I had diligently studied every first aid manual and home diagnostic and nursing book that I could find. The doctor, I thought, would expect his helper to have at least a rudimentary knowledge of such things. How fortunate that I had done so! Because of the doctor's chronic incapacity, I needed every scrap of knowledge I had acquired. Indeed I could have used much more. One particularly wild experience stands out.

One night a Filipino employee came to our little cannery clinic, complaining of abdominal pain. Unlike most Filipinos, who tend to be thin and wiry, this man was fat. He had a high fever. After noting his other symptoms, I quickly guessed that his trouble was acute appendicitis. With great difficulty, I roused the doctor. After several cups of coffee he was able to focus on the problem. He confirmed the diagnosis and said that an immediate operation was necessary. (This was in 1937, before the days of antibiotics.) He told the cannery superintendent, however, that the instruments and facilities available to us at Ekuk were inadequate for the task. I knew that to be untrue. It was obvious that he did not trust himself to perform the appendectomy. The superintendent had become aware of the doctor's alcoholism. He was therefore not inclined to argue. He agreed that the operation should be performed elsewhere—and by someone else!

A bush pilot was called by radio to fly the patient, the doctor, and me to the closest medical station. It was at Dillingham, a small settlement about fifty miles away on the other side of the Nusha-gak River. The tide was low, so we half carried, half dragged the moaning Filipino through hundreds of yards of knee-deep mud to the waiting floatplane. We repeated the process with the poor fellow on our arrival at Dillingham.

We found the Dillingham hospital dark and deserted. Eventually we found the old Aleut caretaker. He told us that the government doctor and the nurse were away in the interior fighting an outbreak of typhoid. They would not return for many days. He had the keys to the little hospital, though, and could start the generator to give us lights. We had run out of options. The operation had to be performed then and there.

The doctor was by then sober, but trembling violently. With the Aleut's help, we found the instruments and the ether. We stripped off the terrified patient's muddy clothes and stretched him out on the table. I was to administer the ether, and was equally terrified. The doctor gave me instructions. "Drip the ether slowly onto the mask," he said. "Every few minutes, peel back the man's eyelid, and shine a flashlight into his eye. If his pupil contracts but the eyeball doesn't move, keep dripping the ether at the same rate. If the eyeball moves, drip faster or he'll soon come out of it. If the pupil doesn't contract, slow down or you'll kill him!"

I started dripping the ether. Soon the man went to sleep. The doctor made a deep incision in the fat belly. It opened like a ripe watermelon, and I got sick. The doctor yelled, "Keep that God-damned ether going, kid. We can't stop it now!" So the operation proceeded. The shaking, perspiring wreck of a doctor kept reaching into the incision, and pulling things out. He would push them back in, saying, "No, damn it, that's not it!" The frightened kid puked into a bucket, dripped the ether and shone the flashlight into the poor wretch's eye. The old Aleut eskimo looked on with horrified fascination. The scene, which must rival any from Doré's illustrations of Dante's *Inferno,* lasted *four hours.* That was the eternity between the first incision and the final stitch after the diseased appendix had been located and removed.

Miraculously, the patient survived. And I, at age 15, had learned something that awful night. There are occasions when you can't say, "This is too hard. I've had enough. I quit!" There are times when duty or circumstances require you to see the job through, no matter what.

3

The Dream Comes True

Soon after we had arrived in the States from Australia, I sent off to the Naval Academy to find the requirements for entry. A large packet came back in the mail from Annapolis. It set out all of the academic and physical requirements and included sample entry examinations. I could see that much hard work in preparation would be required.

The big hurdle, though, would be the obtaining of an appointment. The information packet merely told how many appointments each senator and representative could grant. It gave no clue as to how one could go about getting one. I soon found out that the appointments were parceled out on a political basis. They were a means of repaying political debts or obtaining political support. True, members of Congress generally tried to appoint boys who possessed the mental and physical traits that would get them into the academy and lead to a successful career in the navy. In those years, however, there were always a great many more qualified applicants than available appointments. In my case it was ludicrous even to think of a politician so desperate as to need to curry the favor of my family. We were not yet even citizens. We didn't know *anyone* with the slightest influence in any field. All my letters of inquiry were brushed off with form letter replies.

But I had time. I made certain that my school courses covered the areas of mathematics, physics, English, literature, and history that form the basis for the entrance examinations. I studied hard and sent off to Annapolis each year for a new set of sample exams. They were a good measure of progress. Finally, I learned that some appointments to the academy are made each year from among enlisted men of the fleet. I therefore determined, if no other avenue opened up beforehand, to enlist in the navy and try for one of those appointments.

Then lightning struck! A notice appeared in the Seattle newspapers that Senator Homer T. Bone of Tacoma had made an unprecedented decision. He would award one of his appointments to the Naval Academy on the basis of a statewide competitive examination. The test was to be administered by the U.S. Civil Service Commission. The nearby town of Renton was designated as the testing place for the Puget Sound area. On the appointed day, about 200 boys showed up at Renton. I found out later that some 400 had taken the exam throughout the State of Washington.

In a state of nervousness and high excitement, I scanned the tests. To my relief, I saw immediately that they were patterned closely after the sample exams with which I had become so familiar. That the examination thus favored advance preparation over intelligence was indeed fortunate. With so many competing candidates, many would surely be smarter. Few if any, however, could have been as well prepared!

But doubts and fears arose during the weeks of waiting for the result. What if the examination were to be considered by the senator as only one factor in his decision? The announcement in the newspaper had not been entirely clear on that point. Would he award the appointment, for example, to one who had not only done well on the exam, but also was a fine athlete *and* whose father had contributed generously to the senator's campaign for election?

When finally a franked enveloped came in the mail with Senator Bone's name on the outside, I was almost afraid to open it. But there it was! The senator congratulated me for having stood first among those who took the test. He offered me a principal appointment to the United States Naval Academy at Annapolis, Maryland. He asked, unnecessarily, that I inform him promptly as to whether or not I would accept the appointment.

"Go and tell your father," mother said after we had read and reread the letter to be sure that there was no mistake. With joy almost unbearable, I ran the few blocks to my father's little studio in the Wallingford district, and burst in upon him and his startled young violin student. "Dad, I'm going to Annapolis!" My father shouted his pleasure and hugged me. I saw that his eyes were filled with tears. So were mine.

Included with the senator's letter was a guide for appointees, which had been prepared by the Naval Academy. It pointed out that while the physical examination for entry was given only at Annapolis, appointees were entitled to a free advisory physical exam at the naval hospital nearest their homes. While I knew of nothing wrong, it seemed a good idea to take them up on that. So I telephoned the naval hospital at the Navy Yard at Bremerton, an hour's ferry ride across Puget Sound from Seattle, and made the arrangements.

The time was set for 11:00 A.M. on the following Saturday. Then came a bit of bad luck that almost cost me the academy appointment. The street car that I planned to catch was late, and I missed the Bremerton Ferry. The next ferry was an hour later, so I arrived at the hospital just before noon. My appointment was with a Dr. Funk, and I met him coming out of his office with his golf clubs. I could see that he was intensely annoyed at my late arrival. I wish he had said, "Well, look, let's make another appointment. I'll see you next week." Instead he said, "All right, come in. Let's get this over with." He then quickly found eighteen disqualifying physical defects. I can only remember now that he found that I was underweight, had deficient chest expansion, a disqualifying overbite, a heart murmur, was color blind, and was suffering from "congenital asthenia." That last one had a ring of fatality to me. I found out later, however, that it merely describes a generally poor build. I would have to agree that at that age I was pretty scrawny. The rest of the defects I have mercifully forgotten.

The effect was devastating. My dream of the academy seemed shattered beyond hope. Beyond that, my life expectancy appeared suddenly curtailed—I suffered my first intimation of mortality: I returned to Seattle in a state of shock.

My parents, fortunately, were far more outraged than worried. They assured me that I was a healthy lad, and that the doctor had to be wrong. An appointment was quickly made with our family doctor, who gave me a thorough examination. At its conclusion he said, "I can find nothing wrong with you. You are in good health. I hear no hint of a heart murmur. All you have to do is eat more and build yourself up a little. Your skinny physique is fairly typical of boys of your age."

He did, however, caution me to check up on the potential color blindness problem. Having no means to test me, he made an appointment for me to see an eye doctor. The ensuing tests showed that I was indeed deficient in color perception. The doctor said that he thought it was serious enough to disqualify me for the Naval Academy, but he couldn't be sure.

Soon after this, I got a letter from Senator Bone. Enclosed was a copy of a letter he had received from Dr. Funk reporting the results of my physical examination, and advising the senator that the chances of my getting into the academy were nil. Dr. Funk's letter also had a notation that a copy had been sent to the Medical Department of the Naval Academy.

Bone said that he had decided not to withdraw the appointment, but questioned whether it was wise to subject my family to the expense of a trip back to Annapolis in light of Dr. Funk's findings. He reminded me that my travel would only be reimbursed if I were admitted to the academy. Finally he asked that I let him know soon so that he could give the appointment to someone else if my decision was to relinquish it.

After much soul searching, I concluded that the road had been too long and too hard to give up without seeing it to the very end. So I wrote Senator Bone that I would go to Annapolis and take my chances.

Rather than leave it entirely to chance, however, I allowed time on my trip back east for a week in Washington. There I spent every day in the Library of Congress studying all about color vision. I found that it never changes from the time one is born, so nothing can be done to improve it (or hurt it, for that matter). Color deficiency occurs mostly in men but is transmitted through the mother. Red-green blindness is the most common deficiency, and is what I had. This didn't mean that I couldn't tell the difference between red and green in traffic lights or ships' port and starboard running lights, for example. These colors appeared to me to be as bright and distinguishable as they should be. The deficiency only showed up in tests that can reveal an inability to distinguish between very subtle shades of those two colors. I was convinced that my "deficiency" was purely the invention of those who had devised the tests and that I could see colors as well as I needed to. My experience in all the years since then has proven that to be true.

The Library of Congress had books containing all of the tests that had ever been devised. I studied and re-studied them until my head and eyes ached. Then I went to Annapolis to face the examiners. They were waiting for me. Having been tipped off by Dr. Funk, they gave me a thorough going over. By that time I had put on some weight and had been exercising diligently, so I looked a little better. Several doctors listened to my heart but apparently heard nothing amiss. They were equally careful in all of the other areas identified in the Bremerton physical examination. I passed everything except the color tests. There they caught me. Because of my preparation at the Library of Congress, I believe I would have gotten by if the doctor conducting the tests had not obviously been forewarned. Rather than flip through a few random pages of the tests as he did with the other boys, he took me through every page and then through again. I stumbled and he had me.

To be fair, had not Dr. Funk found the deficiency, I would not have prepared myself and might have failed even a random test.

I was immediately and formally advised that I had failed to meet the physical requirements for admission into the Naval Academy. I had, however, the right to appeal to a Medical Board of Review. I could avail myself of that right by signing an agreement to accept the board's ruling as final. The obvious purpose of this was to shield the academy from political pressures, since each failed candidate had potential congressional backing.

I naturally requested to go before the board. At the appointed time, about twenty other boys also appeared. All of them had failed to pass the visual acuity test. Each had scored 20/20 in reading the eye chart, but was found to have some degree of myopia when his eyes were dilated. They went before the board one by one and were examined. Without exception, they failed. This dreary and discouraging process went on all day. It was late in the afternoon when the board finished (literally) the last of those boys. Since my problem, color blindness, was different from theirs, I was told to come back the next morning. I passed the night with a sense of impending doom.

The next day I had the board to myself—or more accurately, vice versa. There were five navy doctors, all dressed in splendid white summer uniforms with gold stripes on their shoulder boards denoting various ranks. The testing began. I remember going through the Stillings Pseudoisochromatic test, the Ishihara test, and the Columbian Optical Company test among others. Scared and nervous as I was, I was impressed. These guys really did mean to find out if I was color blind. The board was not the greased chute I had feared from my observations of the previous day. I was excused to wait in an anteroom. Soon the corpsman on duty said, "They want to see you again." We went through all of the tests again, although in a different order. The sequence of being excused and then recalled for further testing went on all morning. Finally the corpsman said, "I shouldn't tell you this, but they're having a hell of an argument. Two are for you and two are against you, and one can't make up his mind. He says you have missed one plate fairly consistently. I have no idea which one it is. He says he'll give you one more chance. If you get it, you're in—if not, you're out."

We went back over the tests from beginning to end. I think I must have seen colors then that I had never seen before, and would never see again! I was excused with no hint as to the result. Very quickly I was recalled for the last time. The president of the board, a navy captain, stood up and cleared his throat. Adjusting his glasses, he glanced down at a paper in his hand and said, "Mr. Kerr, the board finds you qualified." Those words are not an approximation. They are chiseled into my memory. There are times when the expression, "My heart leaped for joy" is the only one applicable. There were no more hurdles! Not trusting myself to speak, I shook hands with the board members, who were all smiling broadly, and rushed out to telephone home.

A day or two later, on 18 May 1941, I took my oath as a midshipman in the United States Navy. My assigned roommate had been a high school football star. He instantly tagged me with the nickname "Andy." His hero had been the great coach at Colgate, Andy Kerr.

Plebe summer passed in strenuous physical activity designed to whip us into shape. We marched, swam, ran obstacle courses, climbed the rope, sailed, rowed, and sweated on the rifle range. I was surprised to find that my ability in those activities was about equal to that of the average member of my class. My surprise was occasioned by a bad inferiority complex in sports that I had developed after our arrival from Australia. When we came to the States, my American contemporaries were already adept at such sports as baseball, football, and basketball. None of these were played in Australia. My inability to play these games "like everyone else" caused me acute and continuing embarrassment. I suffered as only an adolescent can suffer from such things. So it was a grand thing to find on arrival at the academy that we were all being measured in new areas of physical endeavor, and that I was not the klutz that had become my self-image.

At the time my class entered the academy, during the spring of 1941, Hitler had overrun Europe. The Air Battle of Britain was raging, and the Battle of the Atlantic was going badly. Losses from the convoys carrying lend-lease material to England, through attacks by German U-boats, were heavy. President Roosevelt had declared a state of unlimited national emergency. The course of instruction at the academy had been accelerated so that we would graduate in three years rather than the normal four.

Conditions worsened during the summer and fall. The U.S. destroyer *Reuben James* had been sunk by a German submarine while on convoy duty in the Atlantic. The destroyer *Kearny* was torpedoed. Relations with Japan deteriorated badly. Germany invaded the Soviet Union. Nevertheless, I didn't expect the United States to become fully involved in the war as a belligerent. Most of us thought that the U.S. would increase its efforts to provide material support to England, and that this would cause us increased losses in the Atlantic. That was about the extent of the combat duty we expected to see if the war continued.

Then, on December 7th, the Japanese attacked Pearl Harbor. Germany and Italy then declared war on the United States. We, in company with the rest of the nation, heard the news with shock and initial incredulity. The unthinkable had happened, and we were at war.

The pressures associated with our accelerated educational program increased after Pearl Harbor. Our academy experience therefore did not give rise to the degree of nostalgia which others usually have for their campus years. We could never forget that we were preparing ourselves to serve as officers in the navy in what had become a titanic war at sea. Many of our instructors were survivors of ships that had been lost in engagements with the enemy. We were generally restricted to the Naval Academy and its close environs. There were no such respites as the traditional annual cruises to foreign ports. We stood our watches armed with .45-caliber pistols against the possibility of saboteurs. Of course it was not all grim. I liked being a midshipman. I felt a thrill of pride during our parades as we marched past the reviewing stand to the sound of "Anchors Aweigh." Great and enduring friendships were formed. The very pressures gave rise to a strong sense of camaraderie. The occasional light-hearted weekend in Washington or New York, permitted during our last year, was all the more memorable for being so rare. I thoroughly enjoyed my participation in wrestling and gymnastics.

A sense of wonder that I was indeed a midshipman at the

United States Naval Academy never quite disappeared. But there was another less felicitous side to that coin: I never felt, in my deepest heart, that I truly belonged there. Fervently as I wished it to be otherwise, I always had the disquieting sense of being an outsider. My classmates were the *real* midshipmen, occupying their proper place in the grand scheme. I was in some vague way an interloper. My Australian background had set me apart. It continued to do so, although fortunately with diminishing impact, throughout my navy career.

As for girls and dating, my record at the academy was not auspicious. During Plebe year, of course, the institutional barriers discouraged all but the most determined. But even after that, when there *were* opportunities, I seldom seized them. It was not that I didn't want to. I just didn't know how to go about it. I had been very much of a bookworm during the long effort to get into the academy, and was about as inexperienced with girls as you can get. Awkward and self-conscious, I would surely in today's vernacular have been called a wimp! Toward the end of the last year, I began to improve, but by no stretch could I have been called a Don Juan. I had yet to learn that a martini or two does wonders for the shiest suitor.

Looking back, I have a better perspective on what the Naval Academy gave me. I thought then that it was as good an education in engineering as one could receive. I can see now that there were serious flaws. The course of instruction was out of date. There was insufficient attention paid to the fundamentals of math and science. Many of the instructors were poorly qualified. The system often rewarded rote memory at the expense of reason. There was undue emphasis on existing hardware. (I think I could still draw from memory a schematic diagram of a three-stage vapor compressor and a Mark I computer.)

But what the academy did teach us more than made up for all of those deficiencies. It instilled in us the attitude that whatever job we were called upon to do, we had to do it superbly well. It insisted that we had to be more knowledgeable in our areas of responsibility than anyone else. Above all, it pounded into us the competitive spirit. We were graded to a hundredth of a point in almost every subject every day. We were aware that class standing would have an important impact on our entire career. We all felt that if we succeeded in graduating from the academy, there would be no one with whom we could not successfully compete.

The course of instruction at the Naval Academy has since been completely revised. Revolutionary changes have been introduced. How some of the most important of these came about as the result of a clash between Admiral Rickover and the rest of the navy will be told in a later chapter.

While many members of our class achieved success in and out of the navy, the name of only one became a household word: Alan B. Shepard, America's first man in space. Alan was one of the most popular midshipmen in the class. He had a wonderful gift of friendship. We were all delighted to see him selected as one of the original seven astronauts, and to see him, as the "old man" of the Apollo program, finally make it to the moon.

We had one evil genius, J.J. King. The phonetic word for the letter "J" being at the time "Jig," he was first known as Jig Jig King, but soon was called more often Jig the Pig, or simply Pig. He was about as sloppy as a midshipman could be and still remain a midshipman. He worked at it!

Pig was an authentic genius who had been compelled to enter the Naval Academy by his father, a wealthy oil man from Tulsa, Oklahoma. The father was a navy buff, a powerful member of the Navy League, and influential in Oklahoma politics. He had no trouble securing an appointment for his academically brilliant son, who came to the academy under threat of disinheritance.

Pig had no trouble whatsoever with the academic subjects. He roomed with Walker Gardner Bennett II (Benny), who had nothing but trouble. Benny had been an enlisted marine and had secured one of the fleet appointments about which I spoke earlier. Strong on native intelligence, Benny was woefully lacking in academic background. It soon became clear that if he managed to graduate at all, he would stand toward the very bottom of the class. Pig decided that there was an opportunity there. He convinced Benny that with diligence, he could be the "anchor man" of our class. The anchor man is the one with the lowest class standing on graduation. Pig's argument, which Benny found persuasive, was that all members of the class who graduated above the anchor man had expended unnecessary effort. Achievement of the bottom slot was therefore worthy of a serious endeavor. Benny decided to go for it, and the Pig got the rest of us interested in the project. It was a touchy proposition, because with one false move, poor Benny would be out. He went before the Academic Board many times, and was always able to talk his way to another chance. The time came, however, when it was obvious that he would never survive another appearance before the board. His only hope was to be sick when examination times came so that he could take delayed exams. In that way, we could coach him and get him through. We had done this successfully several times, with Pig orchestrating the performance. As the last examinations before graduation approached, however, Benny was warned that the doctors were wise to him, and would not be sucked in again. It seemed clear that the Pig had played it too close. Benny was doomed.

The morning the examinations were to start, Benny showed up at Sick Bay (the dispensary) pleading illness. He was laughed at by the corpsman on duty: "Mr. Bennett, you know that you can't get away with this any more. The doctors are on to you. You've had it." "No, no," said Benny, "I'm really sick. I was throwing up all night, and I have terrible stomach pains." The corpsman took Benny's temperature, along with that of each of the other midshipmen who were waiting to see the doctor. He was shocked to see that it was 104 degrees. The doctor then examined Benny and found him doubled over in apparent pain with his abdomen as rigid as a board. A blood count was taken and showed a great excess of white blood cells. It seemed a clear case of appendicitis. Benny was bundled off to the hospital with an appendectomy scheduled for that afternoon. During the day, however, his condition dramatically improved. His temperature was normal and his abdomen soft. He said the pain was gone. The operation was cancelled. He remained in the hospital a day or two under observation and was then released. We coached him on the examinations and he squeaked by.

Here's how he did it: as he sat in a row of midshipmen, each with a thermometer in his mouth, he kept his hand on the radiator behind his seat. As the corpsman approached he removed the thermometer, holding the bulb in his hot fingers. As he saw the temperature reach 104 degrees, he handed the thermometer to the corpsman. As for the rigid abdomen, Benny had practiced yoga when he was an enlisted Marine on duty at the U.S. Embassy in Tokyo. He was thus able to control his stomach muscles. The blood count was the trickiest part: Pig had read that in the aftermath of a significant loss of blood, the white corpuscles multiply much faster than the red. Benny had simply gone twice through a blood donors' line the day before.

Walker Gardner Bennett II was the anchor man of our class. He proudly held a blue and gold cardboard anchor high above his head when Secretary of the Navy Forrestal called his name to receive his diploma at graduation. He received a standing ovation from the assembled midshipmen. His display of an anchor established a tradition that still exists.

It here seems appropriate to insert another footnote to history so I'll jump forward a few years: Shortly after the assassination of President Kennedy, Chief Justice Warren, at the request of President Johnson, headed a commission formed to conduct an exhaustive inquiry into the affair. In early 1964, Governor Connally of Texas, having been wounded in the same incident, came to Washington to testify before the commission.

After his testimony, he came to the Pentagon and visited me in my office. I was still the special counsel to the secretary of the navy. Although we had been in touch by telephone, this was the first time I had seen him since he had resigned from the office of secretary of the navy in 1962. He had put on a little weight, which he carried well, and was greyer at the temples. He was, if anything, even more strikingly handsome and distinguished, and had of course become more famous. His arm was still in a sling from the effects of Oswald's bullet. He had become a glamorous figure, and the women from nearby offices crowded about to catch a glimpse of him. My own very capable secretary, Colleen Dodson, who was not easily impressed by the good and the great she saw on a daily basis, seemed overwhelmed. "He remembered my name. He shook my hand," she murmured in an awestruck tone to the other secretaries.

Connally and I chatted a while about old times and his experience in the Kennedy assassination. He then asked, "Andy, remember that letter we got from Oswald from Russia? Do you suppose you could find it for me? I'd like to have it for my memorabilia. After all, the son-of-a-bitch shot me!" I told him I'd look for it and send it to him when I found it.

The letter failed to turn up, however, in a search of the files of the secretary of the navy's office. The Marine Corps also came up with a blank. Months passed, and I occasionally called Connally to tell him I was still looking. I had almost given up when the letter was finally located in the United States Archives. I told Archivist Mr. Bahmer of Connally's request. He said that he was prevented by law from giving up the letter. "Law? What law is that?" I asked. Bahmer began a long explanation: The letter, he said, had been an item of evidence before the Warren Commission. It had been discovered, apparently, through a routine examination of Oswald's Marine Corps record. It turned out to be the most comprehensive example of Oswald's handwriting available to the commission. It had been used, therefore, by handwriting experts as an exemplar. The handwriting proved that Oswald had been the person who, under a false name, had purchased the rifle used to kill President Kennedy. It served the same purpose with respect to the pistol used by Oswald to kill police officer Tippet. Tippet was killed when he attempted to apprehend and arrest Oswald on November 22nd, the day Connally and Kennedy were shot.

Bahmer said that the day after Oswald himself was shot and killed by Jack Ruby, a man visited Marina Oswald. He offered to buy the two guns. She told him she didn't have them; they had been taken away by the police. He assured her that the guns belonged to her as Oswald's widow, and that eventually she could get them back. They agreed on the price. He paid and wrote out a bill of sale, which Marina Oswald signed.

He then went to the authorities and demanded his property. He was told that the weapons now belonged to the federal government: they had been seized as contraband because they had been bought under a false name in contravention of the Federal Firearms Act. The man objected. "I've read that Act," he said, "and I don't believe it gives the government that authority." He went to court and was successful. The court held that the government had misread the act. The guns must be returned to their owner.

Robert Kennedy, the archivist continued, was distressed to think that the gun used to kill his brother might end up in a private collection, with probable commercial exploitation. As attorney general, he prepared and had introduced in Congress remedial legislation. It gave the federal government the authority to seize by condemnation items of evidence in assassinations or attempts on the lives of certain high government officials. The proposed legislation was swiftly enacted into law. Armed with the new law, federal marshals went to the purchaser of the guns. They tendered a government check for their catalogue prices—$48.50 for the pistol and $119.00 for the rifle, or whatever the sums were. "Oh, no," the man said, "the laws says I must receive 'proper' compensation. These guns are collectors' items. They're worth millions." So the case went back to court. Eventually the Court of Appeals held that both parties were wrong. On the one hand, there could be appreciation in the value of items that should be taken into account in the required compensation. On the other hand, it would be unconscionable to permit individuals to enrich themselves solely because they possessed items connected with the assassination of a president. For all he knew, said Bahmer, the case was still in litigation. He concluded the story by telling me that the Oswald letter I was seeking had fallen under the described legislation. He had, however, a suggestion. "I can't give you the letter, but we have the means over here to make a copy practically indistinguishable from the original. See if the governor would like that." The copy, when I later received it, was indeed a marvelous reproduction and Connally was happy to get it.

I was fascinated by Mr. Bahmer's account. "Do you know," I asked, "anything about the fellow who bought the guns from Marina?" "Oh, yes", he replied. "His background was summarized in one of the court cases. His name is John J. King. He is a big oil man from Tulsa, Oklahoma. He also made a lot of money in Alaska oil." He then added, "As a navy man, you might be interested in knowing that he is a graduate of the U.S. Naval Academy." "My God," I said, "that has to be 'Jig the Pig' King, the evil genius of my class at Annapolis!" And indeed it was.

4

An Officer of the Line

There is always for me a magic sense of excitement in the air of San Francisco. Life seems to take on a special intensity there. What then could have been more wonderful than to be a new ensign, fresh out of the Naval Academy, in wartime San Francisco? There were hundreds of us there during the summer of 1944, waiting for transportation out into the Pacific to our first ships. I shared a room at the St. Francis Hotel with several classmates. Each morning at 10:00 A.M. we reported to the 12th Naval District Headquarters. Each day, some were directed to report to this or that transport. Those of us who were left went out again on the town for "one more night before we go off to war." After four weeks, we few who remained were wrecks. We didn't care if, in all our lives, we never saw another girl or had another drink. So when finally we were told to report to Pier 44 with our gear, we felt we had heard tidings of salvation.

At the pier we found the Matson liner *Lurline* painted grey and converted to a troop transport. Fifteen of us were assigned to what had been a two-person stateroom. It was now crammed with pipe-frame bunks from deck to overhead. No matter! With a sense of peace and vast relief, I crawled into a bunk and fell asleep. I was awakened by the shout of a classmate. "Andy, look out the port. Look what's coming aboard! Women! Women! Thousands of them!" Shocked and unbelieving, I lurched to the porthole. He was right. Long lines of women stretched down the pier. Five thousand assorted army nurses, USO and Red Cross girls, and WAACs came on board to join ninety ensigns for a voyage that lasted weeks and took us eventually to Brisbane, Australia.

To those inclined to envy our situation, I can say that it was far from perfect. It is true that with so many women, the law of averages ensured that some of them were dandies. But there was no privacy! There were women—masses of them—everywhere. It proved almost impossible to cut one out of the herd, when the herd itself pressed in from every direction!

After Brisbane, we shattered survivors made our tedious way in a variety of craft to Manus Island in the Admiralty Group, just north of New Guinea. There in Seeadler Harbor, we rejoiced in the magnificent sight of a vast armada. There were our ships! There were battleships, cruisers, destroyers, and transports and supply ships of every description. This was the primary staging area for the great operation for the recapture of the Philippines.

Now we would face the test. We were no longer students, no longer graduates on a spree. On the morrow, each of us would be an officer in the ship's company of a United States man-of-war. How will I measure up to this responsibility? There can be no one so self-assured as to face such a moment without some trepidation. To what division will I be assigned? Gunnery? Engineering? How successful will I be as a leader of the enlisted men in my charge? Will I be able to earn the respect of the other officers? Do I know enough to pull my weight aboard a ship seasoned in battle?

These had to be some of my thoughts as I climbed to the quarterdeck of my first ship, the light cruiser *Honolulu,* and announced to the officer of the deck, "Ensign Kerr reporting aboard for duty, sir."

Our first test aboard the *Honolulu,* however, was to survive the arrival interview with the executive officer. We had been told that Commander Olin Scoggins was the toughest and meanest exec afloat, and that he "ate ensigns for breakfast." Several of us had reported aboard at the same time. The first to be interviewed emerged white and shaken and described his ordeal to the rest of us.

The ship's practical joker, Lieutenant (junior grade) Francis Rhett, seized his chance. He had identified one new arrival, Ensign

Tom Casey, as being particularly gullible. Casey was also especially nervous about the interview that was soon to commence. Drawing Tom aside, Rhett proffered this advice: "Look, Tom," he said, "all the things you've heard about Scoggins are true. He is really mean. But there is a way to get around him. He is a vain man and extremely proud of his athletic career. If you mention that, he'll be eating out of your hand." "Great," said Tom, "I'll do it. But what was his sport?" "Grabass," said Rhett, pronouncing the word as gra-BAHSS to disguise its meaning. "Grabass? Grabass?" said Tom, "I've never heard of it." "Well," said Rhett, "it's a very popular sport in the east, particularly in the Ivy League, and Scoggins became a famous star. He won the eastern intercollegiate championship three years in a row. He also is credited with developing the western grip, which revolutionized the game. All you need to know, though, is that Scoggins was one of the all-time greats."

Tom, incredible as it seems, tumbled into the trap. No sooner had he entered the exec's stateroom when he blurted out, "It's an honor to meet you, sir—I've heard about you for years." "Oh," said Scoggins, "What have you heard?" "You're famous," replied Tom. "Everyone knows that you were one of the greatest grabass players of all time." "What?" said Scoggins, not believing his ears. "Yes," said Tom, "We've all heard how you won the eastern intercollegiate grabass championship three years in a row, and introduced the western grip into the game. What an accomplishment!"

"What!" roared Scoggins, "Who told you that?" Tom, thinking only that he had gotten some of the facts wrong, made matters worse by repeating that the commander's grabass fame was widespread. He admitted, however, that Lieutenant Rhett had recently refreshed his memory as to the details of Scoggins's career.

Ordered from the room by an apoplectic Scoggins, Tom Casey spent the next year aboard assiduously avoiding contact with the executive officer. The irrepressible Rhett, his career in tatters, emerged from a period in hack (room arrest) with his zeal for practical jokes undiminished.

There were few Naval Academy graduates among the ship's officers. Most had come from civilian life, with a marvelous diversity of backgrounds. There were lawyers, engineers, liberal arts graduates, a historian, and even a poet. They comprised a splendid collection. Almost without exception, they were fine officers.

Our resident poet was Lieutenant Eugene Turner. His nickname, for reasons unknown to me, was Clean Gene. He endeavored to maintain some proficiency at his calling by collecting limericks. I still have, in a box in an attic somewhere, a faded mimeographed copy of "101 Best South Pacific Limericks" compiled and edited by Clean Gene Turner.

To avoid confusion, we changed Clean Gene's name to Sanitary Eugene when Big John Green, the Clean Marine, reported aboard as second in command of our Marine detachment. John B. Green was a Phi Beta Kappa philosophy major from Princeton. He was also a runner-up All-American football player, and was as handsome as a Greek God. Before joining the Marine Corps, he carried a spear in the chorus of Paul Robeson's production of *Othello*.

To one officer aboard, I owe a special debt of gratitude. Ensign Tom Starr was a classics scholar. He introduced me to the Great Books. His library was amazingly extensive. Under his stimulus and guidance, I read Aristotle and Plato, and the Greek historians, Thucydides and Herodotus. The Stoic and Epicurean philosophers, particularly Marcus Aurelius, were other discoveries. Tom Starr opened a new world for me. Aquinas, Marx, Hegel, Nietzsche, Locke, and Hume all became topics between the two of us, with the Clean Marine often participating. Stendahl, Spengler, Adam Smith, and Machiavelli were all on his list. During my two years aboard the *Honolulu*, they became companions. To me, whose academic background had been largely limited to the technical and scientific, the revelation of the world of those books was tremendously exciting.

By October 1944, less than two months after I had reported aboard, the *Honolulu*, a *Brooklyn*-class light cruiser with a main battery consisting of 15 six-inch guns, was in Leyte Gulf in the Philippines. Our task was to conduct close-in shore bombardment in preparation for and during the landing of our troops. General Douglas MacArthur was aboard a sister ship, the USS *Nashville*, in the same task force. He was poised to fulfil the promise he had made on fleeing Corregidor by submarine almost three years before, "I shall return."

My battle station was in Main Battery Plot, the nerve center for the control of the main battery. It was deep in the bowels of the ship. Access was by a ladder in a vertical trunk running down through several decks. My job there was to operate the Mark I computer, which solved the ballistics problem. Yes, we had computers in naval gunnery in 1944. They were, however, extraordinarily primitive by today's standards. They were entirely mechanical and solved the ballistics problem with much whirring and clicking by means of differential gears and integrating discs. I remember scoffing at the prediction of one of our scientifically inclined officers that one day there would be computers that would do the job electronically. I now realize that sophisticated electronic computers existed even then, and accounted for the remarkable successes achieved by the British and Americans in cryptology. The Mark I computer and its cousins could never have broken the German and Japanese codes!

By October 20, we had been bombarding the landing area along the coast of Leyte for three days. We had been at battle stations much of the time because of Japanese air attacks and were nearing exhaustion through lack of sleep. At 4:00 P.M., there was a lull in the air activity, and "condition two" was announced. In this condition, only half of the ship's company were at their stations, rather than everyone. Just then, however, a freshly brewed pot of coffee was ready in the Main Battery Plot. All of the off-going section, except me, decided to remain for a few more minutes to have a cup. I decided that I'd rather have a few more minutes sleep. After I had climbed up the access trunk past two or three decks, the ship's loud-speakers blasted out with "Set condition Affirm! Underwater attack!" This meant that all watertight doors and hatches had to be closed immediately. Having just passed upward through an armored watertight hatch, I closed it behind me and dogged it tight. At that moment, the torpedo struck. At that same moment the thirteen officers and men I had just left died together in Main Battery Plot.

I recall that my first reaction, upon hearing of the fate of those I had left behind, was shock and grief at their loss. Then followed a sense of wonder that I alone had been spared, and amazement at my luck. Then slowly came a curious and most persistent feeling of guilt. It was as if somehow my escape had been unfair to those who had died. I was unable to free myself of this emotion, illogical though I knew it to be.

The torpedo had been dropped by a Japanese plane that came in low, concealed behind the hills of Leyte. When it first appeared, it was lined up squarely on the *Honolulu*. We were clearly a preselected target. Within hours, Radio Tokyo was broadcasting that the ship in which General MacArthur was embarked had been hit and sunk in the Philippines. The *Honolulu* and the *Nashville* were identical.

The Japanese torpedoes of World War II excited the envy of our professional weapons experts. They ran straight and true, exploded on impact, and packed an enormous load of explosive. In contrast, the U.S. torpedoes, particularly those used by our submarines, were a disgrace. The lives of many of our submariners were lost when they were attacked and depth-charged after their torpedoes failed to explode. We entered World War II with a torpedo exploder mechanism that was so secret that it was issued to our submarines in a sealed box. The box was to be opened and the instructions read only in the event of war.

In using these new exploders, the running depth was to be set so that the torpedo would pass *underneath* the keel of the target vessel. Then, at the right moment, the magnetic field of the target ship was to activate the exploder. The resulting explosion of the torpedo's warhead under the keel was supposed to break the back of the target. To the dismay of the fleet, the exploders turned out to be highly unreliable. The disgust in the voice of an old chief torpedoman was almost palpable when, years later, he told me that the exploder had been devised and tested "by a few trusted civilians." The fleet, in desperation, finally gave up on Washington and, on its own, developed at Pearl Harbor an exploder that worked. The deep distrust of submarine men for the Navy Bureau of Ordnance was later transferred undiminished to its successor, the Bureau of Naval Weapons. The distrust may now have faded. I hope the lesson has not.

The *Honolulu* did not sink. She took an immediate and pronounced list to port and lost all power. The damage was massive. Sixty-five men were killed. The ship was flooded from keel to waterline, and from the bow to the fireroom bulkhead. Skilled and timely damage control saved her. Gradually, minimum power was restored, bulkheads were shored, and she able to limp at a dead slow speed to the repair facilities at Manus Island. She was accompanied on that voyage by another cripple, the Australian heavy cruiser *Australia*. That ship had been struck on the same day, 20 October 1944, in Leyte Gulf in the first positively identified Japanese kamikaze attack of the war.

When the *Honolulu* reached Manus and was raised up in the floating dry dock, the bodies of those who had been killed had been submerged in tropical water for almost two weeks. My grim duty as the only survivor of those assigned to Main Battery Plot was inescapable. As the oily water receded, I climbed back down through the access trunk and into that devastated compartment, to identify as best I could my dead shipmates. The experience gave me bad dreams for years afterward.

There was to be no more combat for the *Honolulu*. After a temporary patch-up in Manus, she returned to the States for complete repairs and the installation of a more modern secondary gun battery. The work was to be done at Norfolk, Virginia, to the chagrin of the crew. Norfolk, at that time, would without doubt have come in first in any navy poll to determine the most dismal liberty port in the United States. The sailors hated Norfolk, and the sentiment was reciprocated. I was therefore delighted when soon after our arrival in Norfolk, I was sent to Newport, Rhode Island, to assist in the Honolulu's training program. Many of our men and officers had been transferred from the ship because of the long stay expected in the Norfolk shipyard. The new replacements were trained in Newport so that they could come aboard prepared to undertake their duties when the *Honolulu* was again ready for sea.

The ship's new executive officer, Commander William J. Lederer, was in charge of the Newport contingent. Lederer later became a noted author. His books include *All the Ships at Sea, A Nation of Sheep,* and, in collaboration with Eugene Burdick, *The Ugly American*. He was a remarkable man who, with no schooling beyond grade school, had entered the Naval Academy through the enlisted ranks. He walked with a pronounced limp—almost a hop—spoke with a serious stutter, and had incredible energy. A prodigious worker, he was driven in two directions at once: to be a successful naval officer and to be a successful writer. We became friends.

When our training was completed, Lederer arranged for a special troop train to take the crew from Newport to Norfolk.

We loaded aboard and pulled out early in the evening, and I soon fell asleep. Several hours later I was awakened by Lederer, who was holding a railroad lantern. He said, "Andy, quick, c-c-come with me! I haven't t-t-time to explain." With no time to grab hat or jacket, I followed him out of the car and across the tracks of a railway yard. It was very dark. He ran with his peculiar hop, lantern bobbing, until we reached a lone box car. He said, stuttering and panting, "This box car has all of the sea bags of the men going back to the ship. Don't let it out of your sight! Get it to Norfolk!" And with that he was gone, the lantern disappearing in the blackness. What the hell happened? Where the hell was I? There was no one to answer these questions.

I groped my way into the box car and could feel that it was, indeed, filled with sea bags—sailor's duffel bags. When no one came and nothing happened for an hour or so, I slept the rest of the night stretched out on top of the bags. I was awakened early in the morning by a railroad detective. I convinced him with some difficulty that I wasn't a hobo dressed in an ensign's suit, minus hat and jacket. He told me that we were in the marshaling yards outside Philadelphia, but he had no idea how the car got there. I explained that I couldn't leave the box car. He promised to check with the station master to see about getting me to Norfolk. He never came back.

After several hours, a group of workmen came within hailing distance, and through them I got a message to the station master. His man came out and explained that the night before, the baggage car of the *Honolulu* train had developed a bad bearing. The sea bags were shifted to another car that had been pulled up on an adjacent track. It had then become necessary, because of the emergency movement of high-priority rail traffic, to move the box car to its present location, and to move the *Honolulu* troop train out immediately. The alternative that had been presented to Lederer was that as much as a day's delay could occur if he wished to unite the train with the new baggage car. He decided to move. My sudden assignment was the result.

For the near ultimate in frustration, try hitch-hiking a box car full of sea bags in wartime without credentials. Sometimes I would only make a few miles before getting unhitched. More than once I found myself going in a direction away from Norfolk. It seemed that whenever I went to sleep, I'd wake up on a siding and have to start through the entire routine again. I saw the wisdom of Lederer's order not to leave the car. It would, otherwise, surely have disappeared without a trace.

On reaching Norfolk, I managed to get a navy yard diesel engine to take us right out on to the pier alongside the *Honolulu*. The crew, whose gear had been missing for three days, had gotten word of the approach of the box car and were lining the ship's rail. I stood triumphant in the open door, black from head to foot from soot and cinders, and acknowledged the cheers of the crew with a huge grin. It was a grand moment.

The next few months passed in a kaleidoscopic blur of movement and training as we readied our rebuilt ship and her crew for combat. From Norfolk to Newport to Guantánamo we sailed and back again with gunnery practice, readiness inspections, and drill!

drill! drill! The war in Europe had ended, but it continued with increased ferocity in the Pacific as Nimitz and MacArthur pressed closer to the Japanese home islands. Then suddenly came Hiroshima, Nagasaki, and the surrender ceremony of September 1945 aboard the battleship *Missouri* in Tokyo Bay. General MacArthur, in accepting the Japanese surrender, announced the end of the global cataclysm that had begun six years before with the words, "These proceedings are closed."

Many Americans suffer from a sense of guilt from our use of the atomic bomb against Japan. I don't. My feelings have nothing to do with revenge or retribution for the Japanese attack on Pearl Harbor. Not at all. Rather, I believe that our demonstrated readiness to use the bomb almost certainly saved countless Japanese and American lives. The attacks by swarms of kamikaze aircraft and the fanatical defenses of Okinawa and Iwo Jima as we closed in on Honshu showed what we could expect in an invasion of the home islands. The defenders of those outposts of the crumbling Japanese empire elected to die to the last man rather than surrender. They died not by hara-kiri, but in bitter fighting, during which we suffered heavy losses. The refusal of Japanese soldiers to surrender in hopeless situations was not new. Earlier in the war, however, one might have seen a military justification. A policy or ethic of a fight to the death might, to the Japanese mind, contribute to victory. But by the time of Iwo Jima, there could be no victory for Japan, and the Japanese knew it. Their navy had been destroyed, and our submarines had sunk their merchant fleet. Any troops outside Japan that had not been defeated were isolated and neutralized. Their industry was under intense air bombardment. They had run out of oil. And still they fought to the death.

The end of the war was followed immediately by a public demand for rapid demobilization. The cry heard everywhere was "Bring the boys home!" In response we set about dismantling, in great haste, the most powerful military force in history. We did this in the naive belief that all possible enemies had been defeated, and that the victorious great powers would live henceforward in peace and harmony!

The *Honolulu* was ordered to go to the Philadelphia Navy Yard to be "moth-balled." This was the popular name for the process whereby ships were sealed and dehumidified. Their topside equipment was cocooned in plastic, and their machinery below decks was coated in grease. Thus preserved, fleets of once-mighty warships were then rafted together in ghostly assemblages in remote bays and rivers, needing few men to tend them, and where fewer still would pass and reflect on their former glory.

When ordered to Philadelphia, the *Honolulu* was in New York City for the Christmas holidays. The commanding officer, Captain H.F. Pullen, was in receipt of orders to another command. Rather than bring aboard another four-stripe captain, the navy decided to give temporary command to the executive officer, Commander Lederer. He was to take the ship from New York City to the Philadelphia Navy Yard, and there supervise the moth-balling process.

On the afternoon of 7 January 1946, tugs eased the *Honolulu* from her berth at the 10th Street pier out into the Hudson River. Our route for the short trip was to be around Sandy Hook then south off the New Jersey coast. We would then round Cape May into the Delaware River and arrive in Philadelphia during the morning of January 8th—an overnight passage. The weather was cold but clear with light wind and a slight sea. Commander Lederer's brief tour in command at sea of a major warship should have been a piece of cake. It wasn't. At approximately midnight off Cape May, the *Honolulu* collided with the U.S. submarine *Argonaut,* and the career of Commander William J. Lederer as an officer of the line was finished forever.

In my later experience as a navy lawyer, I was frequently involved in investigations into the causes of such misfortunes as ship collisions, groundings, and sinkings. I observed that these disasters were seldom caused by a single major incident or error. In almost every case, several minor events combined to cause the casualty. Each single event would be relatively insignificant. The absence of any one of them, however, would have broken the chain of causation, and the tragedy would not have occurred. Of this, the *Honolulu-Argonaut* collision stands as a class example.

The captain's Night Order Book on that evening gave the usual standing orders to the officer of the deck (OOD): the captain (Lederer) was to be called if any ship closed within a certain range, or was determined to be on a steady bearing, or if anything occurred that was abnormal or not understood, et cetera. It contained, that is, all of the instructions and cautions customarily given by a captain when he retires for the night. In addition, Lederer wrote that he wished to be called when Cape May Light reached a certain bearing, and that the OOD should be particularly alert to detect and avoid fishing vessels in the vicinity of Cape May.

The officer of the deck on the four-hour watch before midnight was Lieutenant Joe Willenbring, an able and experienced reserve officer. He was an old hand aboard the *Honolulu* and was standing his last watch in the navy. He was to be released to civilian life on our arrival the next day in Philadelphia.

Sometime during the evening, probably around eleven o'clock, the lookouts reported a group of faint white lights on the horizon off the starboard bow. They were soon spotted by Willenbring, who asked the junior OOD, Ensign Al Meints, to observe them through the bridge pelorus. The pelorus is a device by which the compass bearing of an approaching ship can be measured. If, over a period of time, the bearing remains the same,—i.e., it is a "steady bearing"—the ships are then known to be on a collision course. The device is fitted with binoculars with cross-hairs to enable precise observations. At night these cross-hairs, "reticules," are illuminated.

Meints observed the lights through the pelorus binoculars but had difficulty determining the behavior of the bearing. For one thing, the lights were appearing and then disappearing over the horizon, which seemed to indicate that the contacts were small vessels. Secondly, the reticule illumination suddenly failed, so Meints was unsure that he was observing the same light. It did appear to him, however, that the bearing of the group of contacts was drawing slowly left. He reported all this to the OOD.

About the time of the lookouts' report, the ship's Combat Information Center (CIC) reported to the OOD that a group of small radar contacts had been picked up and were giving intermittent radar returns.

Joe Willenbring put it together: the visual appearance of the distant lights plus the nature of the radar returns indicated small, low-profile ships in a group. What else could they be but fishing vessels, just as the captain had anticipated in his Night Order Book? The CIC officer came to the same conclusion and so reported to the OOD.

Willenbring then reported by telephone to Lederer, "Captain, we have a group of fishing vessels bearing 190 degrees, range 14,000 yards (seven miles), and the bearing is drawing left." "Very well," replied Lederer. "Keep me informed."

At about that time, the engineering officer of the watch reported to the OOD that there was a problem with the steering engine. Although a successful shift to an auxiliary system had been accomplished, Willenbring directed Meints to go aft and check on the progress of repairs to the main steering system. Thus it happened that no further visual bearings were taken on the approaching lights.

CIC, in the meantime, was finally able to determine the course and speed of the contacts, and that a potential collision situation existed. In such cases, standard procedure required that the OOD be informed that he was on a collision course, and that the projected time of collision be given. This was a dramatic way of capturing the OOD's attention, and letting him know how much time he had to take evasive action. The CIC officer, however, was new at his job, and failed to use the key word "collision." He merely recommended a course change.

On the bridge, the time was approaching midnight and the end of Willenbring's last watch. In the U.S. Navy it is customary for a relieving officer to appear fifteen minutes before the end of the prior watch. That time had passed, and Willenbring's relief, Lieutenant Bill Simpson, had not appeared. At about the time that CIC was recommending a course change, Willenbring was calling the wardroom duty steward to find out if his relief had indeed been called. In fact, a mistake had been made. The steward had earlier called the wrong officer, who had mumbled that it wasn't his watch, and had turned over and gone back to sleep. The steward, however, had not understood the muffled response to his call. In his second call to the steward, Willenbring, in a state of agitation, demanded a double check to ensure that Lieutenant Simpson was up and about. Only then did the steward recognize his mistake, and he immediately awoke Simpson. Simpson, however, was unaware of the error. Only after he was dressed did he glance at his watch and realize he was late. He wondered if he could have been called earlier and had fallen back asleep. He rushed to the bridge, full of apologies, "I'm sorry as hell, Joe—I don't know what happened! I really don't recall getting an earlier call. Well, I'm ready to relieve you. What's the situation?" Willenbring answered that he had picked up a group of fishing vessels on the starboard bow and that the range was closing, but that the bearing was drawing left—and that the captain had been notified. He added that CIC had just recommended a course change, but had not reported a collision course.

Simpson then said, "Very well, Joe, I relieve you," the magic words that signify, in the navy, the total transfer of responsibility. He then walked out to the starboard wing of the bridge, blinked, looked again, and saw to his horror that a collision was imminent.

"Hard right rudder! All back full! Sound the collision alarm!" he shouted. It was too late. The submarine *Argonaut* struck the *Honolulu* on its starboard bow, tearing a hole at the waterline, and drowning one of the *Honolulu*'s crew members.

After he had been notified of the sighting of fishing vessels, Lederer had got up, dressed, and awaited a follow-up report. He considered going to the bridge, but reminded himself that the OOD was highly qualified and the report had been unalarming. An appearance on the bridge at that point, he thought, would indicate a lack of confidence in his officers and an appearance of undue nervousness. So he waited in his stateroom. His first indication that things had gone wrong was the vibration of engines going full astern, followed immediately by the collision alarm.

I have put together the foregoing from talks with all of the principals, and from testimony at the ensuing courts-martial. My own watch as junior officer of the deck was not to commence until 4:00 in the morning. I was thus asleep in my bunk when the collision alarm sounded. I recall that the impact of the collision was not unlike the thump of the exploding torpedo that struck us at Leyte Gulf. For one wild moment on awakening, I thought we were back in the war, and had been torpedoed again!

It was ascertained soon after the collision that the *Argonaut* was sailing in company with three other submarines, en route from Panama to the Submarine Base at New London, Connecticut. That in itself was unusual. Submarines almost always travel alone—seldom in company. Thus their number, their low lights, and their small silhouettes all contributed to the mistaken identification.

Those whose lives or careers are blighted by such tragedies are haunted by thoughts beginning, "If only . . . ." In this case, if only the captain had not been so new, he might not have been so concerned with appearances. If only the reticule illumination hadn't failed or the steering casualty not occurred, Ensign Meints would almost surely have detected a steady bearing. He would also have been on hand to keep an eye on things during the crucial time that Joe Willenbring was preoccupied with the lateness of his relief. If only the CIC officer had used the correct terminology—if only it were not Willenbring's last watch—if only Simpson had been called on time—if only the words in the Night Order Book and the almost freak appearance of a group of submarines had not combined to create a misconception.

In the subsequent court-martial, Commander Lederer and Lieutenant Willenbring were convicted of the offense of negligently hazarding a vessel. Lieutenant Simpson was acquitted. His acquittal makes the case unique. Navy tradition places upon an officer who says the words "I relieve you" full responsibility for subsequent events. This is bedrock. I know of no other case in which an officer who had been relieved prior to a casualty was convicted while the relieving officer on whose watch the casualty occurred was acquitted. (There are, of course, cases in which *both* are convicted.) In the *Honolulu* court-martial, however, the court was convinced that *nothing* Simpson did or didn't do contributed in any way to the collision. They felt, in short, that the collision was inevitable at the moment Simpson spoke the words "I relieve you."

Commander Lederer was aware that his career as a line officer was irrevocably blighted by his conviction. He therefore requested to be designated a specialist in public information. In that status, he eventually achieved the rank of captain. His particular field of expertise was Southeast Asia. His navy experience in that area provided him with the background for his book *The Ugly American*.

As the moth-balling of the *Honolulu* neared completion, I prepared a request that for my next duty I be sent to the submarine school at New London, Connecticut. I had formed the ambition for submarine duty while still at the Naval Academy. Our initial assignments, however, were made on the basis of a lottery. The midshipman whose name was drawn first was number one on the preference list, and so on down through the class. Each of us gave our first, second, and third choices of the type of ship to which we wanted assignment—e.g., destroyer, submarine, or battleship. Submarine duty was a popular choice, so only those whose names were drawn early had a chance. My name was drawn well below the middle. I got my second choice, a cruiser.

My request for submarine training had to have an endorsement by the ship's medical officer that I was physically qualified. My friend and shore-side drinking companion, Doc Wilhoit, conducted the physical examination. He found me in good shape. While we were chatting afterward, however, he expressed surprise that I had seemed somewhat nervous. We had been shipmates since before the ship had been torpedoed, and he said that he had never seen me nervous before. I then made an awful mistake. I told him that physical exams always upset me because of my experience getting into the Naval Academy, and I told him the story. He then said, "Oh, oh, color deficiency. I'd better check that." I objected, pointing out that the color vision requirement for submarines was the same as that for the academy and that color vision acuity never changes. He agreed with that, but nevertheless gave me the test. I missed a plate or two. He then insisted that his professional reputation required that he make a note that I had "borderline color deficiency." He said that otherwise a question could later be raised as to the thoroughness of his examination. I was furious—at myself for being so dumb as to raise the issue and at him for taking what I considered to be an unreasonable and unscientific stand. My three years at the academy and two aboard the *Honolulu* without experiencing difficulty had proven to me that the color tests were, indeed, mere clever constructions by ivory tower specialists and that they had no practical meaning in real life.

I now had a big problem. There were always far more applicants for sub school than could be taken, so the selection board could afford to be extremely choosy. Any hint of a defect would make selection of the candidate unlikely. Rejection would make futile any subsequent application. So I angrily told Wilhoit that I would tear up my application. There was no point in sending it in. I'd wait until he or I were transferred. Then I'd be examined, I said, by someone more reasonable.

A few days later, I went with shipmates to dinner at Bookbinders, a famous old Philadelphia seafood restaurant. I ate a gross of steamed clams, and my companions thought that to be exceptional. What I had done solely because I love steamed clams soon became an "exploit" in discussions in the *Honolulu* wardroom.

There could be no such discussion without an automatic reference to Doc Wilhoit. He was, without question, one of the great chowhounds of the navy. He had a metabolism that allowed or required him to eat enormous quantities, yet he was not heavy and he gained no weight. It was always fun to have visitors in the wardroom mess, and watch them gape in astonishment at Wilhoit's prodigious consumption. Navy regulations require the ship's doctor to sample the crew's mess for quality and quantity. Wilhoit took that responsibility seriously. He ate meals with the crew *and* with the officers in the wardroom. So it was inevitable that someone would speculate that Doc could surely eat more than a gross of steamed clams. We were still not speaking, but eventually our respective supporters, seconds if you will, arranged a contest. We agreed on a Tuesday to compete the following Friday evening. Bookbinders was notified to have plenty of clams, and the entire top floor was reserved. All the officers of the *Honolulu* who were not on watch planned to be there. I starved myself that week. Wilhoit maintained his normal diet until Thursday afternoon and then slacked off. As Friday approached, I talked to Wilhoit and said, "Look, Doc, how about us having a side bet on this. Let's say that the loser pays for all the clams, and that if you win, I'll pay you $20.00. If I win, you'll not mention the color thing." He thought a moment and then agreed, "Okay, you're on. There is no way you can win, so I'm not taking a chance. Are you sure that you want to donate $20.00?"

On Friday evening, our table was in the center of the room, and those of the spectators were grouped around. We confirmed the previously agreed upon rules: The neck of the clam had to be eaten, but the skin of the neck could be removed. Butter was optional. We would eat at our own pace, placing the discarded shells in the bushel basket that each of us had on the floor beside us. We were free to look into each other's basket. When one announced that he could eat no more, the other could continue or stop. Only when both had stopped would the shells be counted.

Before we began, I had a single dry martini with a twist of lemon, not an olive. Doc, in a gesture of bravado that I felt was a serious error, had a draft beer. I have never been so hungry.

We began. My pace was much faster. When Wilhoit finally said, "Okay, I quit, I've had enough," I knew that I'd beaten him. With a glance to confirm that my basket had by far the most shells, I said that I also was finished. The shells were counted and divided by two. Doc Wilhoit had eaten just over a gross—150. I had eaten 279. Although I could well have done without it, I finished with a slice of lemon pie. I felt this was necessary to emphasize the conclusiveness of the victory.

Wilhoit kept his word. My application went in without a blemish, and I was selected for submarine training. I count it as no small distinction to be, surely, the only submariner in any navy to have achieved that status through victory in a clam-eating contest.

The five years of service in submarines from 1946 to 1951 were, except for the last several months, wonderful years of personal and professional fulfillment. I matured as a naval officer and gained confidence. The submarine force consisted of the most dedicated and highly qualified professionals that I have ever encountered. Association with so splendid a group called for the best one could do.

The start was auspicious. From Submarine School as a new lieutenant (junior grade), I was assigned to the submarine *Sea Fox* based in Hawaii at Pearl Harbor. The commanding officer was Commander R.E. "Dusty" Dornin, who had been a football and basketball star at Annapolis in the class of 1935. One of the great submarine heroes of World War II, he wore on his chest no fewer than four Navy Crosses, awards second only to the Congressional Medal of Honor. He came to the *Sea Fox* from a tour of duty as aide to Fleet Admiral Ernest J. King, with whom he had attended the Yalta, Teheran, and Potsdam conferences, among others. He knew and told firsthand stories about Roosevelt, Truman, Churchill, De Gaulle, and Chiang Kai-Shek. Tall and raw-boned, his pock-marked face was ruggedly handsome. His voice was a harsh rasp from the ever-present cigarettes that eventually killed him. He knew more about leadership than any man I have ever known, and I idolized him. We all did.

Not long after I arrived in Hawaii, I began to date, and then fell in love with, a wonderful girl. Rusty was the lovely red-haired daughter of Rear Admiral Louis Dreller, who then commanded the Pearl Harbor Naval Shipyard. A recent honors graduate of Swarthmore College, she later told me that she was initially attracted to me because I had read Oswald Spengler's *Decline of the West*. (Thank you, Tom Starr.) I was initially attracted to Rusty for other reasons. By that time, I was somewhat more at ease with girls, but must confess that I found the dry martini to be a marvelous aid to the relaxed enjoyment of a date. I still, however, thought of myself as considerably less than a romantic prize. I was therefore amazed when Rusty consented to have me for a husband. Rusty's mother, however, agreed with my own assessment of my worth. She found it appalling that her lovely and brilliant daughter should marry an insignificant lieutenant (jg) submariner without money or acceptable social background. I found it most disconcerting when she burst into tears each time I came calling.

Nevertheless, Rusty and I were married in the Submarine Base chapel at Pearl Harbor in November 1947. Navy juniors (children of naval officers) usually either love the navy or they hate it. Rusty loved it, and she became a full partner in my naval career. We formed friendships with other navy couples, friendships that had that special closeness and durability peculiar to those made by the young and newly married. We delighted in the gay and romantic social life of postwar Hawaii.

Rusty accepted my bachelor submarine friends. Three of us had been inseparable. John Richard Potter and James H. Cronander were too important in my life to omit mentioning here. My classmate, John, was a brilliant Irishman from Boston. A true renaissance man, he read voraciously, and his mind encompassed in depth the fields of literature, history, poetry, music, medicine, science, and sports. His rooms were always piled high with books and records. John was responsible for my interest in the law. He urged me to read two of his books: one, *A Kaleidoscope of Justice,* was a massive tome. It was a survey of philosophics of law and trial procedures from earliest times. The other was *The Art of Cross-Examination* by Francis X. Wellman. Those books sparked the fascination with the law that later led me to enter law school. John had a leonine head with the beautiful eyes of the black Irish, and a long torso. His legs, however, were so short as to be almost deformed, and he was hardly taller standing up than sitting down. His height was the bare minimum for entry into the academy. Like many short men, he compensated for his lack of height with bombast and a contentiousness that made him many enemies.

Jim was of Norwegian descent and came to Annapolis from Vashon Island in Puget Sound. With gaunt Lincolnesque features, he towered over us at six feet four inches. A genius at mathematics, he was gifted with uncommon common sense and was as pragmatic as John was wild. While little John sought to draw attention to himself with outrageous comments, big Jim tried to avoid notice. He masked his keen mind by affecting, with strangers, the ungrammatical speech of a simple Scandinavian immigrant. The three of us talked for endless hours on every conceivable subject, the discussion usually ending when we were all quite drunk.

The *Sea Fox* ranged widely over the Pacific Ocean. Hong Kong, Tokyo, and Manila became familiar places. Our deployments were frequent and long enough to keep us on a constant honeymoon when we were home, yet not so onerous as to create unbearable domestic strains.

There was, of course, another side of the picture. There was plenty of sweat. We would accept nothing less for the *Sea Fox* than to be number one. This required hard work and long hours. Our World War II diesel-powered submarine was a far cry from the relatively palatial quarters aboard today's nuclear subs. We were hot and cramped. Ashore, we would be recognized instantly by our smell,—"food, feet, fuel oil, and farts." There was a strong element of danger in the operation of those submarines. Each person aboard had it within his power to make a mistake that would cost the lives of all. The risk became acceptable only through the exceptional competence and dedication of every officer and man.

Our pride in the *Sea Fox* set us up for a most distressing incident: We had just completed a long deployment in the Western Pacific. Everything had gone beautifully. We knew that our excellence as submariners was unmatched. We were the best. We found on our return to Pearl Harbor that other values prevailed.

During our absence, a contract had been entered into with a local hog raiser. Every day he was to remove the garbage from the Submarine Base. In return for this service, the garbage had to be separated into two containers. Into one of these was to be placed all garbage edible by hogs. Into the other was to go such inedible items as cans, paper, and egg shells.

The squadron operations officer, a senior submariner with a distinguished wartime record, had been instrumental in negotiating the contract. He had taken it upon himself to ensure that its terms were faithfully executed. He had issued an order requiring each inport submarine to post, on a rotating basis, a watch on the garbage receptacles. It had been promptly dubbed "the offal watch."

The Ops officer bounded aboard the *Sea Fox* as soon as the arrival amenities had been completed. As we fidgeted and squirmed in the wardroom, anxious to join our waiting wives after our six months absence, he explained in tedious detail to our skipper, Lieutenant Commander Gordy Glaes, the importance of properly segregated garbage. He emphasized that the designated watchstander, when it came our turn, should be no less than a responsible petty officer. The watch was expected to exercise good judgment in borderline cases—e.g., was a cantaloupe rind or a potato peel edible or not?

We all tended, at first, to treat the new requirement as a joke. Gordy Glaes sensed trouble ahead, but he was nevertheless adamant. "I'll be damned," he told us, "if I'll assign a *Sea Fox* petty officer to watch garbage pails. If we have to send someone, let it be a properly instructed seaman."

We soon found that it was no joke. The Ops officer himself made frequent and probing inspections. We received several caustic memos detailing instances where he or his assistant had found coffee grounds in the hog food container, or spaghetti leftovers in the other one. He repeatedly complained that the *Sea Fox* watchstander was not of sufficient seniority. He urged that disciplinary action be taken where he perceived that the watch had been lax. Tension mounted. Gordy made sure that the offal watch was properly instructed, but still refused to detail a petty officer. He also refused to take disciplinary action, because he was convinced that our watchstanders had exercised reasonable care. After all, the watch could only judge the propriety of a prospective dump by looking at the surface of the slop pail. What was underneath could only be ascertained after it was dumped into the container—and sometimes not even then. Glaes declined to require that the watch dig around in the proferred slop pails to detect beforehand prohibited items, or to probe into the receptacle to find if anything improper had slipped through.

The Ops officer had an assistant who was a Naval Academy classmate of mine. It befell poor Lieutenant (junior grade) Hugh Murphree to carry out the garbage policies that had become an obsession with his boss. Hugh thus had to make his quota of garbage inspections. The ribbing he took from us, his peers, was unmerciful. There is a particularly nauseous song entitled, "Hector the Garbage Collector." I sang that song at parties whenever Hugh was present, to his intense annoyance. The offal watch continued for many years, although its administration became sensible after the Ops officer departed. It became a Pearl Harbor tradition that when the offal watch list was promulgated each week, a copy was to go to Hugh Murphree, wherever in the world he happened to be. It probably continued until Hugh retired as a captain. For all I know, it continues still.

For Gordy Glaes, however, what started as a joke and had progressed to a matter of principle, finally became a disaster. One day he had left the *Sea Fox* and was placing a bundle of clean laundry in his car. He felt a hand on his shoulder. A quick glance revealed that the hand was covered with slime and coffee grounds, and that it belonged to the Ops officer. "Glaes," he said, "get down there and check that garbage!" Glaes angrily shoved away the loathsome hand. Tempers flared, and the two officers set off to the office of the squadron commodore, Captain Dave White, for a showdown. Captain White, a mild and cultured gentleman, had no stomach for such a confrontation. Seeing from his window the approach of his operations officer and one of his submarine skippers, and determining from their enraged bellows the nature of their dispute, he slipped quickly out of his side door.

The two disputants, thus deprived of an arbiter, and having clearly progressed beyond any chance of rational discussion, took the only remaining avenue. They began to fight. The dreadful commotion in the commodore's office brought others on the run. There they found and quickly separated the two officers, who by then were grappling on the floor.

A more professionally damaging scenario, from Glaes's point of view, can hardly be imagined. Gordy Glaes was subsequently passed over for promotion to the rank of captain. Given his intelligence, competence, and dedication to duty, I can only attribute his failed promotion to this incident. Glaes, however, continued to perform superbly even after having been passed over. He was the rare officer who did not permit himself to become embittered by such an experience. As a result, there is a happy ending. Gordy accomplished the near miracle of being finally selected for promotion to captain the third time around.

During those years in the *Sea Fox,* I had no other ambition but to pursue a career in submarines as long as I could. We were all proud to be in the submarine service. Deep and enduring friendships were formed. I loved the life and found it greatly satisfying. Even with my natural tendency to seek out and identify tomorrow's problems, the future looked good. I was a happy man who had found his niche.

Then on the horizon there appeared a small cloud no larger than a man's hand. I discovered one day that I couldn't hear my watch tick with my left ear. "Oh, well," I thought, "a little wax, perhaps." The ticking came through loud and clear on the right side. Then in only a matter of months, that too began to fade. Now alarmed, I sought on a confidential basis the advice of the submarine force medical officer, Commander Walt Welham. Dr. Welham was the beloved family doctor for all of us at Pearl Harbor. He would make house calls at any hour when a submariner or his wife or child was ill at home and called for help. I knew that I could confide in Walt Welham without endangering my career.

Dr. Welham was a specialist in submarine medicine. Ears, to a submarine doctor, are merely termini for the eustachian channels through which pressure is equalized when depth is increased or decreased. Welham's first thought, naturally, was that my hearing loss could be caused by a constriction to the eustachian tube. This would be akin to the mild deafness most people experience when they have a head cold. He therefore arranged for me to undergo radium treatment at the local navy hospital. Once a week for a month, slender radium-tipped rods were pushed in through each nostril to the vicinity of the presumably offending area, while I sat immobile for ten minutes. The treatment was entirely experimental. It did no good whatsoever. The important thing is that it apparently did no harm either, since thirty-five years have passed and I haven't yet developed cancer of the brain.

Soon after these events, I left the *Sea Fox* and reported for duty in the *Clamagore,* a submarine based in Key West, Florida. My tidy world then began to come apart. After three years of glorious camaraderie aboard the *Sea Fox* under a succession of splendid commanding officers, I found myself in a submarine that was steeped in fear. The captain mistrusted his officers and ruled the ship by close surveillance and frequent reprimands. The officers had quickly come to realize that professional survival required them to "cover their asses" at all times. Rather than a band of brothers, it was every man for himself. There was no joy, no light-hearted banter, no joking in the wardroom. We approached our duties with a grim orthodoxy. There could be no dash, no flair, for any departure from doctrine or any experiment risked the wrath of the skipper. In addition, my hearing was deteriorating rapidly. During that time, my gentle father died at the age of 51, a victim of medical ignorance. His death resulted from an operation that doctors now know should never have been performed. To cap it off, Rusty hated the heat and the squalor and sordidness that characterized Key West in the early fifties. The contrast with our life in Hawaii was too much. We were both miserable. Only my conviction that the *Honolulu* and the *Sea Fox* represented the true navy, and the *Clamagore* was a rare aberration, enabled me to keep faith in a navy career. Without faith, I could not have continued.

There are times when salvation appears in total disguise. In retrospect, my failing hearing was one such occurrence. Long continuation of the *Clamagore* travail could have led to professional or domestic disaster. So, although at the time I viewed my loss of hearing as just one more Job-like affliction, it was undoubtedly a blessing when it required my detachment from the *Clamagore* after less than a year aboard. I was then ordered to a staff job at Key West as a submarine division engineer. My boss was Commander Tom Henry, who was the division commander. He arranged to have me go to the Philadelphia Naval Hospital for a definitive appraisal of my problem. The navy's best-equipped hearing laboratories were there.

The tests at Philadelphia showed conclusively that I had bilateral otoschlerosis. This is a condition in which the small moveable bones of the middle ear are immobilized by bony growths. It is a common form of deafness. I was told that it was progressive, that there was no cure, and that I would end up quite deaf. The small cloud on the horizon had become a dense black thunderhead covering the whole sky.

I had then completed seven years of sea duty since graduating from the academy. My assignment to shore duty was therefore imminent.

I had requested as my first choice the navy's law school program in Washington, D.C. The officers who were selected for that program attended regular morning law school classes at George Washington University or Georgetown Law School. They worked in the judge advocate general's office in the afternoons. It was a three-year program. Successful completion resulted in a law degree and, after passing the exam, admission to the bar.

When I returned to Key West from Philadelphia with the bad news about my hearing, Tom Henry decided that since I would soon be going ashore, there was no need to take any action. Thus it happened that no report was ever made to anyone in Washington about my hearing problem. The whole thing just fell through the cracks! In another month, to my delight and astonishment, my orders came through for the law program. Also about that time I received a welcome promotion to full lieutenant. Everyone in my Naval Academy class had stagnated for a full five years as lieutenants (junior grade), due to postwar cutbacks.

Barring a medical miracle, though, my career as a submariner and as an officer of the line seemed over. I still clung to the hope that somehow I could continue to pursue a career in the navy.

5

Surviving Law School

There are advantages in law school in not being able to hear the professors. I didn't know that at first. I thought it would be a distinct drawback.

I arrived early for my first class at the George Washington Law School that September morning in 1951, to be sure that I had a seat near the front. The class was Legal Method, an introductory course. Professor Benson, the assistant dean of the law school, entered and took his place at the podium. He beamed benignly at the new and nervous students and placed his watch before him. I saw his mouth begin to move. "Ah," I thought, "he's warming up to start the lecture." Then I saw with dismay that the other students were taking notes. I hadn't heard a sound!

I found that kindly, soft-spoken Professor Benson was the extreme. At least at first I was able to hear something of what the other professors said. And as my hearing deteriorated, my lip reading ability improved. From the beginning, however, cohesive note taking was impossible.

To compensate, I worked extra long hours in the law library and at home at night. I concluded that the task ahead would be difficult but do-able. There was no need to panic. But it was clear that without good notes to study, I would not be able in the examinations to recite back to the professors the contents of their lectures. Unless I were to content myself with limping along, which didn't seem to be a great idea, I had to come up with a different approach. The answer began to come in moments of half sleep, half wakefulness in the predawn hours of the morning. I think our minds must continue to wrestle with our most troublesome problems while we sleep. During sleep, the part of our brain involved in that process seems to be wonderfully uncluttered. It appears to be able to sweep aside the cloud of complexities that often obscures the solution from the waking mind. Time and again, the answers to problems that have vexed me for weeks have appeared with marvellous clarity and simplicity during those early-morning hours.

It began to dawn on me that my approach to the law had been completely wrong. I had been looking at it through the eyes of an engineer. The engineer generally seeks answers to well-defined problems: a bearing overheats, a bridge girder must withstand an estimated side load, a solenoid valve fails to operate. My education and naval experience had taught me how to deal with such things. I thought the same problem-solving approach was required in the law. Only the tools of the trade would be different. *Corpus Juris Secundum,* a legal encyclopedia, would replace the slide rule and *The Engineer's Handbook*. I had heard or read nothing to the contrary in my introduction to law school. The course in Legal Method stressed research. It taught how to enter the legal encyclopedias, digests, and law reports to find the cases that would dispose of specified problems.

But there was obviously an earlier step in the process: the problems had first to be identified and defined. My predawn brainstorm was that this basic first step could be far more important than the second. I should therefore concentrate most of my efforts on defining questions, not seeking answers. This approach, I believed, would be more conducive to success through independent study, and less dependent on classroom notes. I came later to realize that it is a superior approach overall in the practice of law.

A second fortunate insight was almost a corollary of the first; law school grades are given solely on the basis of a single written examination at the end of the course in each subject. If I were to concentrate on identifying the issues during these exams, I would have to discuss them in a clear and convincing manner. This required the development of a lucid style of legal writing. I set about that task with enthusiasm. A well-written opinon is, to me, a joy to read. On the negative side, I wanted to avoid the turgid prose that is all too common in legal writing. So I briefed the cases with a critical eye to the literary value of my efforts. I edited the polished the language until I was satisfied that each brief was as elegant and succinct as I could make it.

As the time for the first set of examinations approached, however, I grew increasingly nervous. My classmates were sure that only by citing pertinent cases could a good grade be attained. Grades at law school can have a profound effect on a student's future career, so the stakes are high. We had argued vehemently and often bitterly about the "right" approach to law and examinations. I had staked everything on the issues and language conclusions I have described above, and had scarcely cited a single case. So I awaited the exam results with great anxiety. When they were at last announced, I was dumbstruck. All A's! I had hoped for good results, but nothing like that! It was clear then that I had found the key. I recall shouting at the top of my lungs in sheer exultation as I drove out Route 50 to our little house in Falls Church to tell Rusty the news. As moments of triumph go, it ranks near the top of all those I have been privileged to enjoy.

The approach continued to work. As a result my grades were consistently good and I had the honor and great good fortune to be chosen to be editor-in-chief of the George Washington *Law Review* during my third and final year.

The editorship of the *Law Review* brought many satisfactions and one nasty shock: practising lawyers gain prestige when their articles are published in the *Law Reviews* of the leading law schools. The editor selects these articles on the basis of subject interest, scholarship, style, and the status of the author. He must also develop the tact of a renaissance diplomat as he, a mere law student, blue pencils the immortal words of famous and distinguished lawyers.

One late night in the *Law Review* office, I was working on an article submitted by one of the nation's leading experts on immigration and naturalization law. It was an analysis of the recently enacted McCarran-Walter Act, which substantially revised our immigration laws.

As I read, a statement leaped out at me that meant that I was not a citizen of the United States. It had to do with the maximum age a child could be to gain citizenship at the time his parents were naturalized. Unless the attorney had made a mistake, I had been too old. Cold sweat! I checked the text of the act itself. No mistake! I could remember my father sending off information about our citizenship to the Naval Academy when I won my appointment. I thought, however, it might have only been an affidavit. That would have left room for error.

I then checked the old law. I found, to my great relief, that I had indeed become a citizen under its provisions. The citizenship acquired by a young child on the naturalization of his parents is called "Derivative Citizenship." There was a grandfather clause in the new act that provided that citizenship acquired under the old law would not be lost because of the new changes.

But I could see trouble ahead. I was not a natural-born citizen. Not myself having been naturalized, I had no papers. I had no passport, all my foreign travel having been on navy orders. I could visualize the future dialogue as the immigration people questioned me on return from a trip.

"Where were you born?"

"Sydney, Australia."

"Were your parents American citizens when you were born?"

"No, but they were naturalized in 1937 before I was sixteen years old." (The immigration official at this point consults his handbook of regulations.)

"Look, mister, what are you trying to pull! You just wait in that room over there."

My concern was heightened by a newspaper report about that time. Justice Felix Frankfurter of the U.S. Supreme Court, returning from a trip abroad, had been detained in immigration on Ellis Island because of a dispute as to citizenship. He had been born in Austria and had come to the States with his family as a young boy. He, just as I, had become a derivative citizen. I thought if that could happen to a justice of the Supreme Court, something had to be done.

So I went to see the people at the Immigration Service in downtown Washington. Based on my age and the dates of my parents' naturalization, they agreed that I was a citizen. I asked for a paper to that effect. They said that I should apply for a Certificate of Citizenship, and gave me the necessary forms. The requirements were appalling. Birth and marriage documentation going back to grandparents on both sides of the family were called for. There followed a spate of letters and cables to Australia and Scotland. Some documents could not be found. Gaps had to be filled with affidavits and photocopies of notations in family Bibles. After months of frustrating effort, I got it all together and took the package to the Immigration Service. I said to the lady behind the counter, "I'd like to file an application for a Certificate of Citizenship." She said, "Fine, here are the forms you'll need to complete."

I replied, "Look, I have the forms. They're all done."

She said, "No, you don't understand. You don't just fill out forms. You have to get a lot of documents."

I said, "Will you please look. I've filled out the forms. I have attached the documents. Now I want my certificate."

She thumbed through my papers and turned with a shout toward the back of the room: "Henry, come out! Come and look! Somebody did it! Somebody finally did it!"

The editorial and management experience on the *Law Review* was invaluable. Even more so, however, was the opportunity to work on *Law Review* projects with some of the giants of the legal world. As editor-in-chief, I got to know such men as John Lord O'Brian, Dean Acheson, and Justice Robert Jackson.

I had many talks with the latter about the Nürnberg Trials. Jackson had acceded to a request from President Truman to serve as U.S. chief prosecutor at the trials. This difficult assignment was designed to enhance national and international confidence in the fairness and judicial integrity of the trials. Justice Jackson's acceptance of the task while on leave from the Supreme Court served as a model and precedent for the later assignment by President Johnson of Chief Justice Warren to head the commission that inquired into the assassination of President Kennedy.

Particularly interesting was Jackson's view of the Admiral Doenitz case. Doenitz had been head of the German submarine force during the entire war. In the final days of the Reich, after the death of Hitler in his Berlin bunker, Doenitz briefly donned the mantle of head of the German state in order to surrender to the Allies. He was convicted at Nürnberg of war crimes. These involved alleged violations of international law by submarines under his command. International protocols existed at the outset of World War II that purported to govern submarine warfare. They required a submarine to warn a noncombatant ship and remove its passengers and crew prior to sinking it. This rule is a superb example of the futility of warfare-limiting agreements that have no relation to reality. In World War II, merchant ships were armed and ready to fire on any U-boat that surfaced in the vicinity. Aircraft carriers could speed specialized antisubmarine aircraft to the area in response to radio calls. High-speed surface antisubmarine units might also be just over the horizon. The submarines had barely enough room for their own crews, let alone evacuees from another ship. The only chance for survival of a submarine in World War II was to remain undetected until the very moment of attack. Thus, the protocol rules were totally incompatible with the use of submarines. Any country that believed the rules to be effective would have to forego submarine warfare altogether. This, no belligerent having submarines was prepared or expected to do. The United States, from the beginning, conducted its own submarine warfare in precisely the same manner as did Germany, and for a very simple reason: there was no other way to do it. After reading the evidence against Doenitz, I felt that his conviction had been an injustice. Justice Jackson agreed. He stated that while it was his duty to present the evidence, he felt strongly at the end of the trial that Doenitz should be acquitted and had expressed that view to the court.

During the years of law school, in 1952 and 1953, our two children, Alex and Laurie, were born. It was a rough time for Rusty. Devoting all of my time to the law books, I was no help at all with the two infants. Our little one-bedroom house in Falls Church, so cozy for the two of us, had become unbearably crowded. Rusty's parents lived in nearby Alexandria, but a classic mother-daughter conflict only added to her burden. Navy pay, never munificent, had fallen at that time well below that earned by our civilian contemporaries. By today's standards, we were not much above the poverty level. Even with no social life, no savings, no vacations, and no eating out, my salary barely stretched from one payday to the next. Help for Rusty, then, was out of the question. It was a time of trial for both of us, but I think it was worse for her.

While at law school, I lived in fear that the navy would discover my deafness. I knew that I was not physically qualified to perform the duties of my rank at sea. I believed that if my condition came to the official attention of the Navy Bureau of Medicine and Surgery, there would be no alternative but to separate me from the navy. As a mere student, I had no specialty that could serve as the basis for a waiver. My law school career would come to an abrupt end. Our meager savings had gone into the down payment on the house in Falls Church. With a wife and two children to support, continuation of law school at my own expense would not be feasible. The only career I ever wanted, that of an officer in the United States Navy, would be lost. I could see myself at age 30, deaf, broke, and rudderless. It was a nightmare. Therefore, during the first two years of law school I didn't report for my scheduled annual physical examinations. In my last year, the record caught up with me. Judge Advocate General of the Navy Rear Admiral George Russell had been pestered about me by the Medical Department. He gave me a direct order in forthright terms, "Get your ass over to the Main Navy Dispensary *today!*"

With a dreadful feeling of doom, I obeyed. As I entered the dispensary, I ran into an old friend, Chief Petty Officer Hendricks. He had been the corpsman aboard my last submarine, the *Clamagore*. He told me that he was now on duty at the dispensary. Conventional submarines do not carry doctors. They have a chief corpsman who takes care of all medical problems when the ship is at sea. These men carry a heavy responsibility and without exception are highly competent. Chief Hendricks was the finest I had known.

He was aware that I had left the *Clamagore* because of the hearing problem, and that I had received orders to law school. He asked how I was doing, and I told him. He said, "That's great! You have obviously been able to handle this hearing thing." I said, "Yes, but now I have another problem. I have to have a physical exam, and I know that my ears won't pass. With only six months to go, this could be a disaster. If I can only graduate, I might be able, on the basis of my law school record, to convince the navy not to toss me out."

Hendricks then told me that he was the head of the physiotherapy section of the dispensary and often conducted parts of annual physical examinations. He said, "Look, I'll stick my neck out on this. I can check you off on the hearing test. You've got to promise me, though, that you'll come back right after graduation. Then I'll introduce you to Captain Delaney, who is head of the Eye, Ear, Nose and Throat Clinic here. He's a very sharp doctor and a good guy. He'll know what if anything you can do about your hearing."

So Chief Hendricks checked me off on the hearing test and I finished law school. I returned to the dispensary and was taken to Dr. Delaney. His tests confirmed that my hearing loss was caused by otoschlerosis. Delaney told me that an operation called fenestration had been developed that was often effective in cases like mine. He said that Dr. Robert King, a navy doctor on duty at the naval hospital at Bethesda, Maryland, could perform the operation. He advised me to have it done. I agreed on the spot. I asked, however, if he would delay the arrangements until after I had taken the bar exam about two or three months hence. He said, "Okay, but in the meantime take these pills." I said, "Will they help my hearing?" He answered, "No, but if anyone ever asks what the hell we've been doing about you, I want to be able to say that you're under treatment." I knew at that moment that Chief Hendricks and Dr. Delaney had been in cahoots, bless their souls.

Chief Ellis Hendricks, U.S. Navy, left the dispensary a few years later to report to the White House. There he was the therapist to President Kennedy, whose back problems required daily care.

The day after the District of Columbia bar examination, I was admitted to the naval hospital at Bethesda. The operation was performed on my left ear by Dr. King, and I lay immobile with my head between sandbags for the next ten days. The operated ear had been filled with wax and was heavily bandaged. On the tenth day, the bandages came off and the big wax plug was pulled out. A miracle! I could hear! Sound came pouring in. But my brain had lost its ability to screen out and ignore background noise. For months thereafter, the Niagara Falls sound of a toilet flushing vied with foot-steps in the hall sounding like the approach of the Russian army. The brain gradually regained its ability to discriminate, and my sense of balance returned. With about 70 percent of normal hearing restored to my left ear, and law school and the bar exam under my belt, I was ready to tackle the navy about my future career.

After my convalescence, I appeared before a medical Physical Evaluation Board. It came as no surprise when it found that I was not physically qualified to serve at sea as an unrestricted line officer. My hearing, while much improved, was still well below par. The fenestrated ear was subject to pressure and shock damage that would rule out combat assignments. I asked the board, however, if it would consider granting a waiver if I had my official navy designation changed to that of "Law Specialist." (The navy had no Judge Advocate General Corps at that time.) The board said yes and agreed to hold its final decision in abeyance. I then formally applied to the judge advocate general and the chief of naval personnel for redesignation. Another board was convened, and I was accepted as a law specialist. The doctors then granted the waiver. I was off on a new tack. The year was 1954.

6

The New Tack

Although the doctors had granted a waiver, there were strings attached. I was to remain in the Washington area on limited duty for a year. The effects of the operation were to be carefully monitored. I was therefore available for odd jobs but not a permanent assignment. One of the jobs I got was distinctly odd. I was loaned by the judge advocate general (the JAG) to the chief of naval personnel to assist in a project related to navy morale. The navy at that time was experiencing a disastrously low reenlistment rate. Less than 3 percent were signing up for a second tour. The adverse financial and career cadre effects were staggering. Everyone had a theory as to what to blame. Some said low pay, others said excessive sea duty, and still others said that the prime culprits were overly generous "GI Bill of Rights" benefits. These, they said, made it more attractive to get out and go to school on Uncle Sam than to stay in. A vocal minority insisted that the answer lay in making life more enjoyable for the wives of enlisted men.

My assignment was to work with the latter group. Their project was to expand the role of navy wives' clubs. The idea was that the clubs could make the wives happier. If the wives were happier, their husbands were more likely to reenlist. During the course of the project I met some dedicated women. It soon became apparent, however, that most women are not club women, and that the husbands of those who are were not necessarily the happiest sailors. The prospect, then, of the project having a measurable effect on the reenlistment rate was negligible.

My duties were not onerous. I had plenty of time for independent investigation and thinking about the problem. I gradually eased myself out of the project altogether, while continuing to pursue my own line of inquiry. That is the great advantage of being on loan. No one knows for sure what you're up to!

I began to talk with sailors in the navy's separation centers, who were being processed for return to civilian life. A pattern emerged. In general, these people were not leaving the navy because of attractions on the outside. Often their initially stated reasons were so couched, but further inquiry revealed more important underlying motivations. They were being pushed out of the navy, rather than pulled. They were unhappy with the treatment they had received. They had little feeling of accomplishment or worth or contribution in the navy. The more I got into it, the more interesting it became. The mens' stories over and over again involved an apparent lack of consideration by their officers. They also felt that their superior petty officers—particularly the chiefs, they said—did not seem to be trusted or respected by the officers. This perception dampened any enthusiasm they might have had to aspire to senior petty officer rank.

Speaking to junior officers who were on their way out of the navy, I saw the same pattern. They complained, for example, that they were seldom permitted to handle the ship when coming alongside the dock, the skippers being fearful of damage. Less and less authority was being delegated. It appeared that the navy, in the years following World War II, was providing steadily decreasing satisfaction to its junior members. The obvious conclusion was that there was a leadership failure in the navy, and that it stemmed from the top down. Leadership was still considered in its nebulous, inspirational context, without the war to give it substance. The top officers were working for career advancement without being measured on their ability to manage properly the people below them. There seemed to be no realization that, after all, leadership is essentially another word for management and that proper techniques can be taught and learned. There was no place on an officer's fitness report form to note his ability to manage people.

There were no leadership training programs. Finally, there were no navy directives dealing with the issue. In short, a vast area for improvement existed.

Near the end of the study, I was in Newport talking with the personnel officer of the *Yellowstone,* the flagship of Admiral Arleigh Burke. Admiral Burke was a legendary figure. He had distinguished himself in destroyer warfare in many storied engagements with the Japanese in the South Pacific. He had earned the name of "31-Knot Burke" by the speed with which he habitually closed the enemy. Shortly after my visit he became an equally legendary chief of naval operations. He held that top spot for a remarkable six years.

The personnel officer told me that I must see the admiral before I left. Admiral Burke, he said, insisted on talking with any officer from Washington who visited his command. I demurred at the description of myself as "an officer from Washington" as too grand a title, but to no avail. I found myself in the admiral's stateroom. He greeted me affably and motioned me to a leather chair. It was the damnedest thing! The front edge of the seat forced my knees up so that my feet left the floor. The arms were too smooth and wide to get a proper grip. The back of the seat was a deep pocket. After a short, futile struggle to escape, I was left in a semireclining position with my head tilted back. The admiral, a stocky man, stood close and directly in front of me. He looked down as from a great height. I have never felt so insignificant.

He said, "Well, young man, I understand you're here on some kind of project. Tell me about it."

The last thing I wanted to do was to tell that great man, from my inferior position (literally) that there was a leadership failure in the navy from the top down. He would, however, accept no evasion. I finally blurted it out.

"Bullshit!" he roared. He then gave me a stirring lecture on the *real* reasons why people were getting out of the navy. His voice thundered down as if from the heavens. My responses came back feebly from the depths of the chair as from the bottom of a deep well. In my efforts at advocacy, it was not my finest moment!

The report, however, did catch the attention of Chief of Naval Personnel Admiral James Holloway. He called me to his office to say that he thought I might have hit upon something. In any event, whether it was the report or more probably that the time of the idea had arrived, leadership began to be stressed. Within a year, efforts to improve leadership were being given top priority in the navy. Renlistment rates improved dramatically.

In the spring of 1955, my year in limbo ended. My hearing had stabilized and the doctors were satisfied. I was ready for orders to my first billet as a navy lawyer. Rusty was eager for an overseas assignment. Washington and the law school years had been hard for her. She had been tied down with two infants, born fifteen months apart. Preoccupied with my own problems, I had been incapable of giving the sympathy and support she needed. We had no social life or recreation. On weekends, my time at the desk was interrupted only to perform, with ill grace, essential chores.

Rusty was sometimes asked if that time didn't draw us even closer together. "Hell, no!" she would explode, "it almost wrecked our marriage." She was right.

As the tension slowly eased during the year of limited duty, I realized what an inconsiderate boor I had been and the extent of her forbearance. I was anxious to make amends and agreed that by all means we should leave Washington. I lobbied enthusiastically for the overseas tour she so much wanted. She was ecstatic when the JAG decided to send us to the navy command in Naples, Italy.

We both loved Naples. Rusty, as a student of medieval history and the Renaissance, was in heaven. Always exuberant in her enthusiasms, she found Italy an endless feast for the senses and the mind. She discovered a flair for the language. She delighted in the daily shopping in the markets and her walks of discovery throughout the city. Alex and Laurie, aged three and four, were lodged during the day in an Italian pre-school program. They soon became bilingual, with the ease only shared by very young children. To our amazement, the navy gave us a generous cost-of-living allowance. With that, we found we could afford a spacious and elegant apartment with balconies opening on a magnificent view over the city and the Bay of Naples. To the left was Vesuvius with its plume of volcanic steam. Out in the Bay was Capri, looking in profile like Albert the Alligator. Off to the right was Capo Possilipo with its pine trees. It was breath-taking and we never tired of it. And wonder of wonders, the extra allowance enabled us to have that supreme luxury, a full-time live-in maid! What a contrast to our cramped, austere, and penurious life in Washington!

As an introduction to the normal duties of a navy lawyer, the assignment was ideal. I, as a newly promoted lieutenant commander, was one of several lawyers in a large legal office headed by a navy captain. Our practice encompassed all of the routine legal work that one would find in a navy legal office anywhere. Our legal assistance program for service people and their families was extensive. Being in a foreign land, they had no access to other American attorneys. The scope of their problems was therefore similar to that which would be handled by a civilian law firm engaged in the general practice of law.

One of my responsibilities in Naples was particularly interesting: the legal status of our forces overseas is governed by a series of treaties with the host countries. They are called, appropriately, "Status of Forces Agreements." They deal with such matters affecting our troops as mail, taxes, and import duties. Above all, however, they cover questions of jurisdiction when our people get into trouble. Our Naples command was responsible for handling these questions for all of the U.S. forces throughout Italy. Whenever a serviceman was accused of a crime in Italy, the question arose as to whether he should be tried by court-martial or by the Italians. Although the agreement provided the basic framework for solving such problems, negotiations were often required. These I conducted with the Italians in the Ministry of Grace and Justice in Rome.

The job required a knowledge of the Italian legal system, including the workings of the judiciary. This I acquired in a crash course and through patient counseling by our gifted Italian in-house lawyer, Manlio Cicatelli.

We Americans can be very provincial with respect to the common law, our heritage from England. We tend to think all other systems are distinguished only by their varying degrees of barbarity. I confess to having had the same prejudice. I found that I was wrong. The Italian system is essentially the Cope Napoleon, or civil code, which is the system of France and Germany and to some extent Spain. There are vast differences in substance and procedure between it and the common law. The differences, however, tend to cancel each other out. In any given case, civil or criminal, the outcome is likely to be the same.

For my first major court-martial case, I was sent from Naples to the island of Malta to defend an American sailor charged with murder. What bad luck for the accused, I thought, to have as counsel one so green. In retrospect, however, my very inexperience may have helped. I was grimly determined to do the best possible job, so that neither the accused nor I would suffer from the assignment. I therefore concealed my extreme nervousness, assumed a relaxed and professional air, and got to work.

The outlook was bleak. I found on arrival in Malta that some twenty people had signed affidavits stating that they had seen my client kill the victim, another U.S. sailor, in a crowded bar. The accused had fled the scene and been apprehended by the Maltese police. During the ensuing interrogation, he confessed that he had indeed killed the victim. What was worse, he truculently asserted that he had intended to kill him, and was glad to see him dead.

I interviewed the accused in the brig, and found him hostile and uncommunicative. A black man, his attitude was that everyone was against him, and that nothing he could say would do him any good. After an effort of several days, however, I got through his shell. He then for the first time raised the issue of self-defense. He said that he saw the victim begin to pull a knife, and was sure that he would be killed unless he acted first. I asked why in the world he hadn't said anything about that to the Maltese authorities. He said that when they caught him, he was still mad as hell, and was sure in any event that he would not be believed.

I told him then that he should plead not guilty, and that I would do what I could for him. His prospects were dismal, however, unless we could find at least one credible witness who could substantiate his story. He then told me of a white chief petty officer who had been seated at the same table, who *should* have been able to see the victim begin to draw a knife. Unfortunately, though, the chief had been transferred back to the States shortly after the incident. I reached him on the telephone at his new duty station in Orlando, Florida. He said that he had had a lot to drink, and that there had been a confused melee, but that he had a very strong impression that the deceased had indeed wielded a knife. I then started the machinery to get him sent back to Malta as a witness. There was now a glimmer of hope.

There remained, however, one huge problem: When the accused was captured, he was taken before the chief inspector of Malta, whose name was Federico Bencini. Inspector Bencini, tall and dignified, was Oxford-educated and extremely impressive. He looked and spoke almost exactly like the actor Basil Rathbone playing the part of Sherlock Homes. He had conducted the interrogation, obtained the confession, and was convinced that my client was one of the worst criminals ever to have set foot on the island of Malta. His attitude was so positive and his presence so commanding that I knew his testimony at trial would completely overshadow the defense case, which at best was scarcely overwhelming.

The confession itself was not so much the problem: that could be explained. It was Inspector Bencini who would doom my client.

I then began to think about the British Visiting Forces Act. I had become familiar with this legislation while studying the Status of Forces Agreements. It was an act of Parliament under which the British (and the then-British colony of Malta) could waive jurisdiction in favor of court-martial by visiting forces, where a crime involving only persons or property of those forces was involved. That was the situation here. In practice, the Maltese invariably waived jurisdiction in such cases. Since trial by a U.S. court-martial rather than by a Maltese court was therefore inevitable, I reasoned that any interrogation by the Maltese was in effect as an agent for the American military. That being so, the Miranda-like warnings required under the Uniform Code of Military Justice should have been given. Of course they were not, so I argued that the confession should be excluded. The court accepted that reasoning. Inspector Bencini, baffled and disgusted, was not permitted to testify. I had come to like and admire him, and I regretted that I was unable to explain to his satisfaction the reason I had so objected to him as a witness. He was also unable to grasp the reasoning by which an uncoerced confession, in U.S. law, should be excluded because of the absence of what he viewed as a ritualistic warning.

My client took the stand, and stood up well to cross-examination. The chief was the best kind of witness. Patently sincere, he avoided overstatement and doggedly stuck to his version of the fatal scene. There was, of course, a parade of prosecution witnesses who testified that they didn't see the victim draw a knife. In the end, the accused was acquitted.

Was he guilty? I don't know. The case exemplifies the concept of reasonable doubt. From that experience, I don't have to rely on legal theory to answer the oft-asked question, "How can you lawyers justify defending some guilty bastard and getting him off on a technicality?" The easy answer invokes the presumption of innocence. More to my satisfaction, however, is the impossibility of knowing for sure, beforehand, that the man is indeed guilty, even when he himself thinks he may be.

But in my heart I know there is another side of the picture that is not so good: the acquittal gave me intense satisfaction. I had accomplished the seemingly impossible! But the vice is that it was a personal triumph. That it may also have been a victory for justice was secondary. Therein lies a weakness in our adversary court system. The trials are games—deadly serious games, but games nonetheless. Lawyers are the players and judges the referees. Thus, the outcomes often depend on the skill, ingenuity, and dedication of the attorneys. It is up to opposing counsel to bring out all of the facts, with the judge merely seeing that neither side takes improper advantage of the other.

In the Civil Law countries, i.e., those with systems based on the Napoleonic Code, the lawyers play a far less decisive role. There the judges are responsible to see that justice is done.

Each system has its strengths and weaknesses. In criminal law, I would vote for ours, primarily because it is less susceptible to governmental intervention and abuse. In civil cases, particularly in the tort field, I feel otherwise. There the dice are loaded in favor of the plaintiffs' bar. Class actions and contingency fees have made a small group of rapacious lawyers enormously rich, while tending to impoverish the public through disastrous increases in insurance rates. I think serious consideration should be given to taking tort cases—auto accident and malpractice suits, for example—out of the courts entirely, and placed in the hands of administrative tribunals. That game should no longer be played for the benefit of the lawyers!

O.K., now that that's off my chest, back to Naples.

Naples itself is not notably a tourist city. It is, however, a way-station for those bound for nearby Capri, Pompeii, or the Amalfi coast. We therefore had many visitors. One of these was particularly memorable: One night I was the duty officer at our headquarters on the Via Medina in the center of Naples. The shore patrol officer called and asked to be excused from his duty. His wife was having a baby and he wished to be at the hospital. I told him to go ahead, and to advise his assistant, a chief petty officer, to call me if anything unusual occurred.

The chief called a while later and said that a Captain Harlfinger had telephoned from the Royal Hotel. The captain had asked that the shore patrol officer come to the hotel. He had given a room number, but had declined to give a reason for the request. I told the chief that I would take care of it. I had worked for Commander Fritz Harlfinger several years before in Key West, when I was a submarine division engineer. I was sure this had to be the same officer. How many Harlfingers can there be in the navy? I thought it would be fun to surprise him.

I went to the Royal Hotel and knocked at the specified room. Sure enough, the door was opened by my old boss, Fritz Harlfinger. But he didn't seem at all pleased to see me. Obviously flustered, he mumbled something about getting in touch with me the following morning. Clearly, he wanted me to leave at once. Just then, however, the door was wrenched wide open by a tall, thin, naked gentleman with flowing white hair and a drink in his hand. He had plainly just stepped from a shower. And he was plainly drunk. I recognized him from pictures as a well-known congressman, a ranking member of one of the most important congressional committees. "Is this the shore patrol officer, Fritz?" he said, "Where are the women? Where are the women?"

Harlfinger answered that I was not the shore patrol officer but an old friend. Then came an astonishing transformation. The naked, staggering drunk suddenly became the smooth and confident politician. With hand outstretched, he spoke clearly in a mellow southern accent, "Come in, young man, come right on in! You from the South? No? Washington State, eh? Well fine! Come on in and have a drink!"

I soon learned the whole story. The congressman was well known to be a heavy drinker if not an alcoholic. In Washington, however, he generally stayed on the wagon. Once a year, though, he made an overseas tour, ostensibly to visit U.S. military installations. On those trips he more than made up for his abstemious Washington behavior. The unfortunate military officer assigned as his escort on those sprees had his hands full. His Herculean chore was to keep the congressman out of jail and his name out of the newspapers.

On this particular junket through Europe, his escort officer had suffered a heart attack in Vienna and had died. Captain Harlfinger was at that time the U.S. naval attaché in Bonn, Germany. He had been pressed into service for the remainder of the tour. The congressman had learned that shore patrol officers always had a professional knowledge of the whereabouts of local prostitutes. Hence, at his insistence Harlfinger had made the call that brought me to the Royal Hotel that night. And hence the captain's chagrin at being confronted, during this embarrassing episode, by an old submarine force associate. In my later years in the Pentagon, I frequently encountered Admiral Harlfinger. Neither of us, however, ever mentioned Naples, the congressman, or the special expertise of shore patrol officers.

During my tour in Naples, I observed an interesting point relating to the overseas assignment of U.S. personnel: The navy gave preference to those of Italian ancestry who requested assignment to Italy. The idea was that those with Italian names, or who had spoken Italian in their homes, would make the best people-to-people ambassadors. A great many second- and third-generation Italian-Americans were sent to Italy under this policy. The trouble is, it didn't work. While the rest of us were charmed by the exuberance and joie de vivre of the Italians, these people were embarrassed. They felt personally demeaned when the Italians, with insouciance, peed by the roadside or spoke loudly in church. We could be amused by the artful knavery of the Neapolitans, at least when we were not the immediate victims. The second-generation Italians, however, were shocked and appalled. With rare exception, they came to hate their assignment. Anxious to set themselves apart from the local people, they became arrogant and hostile. They were the worst possible representatives of the U.S. They were intensely disliked by the indigenous Italians. Thus, the benign and superficially logical navy policy was a dismal failure. There is a lesson here for American agencies that have programs in other countries. Too close an identification of the American representatives with the people of those countries can backfire.

Of all the Italians, the Neapolitans are a breed apart. Even other Italians find them impossible to deal with, yet endlessly fascinating. They live for the moment. Short-term benefit is always grasped at the expense of long-term advantage. Talented musicians, peerless bargainers, and charming rascals, they have been conquered by everyone. First came the Etruscans, who were followed by the Carthaginians. Then there were the Greeks, and afterward the Romans. The Moors and the Normans had their turn, as did the French, British, and Germans. There were others whom I have forgotten. The Americans were the most recent. The Neapolitan long ago gave up any idea that he could provide securely for the future. He had to enjoy what he had for today. Anything left could be taken away tomorrow. But he became adept at conquering the conquerors. He would crawl from the rubble, brush himself off, and patch together a presentable suit. Then, approaching the new ruler with a respectful air and an ingratiating smile, he would make a beguiling proposal too good to refuse. Without ever knowing how it happened, the victor would all too soon find himself working to the benefit of the vanquished.

There is no way to get the better of a Neapolitan. You can only do business on his terms. You may think your superior economic position will permit you to force him to do business your way. It won't work. Here's an example: You decide to have a chest of drawers made. You find a *falegname,* a cabinetmaker, and you show him a drawing. He says he can do it and proudly shows you examples of his work. Then because you are an American, you ask, "How much will it cost?"

He replies, "When I am finished, you will like it and you will pay me what you like."

You say that you can't do business that way. You must know the price. You tell him that you are not a rich man and have a limited budget. He does not believe you.

He insists, "You'll be very happy. You need only pay me what you think it's worth."

You persist until he sees that there is no alternative to the acceptance of the job on a fixed-price basis. He reluctantly agrees, and the price is negotiated. You make a partial payment to enable him to acquire materials to commence the job. Congratulations! You have won. But then you find that your project never gets done. It always takes precedence behind the jobs of his other clients who have agreed to his terms. With them, his reward is uncertain. He does his best work, and he hopes for a windfall. In his mind, there is no limit to the possible largesse of his customer. He lives on hope. When you deprive him of that, he loses all joy in the work. When he knows what he will receive, it is spent in advance. After that, there is only drudgery. So he concentrates entirely on the work for his other clients, from whom he dreams of splendid compensation. You make countless visits and nothing is done. There are always excuses. You finally demand you money back. He doesn't have it. He has spent it for your materials, but they have not yet been delivered. You threaten to call the police. He completes the job. It's terrible. You refuse to pay the balance. *He* threatens to call the police. There is much shouting, and his friends, family, and neighbors crowd around. There is an ugly scene. You pay. You lose.

Neapolitan street urchins are adept at sneak-thievery. It is a fortunate traveler who passes through Naples on his way to Capri, Sorrento, or Pompeii who doesn't lose something. More than one American sailor has been seen streaking stark naked across the Piazza Publico in the early morning hours in a frantic attempt to reach the fleet landing before his condition is illuminated by daylight. The urchins have picked him clean, even to his shoes, as he lay passed out from too much vino in a Naples alley.

While I served in Italy in the mid-fifties, there were virtually no crimes of violence by Italians, other than those of passion. Although there was extreme poverty, particularly in the south, one could walk without fear of bodily harm in any quarter of the cities, during day or night. Wives could wander alone through the warren-like alleys of Napoli, confident that they would never be molested. There were, on the other hand, many instances of American servicemen assaulting and injuring Italians. Taxi drivers and prostitutes were frequent victims. Not one incident of the reverse came to my attention.

One comes to realize that there is no real correlation between poverty and crime, particularly violent crime. Even the sneak thievery was more the product of Neapolitan tradition than poverty, since it was not prevalent in other cities that were equally poor. As Italians have become more affluent in recent years, incidents of violence have become more common. During the four years we recently spent cruising the Mediterranean in our sailboat, we heard complaints from local people in many countries about the rise in crime. We are saddened and disturbed, however, to have to admit that our beloved country, the richest in the world, is plagued by crime worse than in any country we have visited. Those who make the facile assumption that violent crime is a product of poverty have never traveled abroad, or having traveled, have been blind to what is there to see.

Occasionally, the misdeeds of an American would become a *cause célèbre*. In such a case, I had to involve our embassy in Rome. My dealings were generally at the chargé d'affaires level. Our ambassador then was Clare Booth Luce. I can recall only one meeting at which she briefly appeared. She did, however, figure prominently in a drama affecting our Naples command. Mrs. Luce was then suffering from an undiagnosed but debilitating malady. She had lost weight and was tired and listless. For a lady of such normally boundless energy, this was intolerable. The U.S. Navy doctors from our command in Naples were called in. They visited her in the ornate Renaissance palazzo in Rome that served as the official residence of the American ambassador. They concluded that she had arsenic poisoning. The arsenic was believed to be flaking down from the ancient paint on the ornate frescoes that decorated the ceiling above her bed. The ambassador was flown to the naval hospital at Bethesda, Maryland, for treatment.

Her husband, Henry Luce, was the long-time president of Time-Life Corporation. *Time* magazine accordingly gave the bizarre story prominent play. A short time later, however, *Time*'s competitor, *Newsweek*, debunked the story. *Newsweek*, purporting to rely on leaked information from navy doctors at Bethesda, reported that the ambassador was merely anaemic. The Luces were made to look foolish. Jokes appeared everywhere about "Arsenic and Old Luce."

While all of this was going on, *Time*'s Rome bureau reporter, George DeCavalho, was independently writing a story about the

U.S. Naval Command in Naples. He had received the cooperation of my good friend, Jim Jenkins, the command's public information officer. Jim, who later served with me in the office of the secretary of the navy, had spent a congenial day or two with DeCavalho, showing him around. When his article appeared in *Time,* it held the Naples command up to ridicule. It implied that the command was a boondoggle existing only to provide recreation and soft living for its members. Jim was shocked. The viciousness of the article made it a devastating professional blow. He called DeCavalho for an explanation, "How could you have done this?" The *Time* man responded that the article, when first submitted to New York, had been rather mild, with only a dash of *Time*'s habitual cockiness. It had been returned twice with instructions to make it nastier.

Jim Jenkins was convinced that our command, whose doctors had started the whole mess, was the victim of the vengeance of Henry Luce.

My tour in Naples convinced me that I should try in the future to avoid working for other lawyers. I would seek assignments in which I would report directly to the commanding officer. I found it tedious and often frustrating to have to work upward through a legal office hierarchy to get one's advice to the client. Furthermore, I concluded that in any given legal hierarchy, the odds were very good that at least one of the lawyers would be insufferable. There is, unfortunately, a large minority of members of the bar who believe that being a lawyer in and of itself confers on one an exalted status. They believe themselves to be entitled *as lawyers* to be treated with respect if not awe. In the main, they are pompous asses. They have created a prototype most damaging to the majority of lawyers who take themselves much less seriously.

The top lawyer in Naples, whom I shall call Captain Harry O'Toole, was a certified member of the offensive minority. From an event of many years later, it appears that he persevered in that capacity. In order to tell the story, I have preserved for him a measure of anonymity. At least ten years after leaving Naples, I had my next contact with Captain O'Toole. I was at the time the special counsel to the secretary of the navy in the Pentagon. Harry O'Toole called me on the telephone from the West Coast.

"Andy," he said, "I heard you were in the secretary's office. I need some advice."

"Sure, Harry," I replied, "How can I help you?"

"Well, I've got a problem with the Physical Disability Review Board."

"Just a minute, Harry," I interrupted, "appeals from that board come to the secretary of the navy. As his counsel, I get involved in that process. So I'd better not talk with you about your case."

"I understand," said O'Toole, "but all I want is advice as to the name of a lawyer in Washington who specializes in disability cases. I'm being retired in a disability status, and I disagree with the board as to the degree of my disability."

I should here point out that the amount of disability, commonly expressed as a percentage, can have an important bearing on one's post-retirement income. This is particularly true with respect to taxation of that income.

"Yes," continued Harry, "the board says I'm 20 percent disabled, and I'm sure that I'm at least 80 percent disabled."

"I'm sorry to hear that, Harry," I said, "but I could help you more if you could give me a clue as to the kind of disability."

"Hmm, well, yes, I can see that," he said with obvious reluctance. "Well, O.K., I'm being retired because of senility."

"Wait a minute, Harry," I said, "I want to be sure that I have this straight. Are you claiming that you're *more* senile than the board thinks you are?"

"Yes, indeed," said Captain O'Toole, "and can you imagine the impertinence of those doctors to question the considered judgment of a four-stripe navy lawyer!"

Our two years in Italy came to an end in the summer of 1957. Harry O'Toole notwithstanding, they were good, healing years. Hardly a scar from the law school days remained. Now we returned to Hawaii where I was to serve as the lawyer for the commander of the Pacific Fleet Submarine Force. It was a dream assignment for one who was still a submariner at heart. I knew the language. I was back with old friends. My fellow staff members were superb professionals for whom I had the greatest respect.

We found a house near the beach in Lanikai, on the windward side of the island of Oahu, and I drove to Pearl Harbor each day with another staff member, Commander Bill Heronemus. Bill, a serious man whose habitual solemnity approached lugubriousness, was a brilliant engineer. Taking nothing on faith, he searched endlessly for a better way to do things.

A submarine engineering specialist, Bill had been involved in the early experimental use of the polyester resins and polyurethane foams in the construction of submarine superstructures. He knew about as much as there was to know of those new and exotic substances, which were just then beginning to have wide application.

One day as we drove together over the Nuuanu Pali—that was before there was a tunnel—Bill mused that there had to be a better way to build surfboards. I was surprised that Bill was interested in surfboards. I shouldn't have been. Bill was interested in almost everything.

At that time, all surfboards were carved from balsa wood. They were then wrapped by hand with resin-impregnated fiberglass. Bill said that this was all wrong from a hydrodynamic, economic, and industrial viewpoint. The boards, he said, should be much lighter. They should therefore have cores made of the new polyurethane foam. An added advantage was that the foam, unlike balsa, would not absorb water if the board's skin were nicked. He said also that he could visualize a vacuum lay-up process whereby the skin could be formed inside a mold, with the foaming resin then poured in to expand and fill the cavity. Then, voila! A bright and shiny completed surfboard would be popped from the mold, needing only the skeg to be attached. And the cost would be peanuts compared to the then-current price of boards.

Bill suggested that for a few hundred dollars we could buy a good surfboard to use to construct the mold, together with the necessary tools and raw materials. He asked if I would join him in perfecting the process and producing a prototype. Visualizing the capture of the world surfboard market, with Heronemus and Kerr the first surfboard tycoons, I agreed enthusiastically to join him in the venture. We pooled our cash, bought a board and the other necessities, and began working in Bill's garage at night and on weekends.

Bill wrote to fiberglass and resin manufacturers such as Owens-Corning, describing in carefully guarded terms what we wanted their materials to do. To keep secret our real goal, he wrote that we had in mind producing insulation panels about 10 feet long, so many inches thick, and so many feet wide. He also described the process we intended to use. The replies were uniformly encouraging. "Yes," wrote the suppliers, "our product is just what you need."

Well, everything went wrong. For example, the mold release agents didn't work, and the skin stuck to the mold. There was no adhesion between the foam and the skin. The foam never did behave as it should: it was supposed to expand and fill the cavity at a uniform density. It would, however, end up as dense and hard as a rock at the bottom, with nothing but air at the top. We tried everything. An entire year went by with endless failure and frustration.

The more failures we met, the more Bill was determined to succeed. He felt that his reputation as an engineer was at stake. "I *know* this is the right way to build surfboards," he would say. "We can't give up. There's got to be a way to make these materials work."

My reputation as a lawyer was not at all at stake. I only continued because I hated to let Bill down. My home life was taking a hell of a beating. Rusty had long since lost all patience with the project. When I wasn't at work at Submarine Headquarters, I was in Bill's garage. We were pouring money we could ill afford into what had become a bottomless pit. So at last I quit, telling Bill he could keep my share of the investment. Bill, salvaging something of his self-respect, finally devised a means to produce foam slugs, which he sold to surfboard makers. He was never able to produce a complete board by the process he had envisaged.

Later we found that we were simply ahead of the state of the art. There were temperature, pressure, and humidity constraints unknown at the time. Manufacturing and quality control processes for production of the resins themselves were later improved, so that the materials became more predictable in their behavior. Sophisticated devices for the measurement, mixing, and application of the materials were later developed. Thus, within a few years of our fiasco, every surfboard in the world was produced almost precisely as Bill had foreseen.

Bill Heronemus is now a respected professor of engineering at the University of Massachusetts at Amherst. He is also one of the world's greatest authorities on windmills. I hope that Bill will forgive me if I observe that he always did have a strong quixotic streak in his character!

The loss of a submarine, the *Stickleback*, was the most devastating event to involve the submarine force during my tour with the Pacific Submarine Command. And in no other case were both my experience as a submariner and my training as a lawyer called so fortuitously into play.

The U.S. submarine *Stickleback* sank after colliding with the destroyer escort *Silverstein*. The two ships had been engaged in a training exercise in the submarine operating area south of Pearl Harbor. My Naval Academy classmate, Lieutenant Commander Quinley (Dutch) Schulz was skipper of the *Stickleback* at the time.

I served as his counsel during the formal investigation into the loss of his ship.

During the exercise, the *Stickleback* had been operating submerged. She was struck and sunk after she popped unexpectedly to the surface—i.e. "broached"—directly in front of the destroyer. The latter, it was generally agreed, had no chance to avoid the collision.

The *Honolulu-Argonaut* collision was a classic example of a disaster resulting from a concatenation of relatively minor incidents. The *Stickleback* case exemplified the much rarer situation in which a single decisive event places the fate of the vessel in the lap of the gods, beyond the reach of any purposeful redeeming human action.

The sequence of events that preceded the broaching of the *Stickleback* was as follows: Her commanding officer had ordered the ship's speed increased to the maximum. To accomplish this, the two electricians (controllermen) who controlled the submarine's two main propulsion motors had to shift from parallel operation of the main batteries to the series mode. Inasmuch as this suddenly doubled the voltage to the main motors, the shift had to be accomplished with great precision. Otherwise, an unmanageable surge of current could result. One of the two controllermen was performing the operation for the first time, under the tutelage of an experienced electrician's mate. At a critical point in the evolution, the controllermen had to simultaneously increase the field current in their respective motors. Although the trainee had observed the operation several times, and was being coached, he inexplicably turned his rheostat the wrong way, thus *decreasing* the field. The supervising electrician immediately saw the error, and reached for the rheostat. But the damage was already done. The resultant current surge kicked open the main circuit breakers, causing a total loss of all power throughout the ship. The lights went out and all auxiliary machinery stopped. As the diving planes happened to be in the down position when power was lost, the ship rapidly took a large down angle and plunged toward its test depth. When power was lost, the captain ordered the ship's control systems shifted to the hand-operated mode. This takes time, however, and since the submarine was dangerously increasing its depth, he ordered its ballast tanks to be blown. This stopped the downward plunge, but caused the *Stickleback* to broach. She was immediately thereafter struck broadside by the *Silverstein*.

The captain of the destroyer, Commander Charles Shuford Swift, acted with remarkable coolness. Realizing the catastrophic damage the collision had caused the submarine, he did not back clear, as would have been a normal instinct. He kept the bow of the *Silverstein* partially plugging the mortal wound in the *Stickleback*'s side, going ahead slowly to maintain that position. This gave time to evacuate the submarine crew from the ruptured and rapidly flooding compartments with no loss of life. Efforts to control the flooding and later to take the stricken submarine under tow, however, were unsuccessful. She sank in 3,000 fathoms of water south of Oahu.

The loss caused consternation at the Pacific Submarine Headquarters. Speculation was rife as to what Dutch Schulz did or should have done. I did not join in the speculation. I thought I knew.

Seven years before, I had reported as chief engineer of the Key West-based submarine *Clamagore*. She was then undergoing extensive modifications to her electrical propulsion system at the Philadelphia Navy Yard.

After our arrival back at Key West, the day came to test the new installation by shifting the batteries from the parallel to the series mode. I stood behind the controllermen to observe the procedure. Everything went smoothly. The speed was built up and the field current increased with the two controllermen acting in perfect concert. Then the big lever was thrown to make the shift from the parallel to the series mode. Wham! The lights went out, the motors stopped, and we took a big down angle. I then heard the tanks being blown, and we were on the surface. We had broached. Fortunately we were operating all alone. There were no other ships in the vicinity.

The commanding officer was furious. Summoning me to the bridge, he demanded to know what we had done wrong. "Nothing, Captain," I responded. "The shift was going like clockwork. Before the lights went out, all of the meters showed readings within normal limits, as far as I could tell." "Well," he said, "let's try again, and this time, for God's sake, do it right!"

I returned to the maneuvering room and said to the two controllermen, "The captain wants us to try again. It seemed to me that you guys did it perfectly. If the breakers trip again, though, let's see if we can remember the exact readings on the meters." We then decided which meters each of us would particularly watch.

The same thing happened! But this time, the stern planes happened to be on rise rather than dive. We immediately broached because of the consequent large up-angle and the speed of the boat.

The commanding officer called me to his cabin. With barely

controlled fury, he said we should wait until the next day to try again. "But tomorrow," he said, "I'll have the squadron engineer ride with us. He'll show you guys how to do it!" In vain I protested that we had not made a mistake, and that there had to be something wrong with the installation.

I have spoken before of my unhappiness while in the *Clamagore*. This incident illustrates the captain's habitual attitude: find someone aboard to blame for every unfavorable occurrence. To add to my bafflement and misery, I knew that even eventual vindication, should it come, would have its dark side. The captain did not react well to being proven wrong.

The next day, the squadron engineer was aboard with us in the maneuvering room, standing behind the controllermen. Again the circuit breakers tripped out. As in the first instance, the planes happened to be on dive. Consequently we took a large down-angle, rapidly increased depth, blew the tanks to save the boat, and broached. In both the second and third attempts, even though everyone was standing by for a possible loss of power, with emergency lights already on, it proved impossible to control the submarine and prevent a broach.

The squadron engineer and I drafted a message to the Navy Bureau of Ships, describing the problem. In a few days, the bureau responded: We were not to make any further attempt to operate in series. Tests had revealed that the circuit breakers, which had been supplied by a new manufacturer, were defective. They were designed to trip at too low a figure. They would be removed from the *Clamagore* and replaced by breakers of the proper design.

The cause of the loss of power on the *Stickleback* was, of course, different: a rheostat had been turned the wrong way rather than it being the fault of defective circuit breakers. But the effect was precisely the same. Thus I knew from experience that under the circumstances, Dutch Schulz could not have prevented the *Stickleback* from broaching.

The Board of Investigation found that the loss of power was not due to the negligence of anyone, including the trainee controllerman. The *Stickleback*'s training program and the precautions taken were held to be adequate. The momentary lapse of the controllerman was found to be a regrettable, but unforeseeable, accident for which punishment would be inappropriate. These findings were reached fairly quickly.

The inquiry into the actions taken by the commanding officer after the power loss, however, took much longer. None of the submarine officers comprising the board had experienced the consequences of a loss of power such as that encountered on the *Stickleback*. My *Clamagore* experience therefore proved invaluable to me in the conduct of Dutch Schulz's defense. In the end, the board exonerated him from all responsibility for the collision and loss of the ship.

There was, however, powerful opposition to the board's conclusions within the staff of Rear Admiral E.W. Grenfell, the commander of the Pacific Submarine Force. The naval tradition of near-absolute responsibility of a commanding officer is very strong. There are many senior officers who feel in their bones that a captain who loses his ship must have done *something* wrong for which he should be professionally punished. Those who have successfully completed tours in command at sea are particularly prone to this attitude. To them, the idea that the captain of a lost ship could go on unscathed in his naval career is anathema.

In the end, Grenfell approved the findings of the Board of Investigation. He concluded that Dutch Schulz was powerless to affect the final outcome—that the fate of the *Stickleback* was indeed in the lap of the gods from the moment the circuit breakers tripped.

Lieutenant Commander Schulz, whose career was saved by Grenfell's decision, went on to command another submarine. After a successful navy career, he eventually retired with the four gold stripes of a navy captain.

Rear Admiral Elton W. "Joe" Grenfell was the first officer of flag rank for whom I worked directly. Known as "Jumping Joe" for his unflagging energy, I learned from him something about the traits that can propel an individual to high position.

Grenfell's ego was enormous. I remember once we were planning a staff picnic. The admiral had decreed the time and place and had named an officer to make the arrangements. The officer made the mistake of asking for alternate instructions in case of rain. Grenfell stared at him coldly. "It won't rain!" he said. It was clear that he viewed the unfortunate officer's request as a direct challenge to his authority. The inference was unmistakable: "If I say we'll have a picnic at 3:00 P.M. next Saturday at the officers beach at Barber's Point, how dare you suggest that it might rain!"

He hated to lose and delighted in direct combat. During World War II he had made a splendid record in war patrols while in command of the submarine *Gudgeon*. This same aggressive spirit was manifested by his obsessive desire to field winning SubPac athletic teams. He would scheme and connive to have promising athletes ordered to his command, badger the coaches incessantly, and attend all the games. He would scream abuse at referees and umpires whose calls were adverse to SubPac teams. More than once he had to be physically restrained from assaulting such officials.

Fiercely ambitious, he loved the limelight and was adroit at maneuvering for press coverage. He hated to be upstaged. He considered himself the embodiment of the spirit of submarines and would brook no equal in that field. He thus viewed his opposite number, the commander of the Atlantic Submarine Force at New London, with unconcealed contempt. He was immensely gratified when later he was promoted to vice admiral and was appointed to the newly created super-submarine command at Norfolk: the New London admiral then became his subordinate.

His insistence on the role of "Mr. Submarine" accounted partly for his attitude toward Admiral Rickover, whom he detested. Rickover, of course, was at the time outshining most of the admirals of the navy. It was particularly galling to Grenfell, though, to be upstaged in the area he had staked out as his exclusive domain—submarines. His antipathy toward Rickover, however, did not extend to Rickover's people or their accomplishments. For example, he liked and admired commander Bill Anderson, skipper of the first nuclear submarine, the *Nautilus*. He spent many hours working with Anderson prior to the departure of the *Nautilus* from Pearl Harbor on its historic voyage under the ice at the North Pole, and exulted in its triumph.

No intellectual, he was probably not even above average in intelligence. He was, however, a shrewd judge of people and surrounded himself with exceptionally able assistants. He was tenaciously loyal to those he had personally selected. For all of his flamboyant forays and diversions, he was devoted to one overriding passion—the selection, training, and management of people. And in that area he was superb.

Thus, in Jumping Joe Grenfell I saw that drive, ambition, ego, and commitment to goals can far overshadow intellect in the pursuit of power. And for all his maddening quirks, the Submarine Force was the better for having had him around.

7

Dipping a Toe
in the Pentagon Pool

After three years on the submarine staff, I was ordered in 1960 to the judge advocate general's office in the Pentagon. En route, however, I was to attend the six month's course at the Armed Forces Staff College in Norfolk, Virginia. There I was introduced for the first time to the thinking of army and air force officers concerning conventional warfare.

I discovered that only the navy thought of itself as performing a supporting role. The navy believes that its mission is to keep the sea lanes open for our own use and to deny them to the enemy. This is not an end in itself. With control of the seas, our armies and those of our allies can be transported and supplied, and our own supplies of raw materials are not interrupted. Few naval officers believe that an enemy can be strangled into submission through sea power alone.

The air force believes in "Victory though Airpower." In its view, the navy exists to keep its supply lines open. The army's job is to guard its airfields against ground attack and to seize the air bases of the enemy. The first task of the air force is to achieve air supremacy by destroying the air power of the enemy. Then the enemy is to be pounded into submission from the air.

The army believes passionately that victory is only to be gained by the man on the ground. Men must occupy the real estate of the enemy. All other forces play a subordinate part to this role. This leads the army to regard the principle of unity of command as sacred. Of course, the man at the top must be an army officer.

The foregoing is vastly simplified. It can, however, be used to predict with surprising accuracy the positions that will be taken by each of the services in any given strategic or organizational dispute. I must also emphasize that the discussion applies only to conventional warfare. One does not speak of victory in nuclear warfare; the proper word there is deterrence.

I also found that as staff officers, the army officers excelled. The navy and air force were badly outclassed. There is a simple reason for this. Naval officers, in peacetime, continue to sail their ships. Air force officers fly their planes. Army officers go to school. The navy and air force can continue to train under simulated, but fairly realistic, wartime conditions. The army's ability in this respect is extremely limited. In peace, therefore, the army trains in the classroom. Its officers become superb at staff studies and the making of presentations. Give them a pointer, an easel, and an array of charts and graphs, and they can't be beaten. The good students advance in rank, and the brightest advance the fastest. Alexander Haig, whom I knew in the Pentagon as an aide to Secretary McNamara, was a product of this system.

Prior to the end of the course at the Staff College, I received a call from Rear Admiral Roy Benson from Pearl Harbor. He had taken over command of the Pacific Submarine Force from Grenfell. He said that there had been a disastrous fire aboard the nuclear submarine *Sargo* at the Pearl Harbor Submarine Base. Could I come immediately to Pearl Harbor to act as defense counsel to Captain Bill Parham, the skipper of the base?

In the years to come, I learned to expect such calls. Chance had made me the only law specialist in the navy who was also a qualified submariner. This combination was deemed advantageous by those caught up in the proceedings that normally follow submarine disasters.

I arrived in Hawaii to find that the board investigation had been in progress for several days, but had adjourned to await my arrival. A review of the record of the proceedings to that point revealed why Captain Parham had, just prior to the adjournment, been declared by the board to be an "interested party." An "interested party" is one whose career could be affected by the outcome of the investigation. As such, he is entitled to be represented by counsel.

The evidence already adduced showed that the *Sargo* had been at a Submarine Base dock on the evening of the accident. Her oxygen banks were being charged from a portable charging rig that had been supplied by the base. Nuclear submarines need to carry a plentiful supply of oxygen because their nuclear propulsion enables them to operate completely submerged for long periods. They thus do not need to come to the surface as do conventional submarines, which have to come up to charge their batteries. But while conventional submarines can replenish their air supply during their periodic visits to the surface, the nuclear subs must replenish the air breathed by the crew from the oxygen supply carried aboard in tanks.

The charging of the *Sargo*'s forward bank of tanks had been completed without incident. The Submarine Base chief petty officer in charge of the rig then moved it along the dock so that the charging hose could reach the aft group of tanks. The hose ran from the rig down through the *Sargo*'s after torpedo room hatch to the charging manifold in the torpedo room.

Shortly after the charging operation was resumed, the chief noticed frost appearing on the charging hose, indicating an abnormally low temperature. He shut down the rig and called for a base electrician to check its controls. He was told that it would be several hours before a qualified man would be available. There was a degree of urgency in the charging operation because the *Sargo* was due to depart early the next morning for a lengthy deployment to the Western Pacific. A few hours delay in charging would delay its departure. *Sargo* people expressed their impatience to the chief. He therefore decided to see what he could do on his own. He made a small change in the electrical connection in the control box, and restarted the rig. Everything seemed O.K. so he resumed the pumping operation. Only in retrospect was it determined that the chief's small alteration had resulted in the deactivation of two important safety features—the low temperature and high over-pressure cutouts. Unaware of this, he continued to pump oxygen to the *Sargo*'s tanks, watching as the pressure slowly approached the required limit of 3,000 pounds per square inch. Suddenly, however, flames began to shoot out of the after battery hatch. The charging hose, itself afire, snaked out of the hatch and whipped wildly about and broke off before the rig's pump could be stopped.

At the charging manifold aboard the *Sargo,* oxygen at nearly 3,000 psi was flowing unchecked from her tanks into the after torpedo room, feeding a fire that apparently started when the hose broke. With this enormous quantity of pure oxygen, everything even slightly flammable was burned. The heat was intense. Even torpedo warheads were melted, and their explosive cargo (torpex) was later found strewn about in charred chunks. That it failed to explode seems a miracle.

The *Sargo* petty officer on duty at the manifold had insisted on keeping closed the watertight door leading forward from the torpedo room. Several times during the charging operation he had refused requests from shipmates to open the door to give them access to their bunks or lockers. His adherence to this safety precaution prevented the fire from spreading immediately to the rest of the submarine. It also precluded any chance of his own escape. He was burned to death. A roaring tower of flame like a great blow torch shot into the sky from the *Sargo*'s after torpedo-room hatch. While the remainder of the submarine had been given a temporary reprieve by the closed torpedo room door, it might only be a matter of minutes until the frightful heat ignited something on the other side: The door itself was already glowing cherry red. The reactor compartment would be in line to go.

The *Sargo* duty officer quickly took the only action that could save the boat. He ordered all other hatches shut, then the immediate flooding of the submarine's ballast tanks. In effect, he dove the submarine at the dock. Sea water then rushed into and completely flooded the after torpedo room through its open hatch, extinguishing the fire.

With these facts established, the board believed the cause of the fire to have been the unwitting deactivation of the rig's safety features by the chief. They reasoned that this must have resulted in damage to the hose, thus causing its failure and the ensuing fire. There seemed no other possible explanation.

The inquiry did not stop with the determination of the chief's mistake. As in all such cases, the "why" is examined from every angle. How qualified was the chief? Who assigned him to the rig, and on what basis? Should he have been supervised? What were his instructions with respect to repairs to the rig? What training programs were in effect? What operating instructions had been issued? What safety precautions, et cetera? And as in all such cases, hindsight revealed things that could have been done differently or better. All of this, of course, was within the province of my client, the commanding officer of the Submarine Base. Hence the decision of the Board of Investigation to name him an interested party.

My first task was to examine critically the chain of causation. True, the chief had made a serious error. But did that in fact *cause* the fire? The board could see no other explanation. At that point, after reading the record and talking with all of the parties, neither could I. Nevertheless, that did not mean that there *was* no other explanation. Here I was assisted by a stroke of very good luck: a piece of the charging hose about 5 feet in length had been recovered after the fire. I sent it to the lab at the Pearl Harbor Naval Shipyard and asked that it be given a hydrostatic test to 4,500 psi. This would test it to 50 percent above full charging pressure. The piece of hose held that pressure! I then asked that it be slit open and the inside surface examined microscopically throughout the entire length. The report came back that the interior of the hose was intact and undamaged. Experts then assured me that this established that the alterations to the rig did not cause damage to the charging hose.

However, it was undisputed that the hose had indeed failed somewhere near the manifold, since its broken and flaming end had been seen whipping about. If the alterations had not caused it to fail, what had? Perhaps, I thought, the hose had not been suitable for charging oxygen at high pressure. It was, if I recall correctly, Aeroquip 409 series hose. A call to the navy's Bureau of Ships in Washington, D.C., gave me the information that Aeroquip 409 series hose had been designated as the proper hose for charging the oxygen banks of nuclear submarines. I was much relieved, for had the hose been of an unauthorized type, the Submarine Base would be back in the soup!

Although the outlook for my client was now much brighter, his reputation would not be untarnished unless the actual cause of the failure could be determined—and further that it be shown conclusively to have been beyond his control. At this point, I could prove to the board only that the base had used the proper charging hose, and that the error in modifying the control circuits had not caused the failure. But after all, the hose *did* fail. Therefore, the suspicion could linger that something else had been done wrong by the Submarine Base.

A call to the headquarters of the Union Carbide Company in New York City struck pay dirt. That company was a leading supplier of oxygen, and I was referred to their top expert. He said that there had been fires at Union Carbide resulting from the use of Aeroquip 409 hose for oxygen charging. As a result, its use for that purpose had been discountinued. He expressed surprise that the Bureau of Ships was still prescribing that hose, since its use for high-pressure oxygen charging had generally ceased in the oxygen industry. He was willing to come to Hawaii to testify to that effect.

Finally, the Union Carbide expert explained the mechanics of the failure. He said that all flexible hosing tended to develop pin-hole leaks through which oxygen bleeds out in small quantities. The trouble with the 409 hose, he said, was that the reinforcing mesh imbedded in the hose was high carbon steel. The oxygen bleeding through the mesh would react with it, causing the pin-holes to be enlarged. Tiny jets of oxygen, through chemical reaction and friction, could raise the temperature of the mesh to the ignition point. The resulting fire could burn along the hose like a fuse, causing it to fail. He said that the proper flexible hose for the purpose should have stainless steel mesh for reinforcement.

The ensuing testimony resulted in the complete exoneration of Captain Bill Parham and his sub base people, and everyone else at Pearl Harbor. Admiral Benson was pleased with the outcome: only a remote entity—the Bureau of Ships—was seen to be at fault.

The combination of initial skepticism, a lot of luck, and a bit of perseverance had paid off. The case is a fine example for the proposition that first appearances can be highly misleading.

On my return from Pearl Harbor and the *Sargo* case, I stopped briefly in Norfolk to collect my family and a Staff College diploma that had been awarded in absentia. I then, with considerable trepidation, reported to the JAG's office in the Pentagon. Still too junior to head a JAG division, I could therefore expect an assignment well down in that organization. Thus, I had to face what I had determined to try to avoid: working for another lawyer within a hierarchy of lawyers. Fate, however, in the form of Rear Admiral William C. Mott, came to my rescue.

Bill Mott was a maverick within the navy legal organization. He had been an aide in the Roosevelt White House and counsel to the chairman of the Joint Chiefs of Staff (JCS). In ego, dynamism, and loyalty to his people he matched Grenfell, but there the resemblance ceased. Where Grenfell was a rough gem, Mott was highly polished and multifaceted. He was a splendid orator and was much in demand on the speakers circuit. He made a small fortune from his appearances, and continued this moonlighting practice even after he became an admiral. He had a cocky and engaging charm that often clashed with a maddening nonchalance. He would, for example, skirt the edge of a conflict of interest between his duties as judge advocate general and his speaking engagements with a blithe indifference I found amazing. A born politician, he had an unerring instinct for the levers and pressure points of power. Although he was the judge advocate general of the navy, I never saw him take the slightest interest in any issue of military law, or, in fact, any issue of law that did not have political implications. He had concluded, I think rightly, that he could leave the routine legal issues to underlings. His career assignments had been almost entirely outside the JAG organization. He had become JAG through the intervention of Secretary of Defense Thomas Gates over the vehement objections of the JAG regulars. They detested him.

I had never met Admiral Mott before reporting to the JAG's office. He informed me later, however, that he had followed my law school career with interest. Also, he had been deluged with fulsome reports of my abilities from Admiral Grenfell, who was nothing if not an exuberant booster of people he liked and had selected for his staff. So, when not long after I had reported, Mott required three officers for an extended special project, I was one of those for whom he sent. The project involved a study of the organization of the U.S. Defense Establishment. Here is the background:

The military services had been buffeted by a series of organizational crises ever since the end of World War II. The United States military effort in that war had been managed by a committee. It consisted primarily of Admiral Ernest J. King, who ran the navy, and General George C. Marshall, who ran the army. Their only common superior who could resolve disputes was President Roosevelt. It was a miracle that it worked. At the end of the war there was a demand for "unification" of the armed forces. As a result, after extended hearings, Congress enacted the National Security Act of 1947. Before the act we had a Department of the Navy and a War Department. After the act we had Departments of the Navy, Army, Air Force, and Defense and a Central Intelligence Agency. So much for unification!

James Forrestal was the principal architect of the new arrangement, and he became the first secretary of defense. He visualized the Department of Defense as a small coordinating body consisting of perhaps forty persons. It hasn't worked out that way. The Defense Department was progressively strengthened by amendments to the act in 1953 and 1958. Now there is a cast of many thousands.

During the presidential campaign in 1960 between Richard

Nixon and John Kennedy, organization of the military was once again a major issue. There were charges of waste, inefficiency, duplication, and inability to make decisions. Kennedy assigned part of the blame for the so-called "missile gap" to shortcomings in our military system. There were planks in the platforms of both parties promising reforms. After the election, President-Elect Kennedy appointed a committee to study defense organization. It was headed by Senator Stuart Symington. He had been the secretary of the air force in the Truman administration. He was asked to complete his study and make his recommendations before Inauguration Day. This indicated that Kennedy viewed the problem as serious and the need for action urgent.

The Symington report was delivered to the president-elect at Palm Beach in December of 1960. A summary was released to the press. It called for complete reorganization of the armed forces along "functional" lines. The meaning of this was not made entirely clear. It was taken, however, to presage the eventual disappearance of the traditional divisions between the army, navy, and air force. Emerging in their place would be such entities as strategic, tactical, and supply forces all comprising a single military service. There was no ambiguity, however, in the Symington proposal that there be a single chief of staff, to replace the chairman of the Joint Chiefs of Staff. The chairman was, and is, indeed just that—the chairman of a committee. He has no power of decision. If the Joint Chiefs fail to agree, they can restudy the problem, sit on it, or refer it to the secretary of defense for decision. Under a single chief of staff, the military would speak with a single voice—his voice.

The arguments pro and con the single chief concept had raged for years. The Symington report was undoubtedly influenced by General Maxwell Taylor's book, *The Uncertain Trumpet*, which had been published in 1959. General Taylor had retired from the position of army chief of staff earlier that year. His book was a strong plea for a single chief of staff system. Remember the army insistence on unity of command?

The navy, the most traditional of the services, reacted to these recommendations with horror. It could visualize the beloved navy blue uniform replaced by a suit of neutral grey common to all services. It could see its ships and fleets and aircraft under the immediate command of army and air force officers. It was sure that the single chief would be an army officer because of the army's philosophical dedication to that concept.

Admiral Arleigh Burke, the chief of naval operations, called Admiral Mott. "Bill," he said, "We've got to do something. It looks like we're in for some kind of reorganization for sure. If all we can do is oppose the Symington plan, I think we'll lose. What we need is a constructive counterproposal. How about putting some of your lawyers to work on this." Mott called in three of us. One was Lieutenant Frank S. Johnston, a recent top graduate of Georgetown Law School. Another was a civilian lawyer employed by the JAG's office, Ziegler Neff, an old friend of Admiral Mott. I was the third. As our charter, Mott related the above telephone call from Burke.

We worked like beavers for a month. In our inexperience and naiveté, we saw ourselves involved in a project that could determine the future shape of our military establishment, and thus affect the history of our country. This was heady stuff! Fortunate for the intensity of our effort, we were not then aware of the number of such studies in Washington that had come to naught.

Our first conclusion was that the critics were right—up to a point. Under existing procedures there had been waste, inefficiency, duplication, and inability to make decisions. Interservice rivalry had to bear a good part of the blame for these conditions. For example, the Joint Chiefs of Staff were often in disagreement on the big issues of the roles and missions of the services, their force levels and weapons development. On those issues, they argued interminably. Many of them remained unresolved for years. The system also was conducive to logrolling. One chief would agree to another's program in return for support of his own.

Yet, we concluded, interservice rivalry is not *per se* a bad thing. There can be important benefits from the competition of ideas. Only when out of control is it harmful. Properly channeled and controlled, it would merely result in alternatives being offered to a decision maker.

The decision maker, we argued, should not be a single chief of staff. Because of his background and experience, the single chief would tend to favor the military philosophy of his own service. A dangerously one-sided national strategy could result. Also, civilian control of the military would be endangered by the very fact that the military would indeed speak with a single voice: Congress and the Executive would not have the opportunity to weigh and evaluate competing proposals. At the end of this spectrum is the danger of the emergence of a man on horseback.

We concluded that the appropriate decision maker, in practice as well as theory, should be the secretary of defense, subject of course to the ultimate authority of the president. The legal framework already existed. The 1958 Amendments to the National Security Act had given the secretary all the authority he needed to manage the Department of Defense efficiently. The difficulty was that this authority had not been fully utilized.

The last secretary of defense in the Eisenhower administration, Thomas Gates, had made a significant start: he had begun to sit with the Joint Chiefs when important disputed questions were under discussion. Much, however, remained to be done. Procedures had to be established whereby the secretary could inform himself of the nature and status of *all* important issues. He therefore had to have an adequate staff so that he could make independent evaluations. He could then control the decision process. He could encourage debate or put an end to it. Interservice rivalry would thus be brought under control to serve a useful, not destructive, purpose.

In opposition to the Symington proposals, then, the navy should stress the disadvantages and dangers of the single service and single chief of staff concepts. Next it should argue that the faults in the current system could be remedied through effective management by the secretary of defense, who already had sufficient legal authority. Therefore, no additional legislation was required. Lastly, we recommended that the navy support procedural and staffing changes whereby the secretary of defense could in practice make the necessary decisions.

Our report was voluminous. Admiral Mott was pleased with it. Admiral Burke was not so pleased. We summarized the report for the latter at a meeting attended by his principal staff officers. I was chosen to make the presentation. He smiled and nodded as I recounted our arguments for retention of the separate services, with their proud traditions. He beamed at our exposition of the evils of a single chief of staff system. But when I got to the part about strengthening the hand of the secretary of defense, he began to frown. When I reached the idea that the secretary had to have a staff adequate to make independent evaluations, he got to his feet and roared, "Bullshit!" I had a strong sense of *déjà vu*. My dialogues with Admiral Burke seemed to have developed unfortunate limitations.

It was now clear, though, what Admiral Burke had meant when he asked Mott to come up with "constructive counterproposals" to the Symington report: He really wished to preserve the status quo, while assuming a progressive posture. The picture comes to mind of a man leaning forward at a 45-degree angle with his feet planted firmly in concrete!

Our report was completed during the first weeks of the Kennedy administration. Robert McNamara, coming from the presidency of the Ford Motor Company, was attempting to get his arms around the job of secretary of defense. He had brought with him to the Pentagon his so-called "whiz kids." They were already creating shock waves within the military services by their probing into established and proposed weapons programs.

Soon after taking office, McNamara called for a briefing on defense organization. Rear Admiral Mott was an expert in that field. In a day-long meeting with McNamara, Mott presented a comprehensive picture of the development of the Defense Department. He gave the pros and cons of the various proposals for change. McNamara then asked Mott, "Who is it in the office of the Secretary of Defense that I look to for advice on organization?" Admiral Mott replied, "Mr. Secretary, you have no one." McNamara was incredulous. "What, here I'm supposed to run the biggest business in the world, and you tell me there's no one on my staff with the job of keeping my organization under review?" "That's right, Mr. Secretary."

Within the next few days, McNamara established an "Office of Organizational Studies," headed by Sol Horowitz. Its purpose was to determine the changes in organization necessary to permit McNamara to manage the Department of Defense. It was manned by bright and experienced army, navy, and air force officers at the lieutenant colonel level who knew how the Pentagon worked. Commander David O. "Doc" Cooke, who was Mott's assistant, became the navy member. Twenty-five years later, Doc Cooke is still there. Now, however, he is the assistant secretary of defense for administration. I took over from him as Mott's executive assistant. I thus continued to be spared the frustrations and drudgery that I felt, rightly or wrongly, otherwise awaited me within the depths of the JAG organization. Life with the brilliant and ebullient Bill Mott was always fascinating, often maddening, but never dull.

Robert McNamara became, from the outset, an extremely strong secretary. His "whiz kids" helped him to evaluate plans, policies, and programs. He called for reports and studies by the hundreds. He established machinery to put the secretary of defense, for the first time, firmly in control of the decision-making process. He thus changed the Pentagon irrevocably. In the process, of course, he became controversial. He projected an image as a human computer, unconcerned with human feelings. With his thin brown hair severely combed back and parted in the middle, he would stare unemotionally through his round, steel-rimmed glasses at his visitors. He wasted little time with civilities, and was often impatient with the high-ranking officers who met with him. He seldom if ever informed them in advance of his decisions—and having decided, he did not share with them his reasoning. I shall have something to say in a later chapter of the great trouble these habits were to cause him. He thus came to be disliked and opposed by most of the Pentagon's officers, who considered him a brash and arrogant meddler in the areas of their military expertise.

Congress, too, eventually came to resent him. He never showed awe and seldom deference toward the powerful congressmen with whom he dealt. He lectured to them, and overwhelmed them with his encyclopedic knowledge of defense facts and figures. His habitual air of condescension was particularly bruising to their delicate political egos.

So, soon after he took office, the Washington hounds picked up his scent. They ceased snapping at the harassed military services, and went baying off after Robert Strange McNamara. Although there were some grumbles that the secretary had become *too* powerful, these complaints were directed toward McNamara as a person. No one seriously proposed stripping the secretary of any of his powers. And during the eight years he held office, no voice was heard calling for reorganization of the Department of Defense. There is no record that the Symington report was even discussed within the Kennedy administration. It just faded away.

Our report, I'm sure, can claim no credit or blame for this result. McNamara needed no such impetus to convince him to take charge. After he took the reins, a quarter of a century passed without serious proposals for legislative changes affecting the Department of Defense. I have heard recently, however, that Senator Goldwater has revived the old charges: There is waste, inefficiency, duplication, and inability to make decisions. All of this, he says, has its roots in harmful interservice rivalry, and the answer is—what else?—the creation of a single chief of staff. The more things change, the more they remain the same!

There must be now, somewhere in the bowels of the Pentagon, eager young naval officers hard at work on a project. They will have been charged by the chief of naval operations to come up with a "constructive counterproposal" to the Goldwater plan.

They will be feeling honor and awe at their involvement in such an important national issue. It is therefore with hesitation that I suggest that they dust off that old report of ours—if they can find it!

Soon after these events the Bay of Pigs incident occurred. We in the JAG's office only knew what we read in the papers. I wish it could have remained that way.

In the immediate aftermath, President Kennedy assumed personal responsibility for the fiasco. He then, however, asked General Maxwell Taylor to conduct an inquiry into the operation. Its ostensible purpose was to find lessons for the future. Assisting General Taylor were Robert Kennedy, the president's brother and attorney general; Allen Dulles, the head of the CIA; and Admiral Arleigh Burke, the chief of naval operations and, as such, a member of the Joint Chiefs of Staff. The composition of the panel gave representation to all potential blamees. Bobby Kennedy could protect the president, Arleigh Burke the military, and Allen Dulles the CIA. If the objective of the committee was to find a scapegoat, it would have a difficult time. The Taylor group met in the office of the attorney general. On his return to the Pentagon after the third day's session, Admiral Burke called the JAG. He said he had an urgent job for a lawyer. Mott sent me to Burke's office. As I walked in, I found to my surprise that the admiral seemed pleased to see me. He even greeted me by my first name, which I didn't realize he knew. He said, "Andy, there have been some hints that the navy didn't do its job in the Bay of Pigs operation. I know that it did. I want you to analyze the operation from the navy's point of view and prepare a brief I can use with the Taylor committee." He told me that a complete file was available to Flag Plot, the CNO's War Room. It was then about 6:00 P.M. I asked when he wanted the brief. He said, "I have to have it at 9 o'clock tomorrow morning to take with me to the next session." I felt that it was my turn to yell "Bullshit!" but I restrained myself.

The word "file" was a misnomer. There were cartons of papers in Flag Plot. Everything related to the Bay of Pigs was there. There were operation plans and comments thereon, minutes of meetings, memoranda of conversations, records of phone calls, and piles of dispatches. I dove in. By about 3 o'clock in the morning, I had the picture. Hindsight of course, helped to hasten an understanding that the operation was seriously flawed. It was predicated upon grossly erroneous intelligence. Beyond that, there was executive vacillation and indecision in its execution. Adlai Stevenson in New York had been almost frantic. He had been misled to make false denials in the U.N. and felt himself to have been badly compromised. During the operation itself the president was in semi-isolation at his country estate, Glen Ora, in Virginia. He was attempting to maintain the fiction that the invasion was solely the work of Cuban exiles. Secretary of State Dean Rusk, undoubtedly responding to pressure from Stevenson, managed to get through on the telephone to the president. He convinced him to cancel a scheduled second air strike against Castro's airfields. Richard Bissel and General Cabell of the CIA were unable to reach the president to urge reversal of that decision. Whether the invasion would have succeeded had the originally planned air strikes been carried out is doubtful. Their cancellation in the middle of the operation simply made success even more unlikely.

It was clear that the naval forces involved, primarily the aircraft carrier *Essex,* had complied exactly with the operation order. There had been no mistakes made by U.S. military forces. At 8:30 A.M., Admiral Burke came to Flag Plot. I had completed the brief, but it had not yet been typed. The admiral took the sheaf of yellow lined pages. I said I would stand by in my office for any questions.

I then heard nothing. Light-headed from lack of sleep, I called the CNO's office at the end of the day. I was told that the admiral had returned from the Justice Department and had gone home. I felt badly treated indeed. Two days later, Admiral Burke called again, this time to me directly. He said, "Andy, I've been meaning to call you. Your brief did the trick. Now can you come to my office? I've got another job for you."

Again it was late in the afternoon. He told me that questions had been raised that day as to the performance of the Joint Chiefs of Staff. He asked that I reexamine the operation from their points of view and prepare another brief. You guessed it! He wanted it by 9 o'clock the next morning.

The job this time was somewhat easier. I didn't have to start from scratch. The involvement of the JCS was primarily in the study of and comments on the CIA plans. The JCS had acquiesced in the plans on the stated assumption that the CIA intelligence estimates were correct. They had further emphasized that success of the air strikes was critical, and that the planned strikes were the minimum required. In other words, the JCS had said, "*If* your intelligence is correct that the invasion will set off a full-scale revolt against Castro; and *if* the planned air strikes are conducted and are successful, there is a good chance that the plan will succeed."

I prepared the brief and had it typed before the admiral arrived. I gave it to him with my home phone number in case he needed more information. He did call me at home at the end of the day, but to thank me graciously and to say that the brief had succeeded in its purpose.

All subsequent contacts with Admiral Burke were congenial. On the eve of his retirement a short time after, he invited me to dinner at his quarters at the Naval Observatory. He wanted me to listen to a proposal from his other guests for post-retirement employment. Over brandy, when the others had departed, I advised him not to accept. I thought the aims of the group were suspect and that his good name would be in jeopardy. He listened carefully and then agreed. The days of shouting "Bullshit" to my conclusions seemed at last to be over.

8

John B. Connally

President Kennedy's favorite candidate for the secretary of the navy spot was Franklin D. Roosevelt, Jr. McNamara had insisted, however, that he be able to choose his own top people. Roosevelt was a close friend of the Kennedys. As navy secretary he would, therefore, have had direct access to the president, being thereby able to bypass the secretary of defense. McNamara would have found that prospect intolerable. He was nothing if not the boss.

John Connally, a Texas lawyer and rancher, was a protégé of Lyndon Johnson. While neither ever spoke of it, it seems likely that Connally was Johnson's candidate. It is clear that he was acceptable to McNamara. Like Kennedy and Johnson, he had been a naval officer in World War II.

Connally quickly demonstrated that he did not intend to be a figurehead. He intended to run the navy. His path was eased considerably by the retirement of Admiral Arleigh Burke shortly after he took office. There inevitably would have been serious clashes between the strong and crusty chief of naval operations and his activist civilian boss. Connally was thus able to select the new CNO. He chose Admiral George W. Anderson, the commander of the Sixth

Fleet in the Mediterranean. He made highly visible visits to all of the top contenders before making his choice. The point was not lost: The new CNO was indebted to him. That ensured at least a honeymoon period.

Connally also made an unprecedented "State of the Navy" address to all of the naval officers in the Washington area. For this, he obtained the use of the DAR Hall in the District of Columbia, across the Potomac from the Pentagon. It was the only nearby arena large enough to accommodate so many people. His presentation was a tour de force. No one present could fail to feel the strength of his personality. Officers who would never see the CNO had seen and heard the new secretary of the navy. There could be no doubt. He was in charge.

Almost immediately after becoming secretary, Connally brought to his staff an old friend and law school associate, Captain Joe Munster. Joe was one of the senior law specialists in the navy and a respected legal scholar and author. Connally created for him the position and title of "special counsel to the secretary of the navy." Soon thereafter, however, Munster was offered the position of tenured professor of law at the University of Texas Law School. He then retired from the navy to take that job. By that time, Connally was accustomed to having his own lawyer on his personal staff. He therefore asked the JAG to recommend a slate of five officers from which he could select a replacement.

Admiral Mott submitted a list of five captains, to which he had added my name. I was then a brand new commander, and his executive assistant. He said, "Andy, I'm sure that Connally wants a captain as a replacement for Joe Munster. But the fact that you are on the list will be good on your record." I was sure that he was right. I was therefore amazed to get a call from the naval aide to the secretary, Captain William R. Anderson, saying that Connally wanted to talk with me about the special counsel job.

Bill Anderson had been captain of the *Nautilus*. We had been friends since my days in the *Sea Fox,* and later from my time at the Pacific Submarine Command. I suspect that, influenced by friendship and the camaraderie of the submarine force, he may have been instrumental in inducing Connally to have a talk with me. Another fine hand behind the scenes may have been that of my old friend from the days in Naples, Italy, Jim Jenkins. He was Connally's special assistant for public affairs.

However it was brought about, I had my meeting with Connally. It was late in the day, and I waited neverously in the outer office for his last meeting to be over. A group of admirals finally emerged. Connally's secretary, a statuesque Texan beauty, told me to go right in.

I felt utterly insignificant and inadequate. In my world, the secretary of the navy was an awesome personage. If a meeting with the great man himself were not enough, his office could only impress and intimidate. It was huge. Connally sat behind an immense desk at the far end, flanked by the flags of the United States and the secretary of the navy. Behind him on the wall as a plaque was the Great Seal of the Navy Department. The motif of the room was traditional navy blue and gold. A great expanse of gold rug covered the floor. The many French windows that looked out over the Potomac toward the Lincoln Memorial had rich blue drapes. On my right as I entered the room, I saw with surprise a stylized saw horse: On it was an ornate saddle.

As I approached, Connally rose and walked around his desk to greet me. He was a tall and good-looking man, with thick, wavy dark hair, just beginning to grey at the temples. He was dressed in what I would call a subdued Texan style, complete with lanyard tie and boots. With a smile and a warm handshake he said, "I'm John Connally. Good of you to come, Commander Kerr." His voice was rich and pleasing, with the Texas accent unmistakable. He motioned me to a group of comfortable leather chairs around a coffee table. I felt an immediate attraction and a growing sense of ease. I was to see him work the same magic many times in the future as nervous or initially hostile visitors responded to his great charm.

He questioned me at length about my views of the role of a lawyer in the political arena, and outlined the needs he expected his special counsel to fulfill. First, he insisted on loyalty. He wanted a lawyer who would look after his interests and his only. I responded that that was the duty a lawyer owes to his client in any event. If at any time a significant legal or ethical conflict arose, I said that I would inform him. If we could not resolve the issue, I would simply step aside. He could get a new special counsel. He said that he found that to be satisfactory.

He also made it clear that he wanted his lawyer to be a generalist. A narrow, legalistic approach to the job would not do. He assumed quite correctly that few problems would reach his level that would be susceptible to a law book solution. He wanted a counsellor who could advise him on a broader basis.

The hour grew late. We continued the talk in his chauffeured limousine on the way from the Pentagon to his home on Foxhall

Road in the District of Columbia. I was deeply impressed by Connally. I left his house that night with the realization that I wanted the position very much indeed. To be special counsel to the secretary of the navy—and *such* a secretary—seemed an honor almost beyond comprehension! I was therefore overjoyed when Bill Anderson called the next day to tell me that Connally wanted me for the job.

Working for Connally gave great satisfaction. He took his small staff into his complete confidence. He made us—Anderson, Wheeler, Jenkins, and myself—feel that he liked, respected, and trusted us, and that we were important to him. We of course responded with complete devotion.

The inhuman hours normally worked in the more exalted offices of the Pentagon caused the affected wives generally to hate their husbands' bosses. It was different with Connally. They felt that he knew and cared about them. They were right. He thoughtfully included them on glamorous official occasions such as Potomac cruises aboard the secretary of the navy's yacht *Sequoia,* or aboard his private railway car to the Army-Navy football game in Philadelphia. More than once, he interrupted his conversation with a famous senator or supreme court justice to call my wife Rusty over to introduce her and say a word or two about her interests. Our wives adored him.

We met as a group with him early each morning to review the day's schedule. One or more of us sat in on all of his meetings. He consulted us often and invited our suggestions. We all met at the end of the day in a relaxed and friendly post mortem. After that, Connally, Wheeler, Jenkins, and I would often go down to the Pentagon Athletic Club for a game of badminton doubles (Bill Anderson did not play).

A nonsmoker and very light drinker, Connally kept himself in excellent condition. Yet he worried about his health, falling just short of being a hypochondriac. On trips, he carried a medical kit containing a vast assortment of pills for every eventuality. He liked to have a doctor in his party. This may have been wise, since his luck was bad with respect to injuries. Once, while inspecting a naval ROTC unit at a Texas university, he paused and asked a friendly question of a naval cadet who was standing at attention in the parade formation. The young cadet, flustered at being addressed by the secretary of the navy, snapped his rifle to the present arms position. A bayonet was attached. Its tip grazed Connally's right eyeball and penetrated deeply under his eyelid. The nasty wound almost cost him the sight of one eye. On another occasion we were playing badminton at the Athletic Club. Jim Jenkins lost his grip on his racquet during a hard swing. It shot across the court and struck Connally above the left eye, opening a deep gash. We rushed the profusely bleeding secretary to the dispensary, where several stitches were required to close the wound.

We shall never know if his wounds at the hands of Oswald were also due to a stroke of bad luck, i.e., riding next to an assassinee. On the other hand, on that fateful day, it may have been Kennedy who was unluckily riding next to the wrong person!

Since writing the above, we arrived in the Kindgom of Tonga in our sailboat *Andiamo III*. Friends in the United States, who knew of my involvement with the Oswald-Connally correspondence, sent me a book by Henry Hurt entitled "Reasonable Doubt," published by Holt, Rinehart and Winston. A *Washington Post* review that accompanied the book described it as a "major new study of the Kennedy assassination."

Boiled down to its essence, the book appears to me to make three points: First, the official investigations into the assassination were incompetent or worse; secondly, Lee Harvey Oswald could not have been the sole assassin; lastly, no conclusive evidence has come to light that would reveal the nature of any conspiracy or the identity of any participants.

Hurt's case against Oswald as the only gunman is based primarily on evidence that Oswald's shooting skill and chosen weapon were inadequate. In short, he concludes that Oswald was simply not that good a rifleman to have done the job. Hurt quotes Sherman Cooley, who served with Oswald in the Marine Corps, as stating, "If I had to pick one man in the whole United States to shoot me, I'd pick Oswald. I saw that man shoot and there's no way he could have learned to shoot well enough to do what they accused him of."

But what if Oswald was not aiming at Kennedy at all? What if Connally was his real target, and Kennedy was hit only by accident? Then the results would be entirely consistent with the lack of expertise that Hurt postulates. Surely Sherman Cooley, who held Oswald's shooting ability in such contempt, would not want to be seated next to the man at whom Oswald was aiming!

Before reading "Reasonable Doubt," I had always considered the idea that Oswald was shooting at Connally as merely a plausible possibility, based on a known motive. Now, however, in light of Hurt's revelations as to Oswald's marksmanship deficiencies, I have upgraded that possibility to a probability that Oswald bungled the job: He only winged his intended victim, and killed President Kennedy with a wild shot.

I soon found out how broad the responsibilities of the special counsel could be. Only days after I reported to the job, reports reached the secretary's office that a partially decomposed body had been discovered in a shallow lye-filled grave at our big naval base at Guantánamo, Cuba. It was identified as that of a Cuban employee of the base, Ruben Sabeñego Lopez. Agents of the Office of Naval Intelligence (ONI) were conducting an investigation. Those who now expect me to tell how the body got into the lye pit will be disappointed. I cannot for two reasons: first, there are, and always will be, important gaps in our knowledge. Secondly, what we did know was sufficient to cause the entire incident to be classified "Secret." It still remains so. Furthermore, I suspect that as a secret, it may make a better story than if the known details could be laid bare. In any event I can only tell about the process by which approval of the handling of the incident was obtained.

A preliminary report on the ONI investigation reached us on a Friday. Although preliminary, the report showed clearly enough the outline of the problem. Connally saw that the case had serious implications. He asked me to think about it and recommend a course of action.

I agonized over the problem that night and all the next day. It seemed to present a perfect dilemma. Each solution I thought of seemed equally unsatisfactory. By late Saturday night, however, I came up with a plan that I thought would work in theory. Connally would have to be the judge as to whether it could be carried off in practice.

The secretary was spending the weekend at the Naval Hospital at Bethesda, having undergone minor surgery. Some elements of the proposed design required immediate action if the incident was to remain under control, so I went to the hospital early Sunday morning. Connally examined the plan from every angle. Eventually he said that he thought it would work, and that he also could think of no other solution. A keypoint of the plan was that all inquiries would be forever answered throughout the government with "no comment." The secretary knew that it would be difficult to hold that line. Someone would be sure to cave in sooner or later unless the president himself had approved that course of action.

Connally undertook to ask clearance from Secretary of Defense McNamara by telephone. The latter already knew the general scope of the problem. It could therefore be discussed with him on the phone in elliptical terms without breaching security. My job that day was to take the scheme to President Kennedy, after first clearing it with his press secretary, Pierre Salinger, and then McGeorge Bundy, the president's National Security advisor. Connally set up those meetings.

It rained heavily all that Sunday. Connally's driver and I had great difficulty in finding Salinger's house on Lake Barcroft in Northern Virginia. The curving streets constantly changed names. The street numbers were mostly concealed. They also seemed to have no logical sequence. I rubbed condensation from the side window, eyes straining to catch a glimpse of a street sign or house number. The driver's full attention was devoted to staying on the road; the windshield wipers could not keep up with the downpour. How ludicrous, I thought. Here I was, lost in the murk at Lake Barcroft on my first important mission for the secretary. I could visualize the president himself waiting impatiently at the White House, growing more angry by the minute!

Eventually we found the house. Short and rotund, Salinger was in a bathrobe, with a drink in his hand and a big cigar in his mouth. He was working on some papers at a coffee table in the living room, assisted by a very pretty secretary. "Why he looks just like he does on television," was my foolish initial thought. Why shouldn't people look in person like they do on television?

Salinger boggled at the "no comment" feature of the plan. After all, he would personally have to stonewall the White House press corps with those miserable words. The prospect could hardly have been pleasant. Although friendly in manner, he probed in search of an alternative. Eventually, however, he agreed with the plan, and said that I could so advise the president. He then called Bundy at the White House to tell him that I was on the way. First, however, I phoned Connally and found that McNamara was in agreement.

The White House guards were waiting with my pass. This was my first visit. It all seemed unreal. I was yet to fully absorb my new status as special counsel to the secretary of the navy. Here I was on my way to see the president of the United States to discuss a most sensitive subject. It was all happening too fast. Someone else should be doing this! Surely affairs of importance to the country should not depend on the limited abilities of one as inexperienced as I! But before I could reflect further on my unworthiness, I was escorted to the west entrance and shown to the large basement office of the president's National Security advisor, McGeorge Bundy.

Bundy commenced our meeting without introductory civilities. "Well, what is it that Connally wants to do?" His cold and abrupt manner contrasted with Salinger's amiable courtesy. It was apparent that to him I was merely an insignificant messenger with distasteful tidings. I told him what we knew of the incident, and what Connally recommended. As the rest of us had done, he too twisted and squirmed in search of an alternative. I became more comfortable. He was not able to suggest anything we had not considered and rejected. At least, I thought, I won't have to go back to Connally to say that we had overlooked an obvious solution.

Bundy was clearly distressed. He ran his hands repeatedly through his thinning, sandy hair, exclaiming, "This is terrible. Oh, this is terrible. We'll never get away with 'no comment.' It won't work."

When nothing further was forthcoming from him, I asked if that meant that he was disapproving the plan on behalf of the president. He replied, "Oh, no, but at times like this—with these difficult questions—I ask myself 'What would *he* have done?' " He gestured toward a picture on the far wall. I could only see that it was a bearded countenance. I thought perhaps that it was Jesus and that Bundy was seeking divine guidance. While he continued to agonize, I walked over to the picture. It was of Henry L. Stimson, who had been President Roosevelt's secretary of war. I found out later that he had been a father figure to Bundy.

It became clear that Bundy was attempting to avoid a commitment. He said, "If this is what Connally wants to do, tell him that I see serious risks. Tell him that I can't now see any better course, but his course could lead to a disaster."

I replied, "I'm sorry, Mr. Bundy, but I can't go back to the secretary with that. This is his recommendation to the president, and I have to tell him whether the president or someone acting for him says yes or no."

I stuck to my guns, and eventually he left the room to see the president. He returned in about twenty minutes and took me to the Oval Office. A feeling of unreality that had grown throughout the day was now nearly overwhelming. It was as if I was a detached observer of these remarkable scenes, rather than a participant. As a result, I was strangely and unnaturally calm. It almost seemed a natural thing that I was about to discuss an important matter with the president of the United States. Thus I was spared the nervousness that otherwise might have reduced me to a state of babbling incoherence.

President Kennedy greeted me graciously and asked a few questions. He then said that I should tell Connally that he agreed that the plan presented the only reasonable alternative. I asked if his approval specifically included the "no comment" recommendation. He said yes.

I was impressed by Kennedy. He grasped the situation quickly and was prepared to bite the bullet. I appreciated his cordiality and his thoughtful attention. On the physical plane, I was struck by his size. John F. Kennedy in person was a much bigger man than one perceives from his pictures.

I was not impressed with McGeorge Bundy. He seemed too eager to avoid responsibility. I realize this may be unfair. His evasiveness may simply have been an attempt to protect the president. It seemed to me, however, to be an effort to avoid a personal commitment. I was not surprised, therefore, to read years later that his fellow presidential advisors were unable to determine where he stood on the decision to launch the Bay of Pigs operation.

I then returned to Bethesda to describe my day to Secretary Connally. He expressed satisfaction, but said, "Andy, we've got another job to do. We're not home free yet, by any means." He then got Congressman Carl Vinson on the telephone at his home. "Uncle Carl" was the grand old chairman of the House Armed Forces Committee, and one of the most powerful members of Congress. "Mr. Chairman," said Connally, "I would like to ask you to see my special counsel, Commander Kerr, first thing tomorrow morning about a very sensitive matter. He will be at your office as early as you like." Vinson said that I should be there by 7:30 A.M.

The next morning, Monday, I briefed the chairman and his ever-present counsel, Russell Blandford, on the general nature of the problem and our reasons for handling it as we were. Vinson said that he would inform the other committees of Congress that the matter fell under his cognizance, and that all inquiries should be referred to him. Our congressional flank was thus covered.

During that week, the body of Ruben Lopez was turned over to his widow by the navy at Guantánamo. Castro immediately commenced to exhibit it throughout Cuba as an example of an American atrocity. He demanded an explanation. He was notified via the Swiss embassy in Havana that the incident was being investigated, and that he would be informed of the result. The American press thereby became aware of the incident. The Navy and Defense

Departments were inundated with questions. All of the public information officers responded with "no comment." Their uniform obstinacy led one national columnist to describe them as "the bun-faced minions of Arthur Sylvester," the latter being McNamara's press secretary. As such, he was the titular head of the information officers of the Pentagon. I have always thought the phrase to be particularly evocative.

At the White House, Pierre Salinger also held the line. By this time reporters had adopted the title of "Ruben the Cuban" as shorthand for the affair. Eventually the president himself was questioned at one of his press conferences. He refused to budge from a "no comment" response.

All attempts to get Congress involved foundered on the same rock—"That matter is within the jurisdiction of the House Armed Services Committee." Such was the power of Carl Vinson. To those who pressed their inquiries to that source, Russ Blandford passed on the chairman's "no comment."

Weeks went by. The discouraged Washington press corps gradually turned its attention to other matters. During that time, however, I learned the price I had to pay for my involvement in the case of Ruben the Cuban. I came to feel that I was personally and solely responsible to see that nothing went wrong. I spent sleepless nights worrying about what could happen, and whether or not I had taken care of all the contingencies. I felt gut-wrenching fear on reading the morning papers, when some new speculation appeared. I approached each day with a dreadful sense of anxiety, which was only dispelled when I got to my desk and began to work. I was to find that I would pay this price many times in other cases in the years ahead as special counsel.

In the Ruben case, too, important help was precluded. Rusty and I habitually discussed the issues with which I was involved at work. I valued her reaction. In a real sense, she shared the load. She encouraged me when I was doubtful or frightened, calmed me when I was rash, and comforted me in setbacks. The "Top Secret" stamp on the Ruben the Cuban affair denied me this relief.

Eventually the Office of Naval Intelligence submitted a final report on its investigation. As we had anticipated, no significant further light was cast upon the incident beyond what we knew at the beginning. A message was then sent to the government of Cuba via the Swiss. It stated that the U.S. Navy investigation into the death of Ruben Sabeñego Lopez had been completed and that "the death remained unexplained." That statement is literally true. As a last step, I drafted and Connally signed a memorandum to General David Shoup, the commandant of the Marine Corps. The latter had shown an element of unpredictability in the affair. Connally had thought it wise, therefore, to instruct him in writing as to what he should do and should not do in the event of future contingencies. It was well he did. Over a year later, when Connally was the governor of Texas and his successor, Fred Korth, was secretary of the navy, Shoup almost blew the case. Connally's memorandum saved the day. How this and even more dramatic events occurred in the continuing saga of Ruben the Cuban, I shall save for a later chapter.

Some questions reaching the secretary are essentially trivial. They become difficult only because of the identity of the people involved. An example is the case of the statue of Dr. Benjamin Rush.

The problem arose because of the construction of a new bridge across the Potomac River. It was to be upstream of the Key Bridge and to cross Roosevelt Island, a nature preserve named after Theodore Roosevelt. The bridge was to be called, not surprisingly, the Roosevelt Bridge. On the District of Columbia side there was to be the typical maze of cloverleaf approaches. They may be seen today in the vicinity of the Kennedy Center for the Performing Arts. One of these approaches had to cut through the corner of the grounds of the old Navy Hospital on Constitution Avenue. On that particular corner was a statue.

The old building on the premises was no longer used as a hospital. For many years it had served as the headquarters of the Navy Bureau of Medicine and Surgery. One can visualize the scene. The workmen stamp into the office of the chief of the bureau in their muddy boots and hard hats with their surveyor's transits. "What do you want done with the statue, Mac?" A quick answer is given. "Maybe it ought to go on Pennsylvania Avenue. Why don't you check with the Interior Department?" The suggestion was acted upon, and the question reached the attention of the secretary of the interior, Stewart Udall. The fact that it did so confirmed my long-standing suspicion that they don't have enough to do over there. It developed that Udall was not neutral with respect to statues. In fact, he held strong opinions and tended to express them violently when the subject was raised. Statues in the District of Columbia were in fact his pet peeve. In this case, he used the occasion to air his views with the press. He stated that there were altogether too many statues in the District and that they were almost all atrocious. He would, if he could, get rid of most of them. So long as he was in charge of the public lands of the District, not one new statue would be permitted thereon.

It must have been a slow week in Washington. Udall's anti-statue outburst got wide play in the press. Thus, it became known that the statue of Dr. Rush was up for grabs. We in the secretary of the navy's office noted the story with mild amusement. We soon began to pay closer attention. Connally got a call from Governor David Lawrence of Pennsylvania. He asked for an appointment to talk about the statue. Lawrence came with a sizeable delegation from Dickinson College of Carlisle, Pennsylvania. Dr. Rush, it turned out, was the cofounder of that institution. They asked that the navy give the statue to the college for placement on Rush Campus at Dickinson.

Connally, unaware of the future storm, but heeding the sure instincts of the master politician, listened gravely but made no commitment. If there were no more claimants, he could make more points if he were perceived as having had to overcome difficulties in granting their wish. If others appeared, he would not have painted himself into a corner. He ushered the delegation to the door with an arm around the governor's shoulder, assuring them graciously that he would personally look into the matter. I saw the same thing happen many times but was always amazed. He had worked the Connally magic. He had promised nothing, but the group left in high spirits, obviously feeling they had won a splendid victory.

The next person to appear was the secretary of the army. He was accompanied by the army's surgeon general. They urged that the statue belonged in a position of honor at the army's Walter Reed Hospital. They pointed out that Dr. Benjamin Rush had been the surgeon general of Washington's Revolutionary Army. Connally's caution increased.

And well it did, because that was only the beginning. A group came from the government agency responsible for the national institute for psychiatric care, St. Elizabeth's Hospital. They informed us that Dr. Rush was revered as the father of American psychiatric medicine. He was known, they said, as "the first American alienist." The statue should go to St. Elizabeth's.

Then the American Medical Association weighed in. Their case was twofold: First, they revealed that the statue had been a gift from the AMA at the turn of the century. If the navy was through with it, they wanted it back. Second, they believed it appropriate that the statue grace the grounds of Rush Medical School in Chicago.

Several temperance groups appeared. It seems that Dr. Rush is a patron saint of that movement.

Patriotic societies surfaced. Dr. Benjamin Rush was a signer of the Declaration of Independence.

Several women's groups sought and were granted an audience. Their requests were generally for the placement of the statue at one of the women's colleges. Dr. Rush, it appeared, was the first prominent American to advocate higher education for women.

Finally, the people from the Navy Bureau of Medicine belatedly realized that they had offered to give away a good thing. They suggested that the statue should go to the National Naval Medical Center at Bethesda, Maryland.

Our mild amusement had long since turned to aggravation. Connally called me in. He was fed up. He said, "Andy, I don't give a shit where they put that God-damned statue. Just figure out how we can get rid of it, and I don't want anyone mad at me!"

It seemed an impossible task. The outlook was for one happy recipient, with all the rest upset. Each group was convinced that its own request was overwhelmingly meritorious. Yet objectively, no applicant had a clearly superior claim. There was no way we could convince the losers that the winner had a compelling case.

Without much hope, but with the idea that you have to start somewhere, I looked through the cumulative index of the United States Code. To my surprise, there was an entry, "Statues—see Fine Arts Commission." That led me to the act of Congress that had established the Fine Arts Commission of the District of Columbia. Its charter listed several duties. One, believe it or not, was to advise as to the location of statues in the District. There was a light at the end of the tunnel! Then I looked into the relationship of the statue to the navy. Sure, we had it on navy property. But how did we get it and under what conditions? The AMA delegation had said that it was a gift of the AMA but was vague on the circumstances. I checked the archives and found that it had been accepted by President Theodore Roosevelt in a ceremony on the grounds of the Navy Hospital. The president of the AMA had presented it to "the people of the United States." President Roosevelt, in a speech extolling the multifaceted contributions of Dr. Rush to our young Republic, accepted the statue, "on behalf of the people of the United States." Nowhere was there any mention of the navy. I swiftly concluded that the navy did not own the statue. It was not ours to give away. The navy was merely the custodian. Now that it had to be moved, our clear duty was to put the statue in a place selected by the people. One could hardly expect to have a national referendum on the subject. The people, though, are represented by Congress. Now it all came together. Congress in its wisdom had decided not to involve itself in day-to-day problems involving placement of statues. (One is tempted to make a bad pun about the statutory duties of Congress.) It had established a Fine Arts Commission and delegated to it the authority to act on such matters. The answer was clear. The commission, not the navy, must determine the new site from which Dr. Rush could gaze upon the remarkable activities of the inhabitants of the capital city of the nation he helped to found.

I telephoned the chairman of the commission and introduced myself. I then said, "I think you've got a problem." He answered, "We were afraid you might eventually get onto us! Okay, there is no way we can duck it. Toss it over to us."

I prepared a letter that Connally sent to all the claimants. It developed the above rationale as to why the navy was powerless to act. It concluded with a statement to the effect that, "We have referred your request to the Commission, where we are assured it will be given careful consideration."

The entire pack went baying off after the Fine Arts Commission. Connally was delighted. A year later the commission announced its decision. The statue was to be moved ten feet and rotated 180 degrees.

As a postscript to this affair, this was the only case in my experience as special counsel, or indeed in my subsequent legal career, in which the answer to a significant problem popped out of a law book. Maybe that's because, as I said in the beginning, the problem was not, in the grand scheme of things, significant.

Much of every secretary's time is taken up with tempests in teapots. One can look back in amazement that they caused so much fuss and required so much attention. They often arose, however, from the efforts of persuasive and single-minded individuals. They are the people who are tireless in pursuit of a goal that they are convinced the "establishment" is wrongfully determined to deny them. In later years, Marcus Aurelius Arnheiter, in his quest for "justice," plagued Navy Secretary Paul Ignatius. With Connally, it was the case of Captain Cooper Bright and his Wagmight concept.

Wagmight was born during the last year of the Eisenhower administration. It was an idea conceived by three officers who comprised a small think tank in the office of the CNO. They were Captains Wagner, Miller, and Bright. These officers had the reputation of being smart and innovative. Admiral Burke had asked them to think about new ways to approach the navy's technical problems. They had no other duties. They thought up the idea of an inflatable aircraft. The idea went through many iterations and alterations during its life. In its simplest form, however, it involved an aircraft that could be boxed up and prepositioned at advanced bases. When needed it could be pumped up and flown away. They termed the concept Wagmight, which was an acronym for their names, Wagner, Miller, and Bright.

Admiral Burke was intrigued with the idea. He asked the Bureau of Naval Weapons to evaluate it, and it did so. The bureau reported back to Burke that while the idea was technically feasible, it fulfilled no known military requirement. In the vernacular, one would say, "Who needs it?" Burke called in his three innovators and informed them regretfully of the finding. He said it had been a good try, but now they should go back to the drawing board.

Captains Wagner and Miller apparently accepted that decision. Captain Bright did not. He continued to push for acceptance of the idea. He was intelligent, personable, and extremely articulate. He obtained powerful allies outside the navy. One was Senator Margaret Chase Smith. He was also able to interest Senator Lyndon Johnson, who was then chairman of the Senate Aeronautics and Space Committee before he became vice president. Several other key members of Congress were persuaded to his cause. Drew Pearson, the Washington columnist and predecessor of Jack Anderson, took up the fight. Captain Bright was portrayed in the press as a courageous officer with a progressive idea that was being suppressed by a hide-bound navy. The newspapers sought to draw a parallel between the navy's treatment of Captain Bright and its earlier treatment of Captain Rickover. Rickover, it may be recalled, had been instrumental in the development of nuclear submarines. He had, however, been passed over for selection to the rank of rear admiral. The power of Congress and the press combined to save him. He went on to a career that lasted a phenomenal thirty years after that. Eventually he retired as a full admiral.

The press and congressional attempts to liken Bright to Rickover were of course specious. At the time Captain Rickover was passed over, he was already the head of a highly successful program that the navy recognized as essential. At the time of the efforts to make Captain Bright seem a martyr, the latter had only a paper idea, which the navy had evaluated and found useless.

By the time Connally became secretary of the navy, Wagmight had become a time-consuming issue. He therefore determined to get to the bottom of the controversy. Was Captain Bright in fact being persecuted? Had his ideas been given a fair shake by the navy? How useful was the Wagmight concept, anyway? Connally called a meeting of all the navy principals. Present were the chief of naval operations (CNO), the vice CNO for air, the chief of the Bureau of Naval Weapons, the assistant CNO for Research and Development, and many others. The secretary told Bright that he should cover not only the merits of Wagmight, but also any evidence that he had been unfairly treated. He also told the captain that the meeting would go on as long as it took him to present everything he had. The meeting went on all day. Connally, with a sure lawyer's touch, insisted that nothing be left dangling. When Bright made an assertion, the secretary held him to it until it had been tested.

Cooper Bright's family was well known in the navy. His sister, Joy Bright, had been head of the WAVES. One senior admiral present at the meeting had known Cooper from childhood, as well as his sister Joy and his other sister, Honor Bright. There was an emotional moment when this old family friend, with tears in his eyes, cried out, "Cooper, Cooper, how can you make these baseless statements to the Secretary of the navy?"

At the end of the day, the secretary was satisfied that Captain Bright had no case. He concluded that the navy had leaned over backward to be fair, and that the navy had no use for Wagmight. He said, "Captain, I now know everything I need to know about Wagmight. I've been around long enough to know the difference between chicken salad and chicken shit. What you've been serving up to us all day long is nothing but chicken shit!" He also instructed him, on the spot, to cease his promotional efforts.

Later that evening he asked Jim Jenkins and me to draft a statement for the press. That we did. The press release stated among other things that the secretary of the navy had concluded that Captain Bright had printed a brochure at government expense for the apparent purpose of promoting his idea outside the navy. It further stated that Bright had been directed to cease using government printing facilities to support a concept that had no official standing.

The next day, Cooper Bright either brought suit or publicly

threatened suit against the secretary of the navy for libel. He intensified his efforts to obtain support. Thus, Connally's efforts to close out the controversy, one way or the other, had failed.

During the ensuing months, hardly a week passed without Jenkins or me being called to put out a Wagmight brushfire. One of our difficulties was that the Wagmight concept constantly changed. Only the name remained the same. Bright was therefore always able to argue that the various evaluations did not address his current idea. Thus Wagmight was subjected to several further studies. All reached the same conclusion—who needs it? One such evaluation was conducted by the Institute for Defense Analyses (IDA) for the secretary of defense. At the time, I believe that Wagmight had become a short take-off and landing aircraft that could hover by virtue of compressed air accumulators in the wings. The scientist who wrote the IDA conclusions indulged in levity rarely found in such reports: He said that in order for Wagmight to hover for the required time, it would have to deflate to the vanishing point.

Even after all of this, Bright acquired an ally in the White House. He apparently convinced Bobby Kennedy that the navy's treatment of Wagmight could result in a scandal damaging to the Kennedy administration. As a result, Kennedy asked Adam Yarmolinsky, special assistant to McNamara, to investigate. In each department during the Kennedy years, there was one person who was specially trusted to look after Kennedy interests. In the Department of Defense, that person was Adam Yarmolinsky.

Yarmolinsky brought Frank Bartimo, a cool and capable lawyer, into the picture. Bartimo was an assistant general counsel in the Defense Department under Cyrus Vance.

Bartimo commenced his inquiry on the stated assumption that Bright was right and the navy wrong. He therefore declined all offers of advance briefings by the navy. He felt that these would merely be attempts to prejudice him against Wagmight. I was only able to suggest to him that he leave no assertion untested. He spent many hours with Captain Bright. Usually unperturbable, he emerged from the last session with his collar open and tie askew. Red-faced in anger and frustration, he could only mutter, "You can't pin the man down!" His report went back via Yarmolinsky to the White House, "The navy is right, Bright is wrong."

Soon after, I received a call from the naval aide to President Kennedy, Captain Tazewell Shepard. "The president," he said, "is going to issue a statement to the press about Wagmight. It backs up the navy, and will finally end this thing." "Great," I replied, "But you had better believe it won't end it!"

And it didn't. By that time Connally had left the Pentagon. His successor as secretary of the navy, Fred Korth, was summoned to Capitol Hill to the office of Senator John Tower of Texas. I, as resident expert on the history of Wagmight, went with him. Tower demanded an explanation of the navy's "ill-treatment" of Cooper Bright. I went through the whole story. By then I didn't even have to use notes. At the end, Tower said, "I'd like to have something to beat John Connally with back home in Texas, but I see that I can't beat him with this old dog!"

Captain Bright continued his efforts. By this time, however, they centered more on attempts to clear his name, which he believed to have been besmirched by the navy in its public statements. This prompted Secretary Korth to conduct still another review, after which he issued *another* public release. It stated Korth's conclusion that the prior navy press releases were accurate statements of the facts. It added, however, that the navy had never intended to attribute to Captain Bright any other motive than the desire to pursue the development of Wagmight. Nor had the navy ever wished or intended to question his obvious devotion to his country. This seemed to satisfy Captain Cooper Bright, for he and Wagmight at long last faded away.

During the year in which he served as secretary of the navy, Connally was often involved with controversies generated by Admiral Hyman G. Rickover. Admiral Rickover was the great navy original. There never was and probably never will be anyone remotely like him. Brilliant, sly, tireless, blunt, devious, arrogant, foresighted, vain, angry—attempts to define him will forever fail. Father of the nuclear navy, shameless flatterer of Congress, scourge of government contractors, he was near the height of his power when Connally was secretary. Yet at that time, he was approaching the statutory retirement age for officers. He would reach that age, 62, on 27 January, 1962. His enemies in the navy, and they included all of the most senior admirals, thought that at last he was finished. During the summer of 1961, they proposed that Connally order Rickover to accept a deputy. That officer, they said, could then take over in January when Rickover retired. The story, probably apocryphal, is told that on hearing this, Rickover snorted, "Deputy? Deputy? Did Jesus Christ have a deputy?" In any event, he would have none of it.

Part of Rickover's power stemmed from the navy's treatment

of him in the early fifties when he was passed over for promotion. From then on the navy was on the defensive. Rickover was thenceforth regarded in the press and by Congress as one whose great contributions were made in the face of implacable navy opposition. This also became the view of the general public. There was enough truth in it to enable Rickover to nurture his image as the courageous underdog.

Also, he had managed to acquire two hats: He was the director of the Naval Reactor Division of the Atomic Energy Commission (AEC). He was also the assistant chief for Nuclear Propulsion of the navy's Bureau of Ships. These two hats gave him the ability to shift adroitly from one position to another. He could thus attack navy positions from his spot as an official of the AEC without subjecting himself to charges of insubordination. He could also, when it appeared advantageous, speak as a naval officer. Finally, his AEC hat enabled him to gain great influence with the Joint Committee on Atomic Energy in Congress.

Representative Chet Holifield, then chairman of the Joint Committee, paid a call on Connally. "Mr. Secretary," he said, "the Joint Committee wants to know the navy's plan for Admiral Rickover after he reaches the mandatory retirement age." He went on, "The committee feels it would be a tragedy if the country is deprived of the services of the admiral. We feel he should continue to perform the duties that he does now." Holifield then said that if the navy should find any difficulty in doing this within the framework of the existing laws, the Joint Committee wanted to be informed. "We can then," he said, "get started on drafting the necessary legislation to ensure that this is accomplished."

Connally said that of course the navy wished to continue to avail itself of the expertise of Admiral Rickover. He added that he hoped there would be no necessity for legislation. With the familiar gesture of his arm about Holifield's shoulder as they walked to the door, he said, "Now, Mr. Chairman, don't you worry. I'll get back to you soon on this." He then asked me what his options were. I explained that unless the law was changed, Admiral Rickover *had* to be retired on the next January 27. I said, however, that the secretary of the navy had the authority to call him back immediately thereafter in the status of a retired officer on active duty. In that capacity he could be assigned whatever duties the secretary desired. Connally considered other alternatives. All seemed impossible or undesirable. Clearly, Congress would insist on no diminution in Rickover's responsibilities. If legislation were enacted to avoid such a reduction, the navy would lose the possibility of control in the future. Connally therefore decided on the "recall to active duty" approach. He cleared this with McNamara and the White House. He then stole a march on the admiral. He first called on Holifield and obtained his concurrence. Only then did he call in Admiral Rickover. He said, "Admiral, I've given a lot of thought about how we can avoid losing you next year when you become sixty-two. Here's what we would like to do." He then explained his plan and said that he hoped the admiral would continue to serve. Rickover agreed, but said that he wanted to see it in writing. Connally said that it was already in writing. He had withheld signing it only to be sure that the admiral would consent to be recalled to active duty. Only then did Connally show him the order. It recalled the admiral *for a period of two years.* Rickover was upset. He insisted that the recall should be open-ended. Connally maintained, however, that after the age of 62, a periodic review of the ability of any officer to perform such arduous duties as those of the admiral was necessary. He made it clear that he was willing to go on the mat on that issue with the Joint Committee. Rickover, realizing that for once he had been out-maneuvered, reluctantly accepted the decision. The precedent was established. His status came up for review every two years until his final retirement, over twenty years later. Each time, his opponents marched up the hill in a determined effort to unseat him. And each time, for the next two decades, they marched back down again.

On a personal level, I found my many contacts with Admiral Rickover to be invariably difficult. He was always brusk and contentious and apparently incapable of any light touch. The ordinary civilities were beyond him. He reacted equally negatively to praise and criticism. He had a way of disagreeing with even the blandest of assertions so as to make one feel like a fool. His dominant attitude seemed to be one of anger. I thus disliked meeting with him although in the majority of instances I agreed with his positions. I always had a sinking feeling whenever my secretary announced that Admiral Rickover was calling, even though in the abstract I admired and respected him and felt that the navy and the country were indeed fortunate that he was around—and even though I knew that beneath his irritating ways, the crusty old coot regarded me as a friend.

The Rickover controversies that reached the secretary often involved personnel policies. In those disputes, the CNO and his people would say, "All right, we agree that Rickover can call the shots when it comes to technical questions of nuclear propulsion. He has no business, though, interfering in navy personnel matters." Rickover would clap on his AEC hat and reply "Look, I'm responsible to the Reactor Safeguards Committee of the AEC for the safety of the navy's nuclear reactors. I have to ensure that the people who man the nuclear ships have the capacity and training to do a safe job." His safety responsibility also gave him a powerful and often decisive voice as to how and where the nuclear ships operated. This too caused bitter resentment among the navy's line officers.

One acrimonious dispute arose concerning the curriculum at the Naval Academy: After the Soviet Union had sent its Sputnik into orbit, there was general concern that scientific and engineering education in the United States was lagging behind that of the Russians. The navy reacted by modernizing the curriculum at the academy. Many beneficial changes in the content of the various courses were introduced. Also, the academy began to offer majors in several disciplines, in addition to the traditional major in electrical engineering. One of those was a major in nuclear engineering. Admiral Rickover had not been consulted. When he heard of it, he reacted violently. He had personally selected all of the officers who served in the navy's nuclear program. He contended that the scholastic performance of graduates of the Naval Academy was consistently inferior to that of graduates of the good civilian engineering schools. He claimed that this was caused by deficiencies still existing at the academy in the basics of mathematics and the sciences. He said that nuclear engineering was a "hardware" course. What the academy needed instead, he said, was more emphasis on fundamentals. His expression was that midshipmen should learn to walk before they try to run. He insisted that the nuclear engineering course be disestablished. He questioned the qualifications of many of the instructors at the academy. Typical of Admiral Rickover, he didn't stop there. He attacked the Naval Academy athletic program as excessive. This was a pot-shot at a sacred cow. Even worse, he advocated that some of the midshipmen's time then controlled by the Executive Department at the academy be given over to academics. The Executive Department is responsible for discipline and the molding of midshipmen into naval officers. Indeed, it is what makes the academy a *naval* academy rather than an ordinary university. These recommendations, of course, enraged the commandant of midshipmen, the chief of Naval Personnel, and the CNO. They argued for the retention of the *status quo* at the academy. The two positions were poles apart. Neither side would back down. They would not compromise. Resolution by the secretary of the navy was the only avenue available.

A full-scale confrontation took place in the secretary's office. Rickover and his staff faced the CNO and his staff. Instead of six-guns, however, each side had its charts and graphs and large black-tabbed and indexed back-up books. At the end, Connally thanked both groups. He said he wanted to digest what they had given him. He asked that each leave a copy of his entire presentation, including all available back-up material. After they departed, he scooped up the whole pile, gave it to me and said, "Andy, look into this and give me your recommendations."

I looked into it for a good part of the time Connally was secretary. It was one of my earliest projects. I went to the Naval Academy and talked to midshipmen and instructors there. I examined the curriculum, and visited several of the good engineering schools. The effort took many months. I was aided immensely by the mass of material, statistical and otherwise, that the Rickover and CNO sides had left with the secretary.

In the end, I concluded that Rickover was right when he said that academy education was inadequate in the basics of mathematics and the sciences. He was also right in his contention that many instructors were poorly qualified. He was wrong, I thought, in his belief that the Executive Department (and the athletic program) should be down-graded to permit more emphasis on academics. I concluded that the division of a midshipman's time between academics, the naval sciences, and activities controlled by the Executive Department was about right. Within the academic departments, however, there was a compelling need for improvement in the qualifications of the instructors.

The academic instructors at the academy were a mix of civilian professors and naval officers. Over all, these were about equal in numbers. The officers were ordered to duty at the academy on the basis of their excellence as naval officers. Little or no regard was had as to their academic credentials or teaching ability. Many were therefore unqualified in the subjects they were assigned to teach. Others had a proper grasp of their material but lacked the required teaching skills. These shortcomings were the root causes of the deficiencies Rickover had noted. As a minimum reform, then, all instructors in the academic departments should be required to possess the academic qualifications required of professors in top-flight universities. This would require the replacement of virtually all of the naval officers of those departments. This proposed change was not so radical as it appeared on its face. The Naval Academy had always considered itself superior to the Military and Air Force academies in its employment of civilian professors. The latter institutions utilized only military officers. There was thus no *principle* at Annapolis that midshipmen had to be taught academic subjects only by naval officers. The naval sciences of navigation, seamanship, gunnery, etc., should of course continue to be taught by officers. Obviously, all of the members of the Executive Department should be naval officers, and of the highest caliber.

It is one thing, however, to recognize that a first-class faculty is required. It is another thing to acquire it. Academicians have psychic needs greater than most other professionals. Each academic department at the academy was headed by a navy captain. This reduced the civilian professors to the role of mere employees. It seemed clear that that had to change. Academe demands a hierarchy. In no other pursuit, even the military, is that need so deeply felt. Also, the best people in any line of endeavor need a worthwhile career goal. The head of each academic department should therefore be a civilian professor. Then, since each department would be headed by an academic professional, there should be a civilian dean of academics reporting directly to the commandant of midshipmen. Only then would there be a chance of convincing a bright young academician that a position at the Naval Academy was as attractive as a position, say, at MIT or CalTech. It would be an uphill fight in any event. The academic community tends to think of the military as Neanderthal. A convincing case had to be made that the academic environment at the academy should not be so described.

These then were my recommendations to Secretary Connally. They were accompanied by comprehensive supporting documents. The report was topped by a proposed directive to be signed by the secretary of the navy. It required that within three years, all instructors at the academy in non-naval courses have the specified academic qualifications. It provided that the heads of the academic departments be civilian professors of recognized excellence in their fields. Lastly, it directed the establishment of the position of dean of academics, to be filled by an eminent civilian educator. Connally had the study on his desk for a month. He called me in for several discussions. He recognized the potential for controversy presented by the proposed directive. Nevertheless, he seemed persuaded of its necessity, and I thought him on the verge of signing it. Then came a bombshell. He suddenly announced his decision to resign and to run for the governorship of Texas. Within a few days thereafter, he departed. There was an emotional scene as he bade farewell to his staff at the Butler Aviation Terminal at Washington National Airport. He flew off in the secretary of the navy's plane, accompanied by his naval aide, Bill Anderson. His resignation was to become effective at midnight that night. We all felt a sense of personal loss. We had become devoted to the man. In addition, I regretted his failure to sign the Naval Academy directive.

Bill Anderson flew back to Washington the next day. To my astonishment, he had with him the signed directive. Connally had taken it with him in his briefcase and signed it on the plane on the way to Texas. It was his last official act as secretary of the navy.

The reaction to the order was explosive. The navy's admirals, led by Admiral Anderson, the CNO, united solidly against the changes. Hanson Baldwin, the distinguished and respected military writer for the *New York Times,* wrote scathing articles in opposition to what he termed the "civilianization of the Naval Academy." Baldwin was an Annapolis graduate and had many friends among senior naval officers, both active and retired. It was made to seem that every valued tradition of the navy since the days of John Paul Jones was in jeopardy. It was clear that a determined campaign was in progress for the cancellation of the order. The press, fed by opponents of the directive, presented a distorted picture of its provisions. This led to even more opposition throughout the navy and in Congress. Both the *New York Times* and the *Washington Post* denounced the proposed changes in stinging editorials. Completely obscured by the furor was the fact that only the education of midshipmen in such areas as English, history, foreign languages, physics, chemistry, and mathematics was involved. The directive changed nothing in the Executive Department or in the education of midshipmen in the naval sciences of seamanship, navigation, gunnery, etc. Public release by the secretary's office of the text of the order did nothing to quell the uproar. The press seemed far more interested in the fact that there was a controversy than in throwing light upon it.

Connally's successor, Fred Korth, had hardly taken his oath of office as secretary of the navy when he was assailed by demands for cancellation of the order. He listened to the arguments of its opponents. He studied the directive and its supporting documents. In the end he became convinced, as had Connally, of its soundness and necessity. He informed Admiral George Anderson, the CNO, and Vice Admiral William Smedberg, the chief of Naval Personnel, of his decision to let the order stand. They presented a "reclama," Pentagonese for a request for reconsideration. Korth then extended the period during which naval officers were to be replaced by qualified civilians to five years from the three originally specified. Otherwise, the order remained intact and was put into effect without further change.

The months following the promulgation of the other were among the most difficult of my naval career. My role in its preparation was known. I was despised by a good part of the navy. There were erstwhile good friends who would have nothing to do with me. I knew the feelings of a pariah. Only Admiral Rickover was happy with the order. That didn't help me at all with the rest of the navy.

The changes eventually took place. The navy came to realize that the military training of midshipmen had not been reduced. The Executive Department, the departments of the naval sciences, and the athletic program were all seen to be unaffected. Tempers cooled. Within a few years, all agreed that the midshipmen were receiving a better education because of the reforms brought about by the order. Now, twenty-two years later, the navy boasts of its system of education at Annapolis. It is featured prominently in materials designed to interest young men in the Naval Academy. One looks in vain for any hint of the attitudes that once caused the reforms to be so bitterly opposed.

9

What Might
Have Been?

But for Watergate, John Connally would almost surely have become president of the United States. I began to think that the presidency was his goal when he left the secretary of the navy's office. How he intended to go about it, I had no idea. I knew that he had the stature of a president and the drive necessary to achieve that office. I could only guess at his ambition.

When Connally left Washington to seek the governorship of Texas, he was little known outside the navy. A poll of Texans showed that only 2 percent believed he would win over the other five candidates. We who had served with him had no doubt. He would win if he became known to enough people. He was a master of the political process. He was intelligent, eloquent, and charismatic. Tall and handsome, he also looked the part of a great man. The combination was unbeatable given adequate exposure, and absent the development of some crippling liability.

He became politically invincible in Texas and served two terms as governor. He subsequently left the Democratic party to become a Republican. The political philosophy of Texas Democrats, however, was hardly distinguishable from Republicans in general. He was frequently consulted by President Nixon during the latter's first term.

By 1971, Connally had become the secretary of the treasury: Nixon held him in the highest regard. He praised him frequently, publicly, and extravagantly, calling him one of the greatest living Americans. It was no secret that he preferred to have Connally as his running mate in 1972. He concluded, however, that dumping Vice President Agnew would cause him too much damage within the right wing of his party. Soon after Nixon's landslide victory over McGovern, Agnew's corruption as governor of Maryland began to come to light. Nixon sought ways to get Agnew to resign so that he could appoint John Connally as vice president. He was unsuccessful. It was obvious, however, that Connally was Nixon's heir apparent. The Democratic party was in total disarray after the McGovern fiasco. The path to the presidency for Connally was open.

Then came the long nightmare of Watergate. Nixon's ability to influence Congress sank to zero. Because of Connally's shift of parties, he was disliked by congressional Democrats and not yet fully trusted by the Republicans. When Agnew resigned in disgrace, Nixon was informed that Congress would block a Connally appointment as Agnew's successor. He had to be satisfied with Gerald Ford, who had no congressional enemies.

As for being the heir apparent, a Nixon endorsement became a kiss of death. Worse still, the Special Prosecutor's Office, a creature of Watergate, began to act like a runaway grand jury. Having successfully nailed so many cabinet-level scalps to the wall, it sought one more—Connally's. It brought him to trial on a charge of bribery by a dairy industry lobbyist. The charge was predicated solely on the unsubstantiated testimony of the latter, whose name was Jacobson. He was a convicted perjurer. Furthermore, the Special Prosecutor's Office had agreed to drop another charge against Jacobson in return for his testimony against Connally. A more dismal example of excess prosecutorial zeal can hardly be imagined. Watergate fever had apparently infected the prosecutor's staff to the extent of destroying its professional judgment. Aside from the absence of evidence save the word of a perjurer, the charge made no sense. Connally was several times a millionaire. It was absurd to think he could be tempted by a bribe such as that charged. Secondly, although Connally had political enemies, his integrity had never been questioned. But most importantly, it was unimaginable that John Connally, with his unparalleled political judgment, would make himself a hostage to anyone, let alone one of such questionable character as Jacobson.

Connally, of course, was acquitted. Yet the mere fact that he was charged and tried ended his chance to be president. He could never overcome the widespread suspicion that there was something shady about him. The image of an opportunistic wheeler-dealer, unfair and inaccurate as it was, continued to haunt him. It caused him to lose to Ronald Reagan in his 1980 bid for the Republican nomination.

Connally was not the only incidental casualty of Watergate. Senator Edward Kennedy was another. The national reaction to evidence of wrong-doing by its top officials was one of revulsion. In the election of 1976, only a candidate with no trace of scandal in his record had a chance to win. Ted Kennedy had his Chappaquiddick. The country had just rid itself of a president for covering up a crime. It could hardly be expected to elect another who was widely believed not only to have covered up a crime, but also to have committed it. Kennedy wisely did not even try for the nomination.

Jimmy Carter was the big Watergate winner. He came from nowhere and ran against Washington. He projected an image of freshness, honesty, and sincerity. By skilled avoidance of any clear statement of his political philosophy, he became all things to all men. Watergate-weary Americans wanted "decency" in the candidate above all other qualities. And that's exactly what they got.

How could Watergate have happened? The break-in to the offices of the Democratic National Committee was, of course, atrocious. It was not, however, of itself of sufficient gravity to topple the government. It would have been so only if Nixon himself had authorized it. There is no evidence that he did. Even Nixon's most implacable enemies have never thought him to be stupid. How, then, could he have allowed it to get so completely out of hand? I call the following my *Unified Theory of Watergate:*

Nixon, in 1971, was far from confident that he would be reelected. He knew that a large part of the electorate detested him. In the best of times, he suffered from insecurity. His campaign slogan for reelection did not even mention his name, presumably because it was a red flag to so many people. The slogan was "Reelect the President." During June, 1971, when the break-in occurred, Nixon did not know who his Democratic opponent would be. That then was the climate when the Watergate burglary took place.

There is not a shred of evidence that Nixon was involved beforehand. I am sure, however, that he must have immediately insisted on knowing who was responsible. He would have found to his shock and dismay that it was John Mitchell. Mitchell had been his law partner in New York and his campaign manager in 1968. He was the attorney general of the United States. "Law and Order" was a top Nixon campaign issue. Here was his close friend and associate, and the highest law enforcement officer in the country, involved in a despicable burglary! What to do? One alternative would have been to fire Mitchell on the spot. It would not have been far-fetched for Nixon to have concluded that such an action could cost him reelection. The Democrats would be handed a bludgeon with which to beat him. He had barely defeated Humphrey four years before. His victory was achieved then only because the street mob in Chicago had dealt Humphrey a blow from which he never recovered. Nixon could not expect such luck again. He also could not have anticipated that he would have such a weak opponent as McGovern.

The other alternative was to cover up. He chose that course. He still, however, had a chance to avoid ultimate disaster. He could, immediately after the election, have fired Mitchell. He could have explained the delay by a desire not to have the electorate "distracted from the great issues."

For one who years before had saved his political life with the "Checkers" speech, this would have presented no great problem. There would, of course, have been a great outcry. But it would have died away. That was Nixon's last clear chance. By the end of his term, the incident would have been all but forgotten.

And, as sure as these things can be, in January 1985, John Connally would have completed his second term as president of the United States.

10

Fred Korth

Connally's successor, Fred Korth, was also a Texan and a lawyer. He came to the Office of Secretary of the Navy from the presidency of the Continental National Bank of Forth Worth. He had been an army officer in World War II. A graduate of the University of Texas Law School, he had practiced law in Fort Worth before becoming a banker. He had not been noticeably involved in politics, nor did he appear to have political ambitions. Vice President Lyndon Johnson was his friend. I have therefore assumed that Johnson had something to do with his selection for the job. However he came to be appointed secretary of the navy, he brought to that office great energy and ability.

Korth was a big, imposing man, slightly stooped, with silvering hair. He had a deep and penetrating voice with a rich Texas accent. His size, commanding bearing, funereal suits, and heavy, black horn-rimmed glasses all combined to give him an air of austerity and dignity. It was almost as if he sought through dress and demeanor to mask his natural ebullience, friendliness, and quick sense of humor. He had a keen mind and was a master of repartee. He loved a good joke and was himself a great raconteur. A man's man, he enjoyed the companionship of old drinking and hunting pals. Yet on the social scene, he was charming and urbane, and much in demand among Washington hostesses. In later years, his impressive appearance and extraordinary wit made him the favorite escort of the fabulous Marjorie Merriweather Post.

In the beginning, Korth seemed less sure of himself with respect to the processes of his new office than had Connally. Perhaps as a former army officer, he was reluctant to assert himself too quickly in a navy milieu. He thus had an early tendency to confine himself to issues that were presented to him for decision. On those issues, however, he exercised independent judgment from the start. His handling of the assault by the chief of naval operations on the Naval Academy Directive, which occurred soon after he took office, is a case in point. His early reluctance to take the initiative disappeared in time. For example, he was well out in front of the then CNO, Admiral David McDonald, in his advocacy of nuclear propulsion for ships other than carriers and submarines. He took charge of that agenda, and deserves much of the credit for the creation of the navy's all-nuclear task forces.

John Connally was a hard act to follow. I had looked to his successor with apprehension. Nevertheless, I soon came to admire Fred Korth as an effective and courageous secretary of the navy and a fine human being, and to value him as a friend.

Connally, of course, left behind much unfinished business. There was the aforementioned directive on Naval Academy education that still had to be defended. The Wagmight pot had not ceased bubbling. A major competition to select a contractor to develop a revolutionary airplane for the navy and the air force had been started during Connally's watch. It became the TFX dispute, which eventually became the dominant issue of Korth's term of office. The case of Ruben the Cuban still had big potential for trouble. Connally had advised Korth only that there was such a case. He had advised him to inquire into it no further!

One controversy that had arisen under Connally came to a dramatic head shortly after Korth arrived in the Pentagon. That was the problem of establishing the position of the U.S. Government toward the "flags of convenience" ships. These were merchant ships that were owned by Americans but were registered under the flags of Panama, Liberia, and Honduras. The shipowners had so registered their ships to avoid payment of American seamen's wages. The National Labor Relations Board (NLRB) had ruled that U.S.

labor law applied to these ships. This meant that the American maritime unions could attempt to organize their crews. Such efforts would be "protected activity" under the Taft-Hartley Act.

The maritime unions were asking the courts to enforce the NLRB ruling. The shipowners were seeking judicial reversal. Several cases were converging on the U.S. Supreme Court. They came from various federal courts having jurisdiction over ports on the east and west coasts and the Gulf of Mexico. Since a single issue was involved, the Supreme Court selected a representative case for review. That was the *Incres* case.

The litigation was ostensibly between private parties—i.e., unions versus shipowners. There were, however, important interests of the United States at stake. The Joint Chiefs of Staff counted the flags of convenience ships as available to the U.S. in times of national emergency. This availability was based upon agreements with the owners and contracts for War Risk insurance sponsored by the Maritime Administration. These arrangements were only possible, however, because they were countenanced by the laws and customs of Panama, Liberia, and Honduras. No established maritime nation would tolerate commandeering of its flag vessels by the unilateral action of the United States. At that time, the merchant fleet registered under the U.S. flag amounted to about 10 million deadweight tons. The flags of convenience ships on the Joint Chiefs' list comprised about 12 million tons. Their critical importance to national defense was therefore obvious. If the NLRB ruling was allowed to stand, the owners would have no alternative but to lay up the ships or transfer them to the flag of an established maritime nation. The harsh realities of world shipping economics precluded their transfer to the U.S. flag. Thus, the ships would be lost to the U.S. for emergency use. The shipping available in national emergencies would be reduced by more than half. U.S. merchant seamen had priced themselves out of the world shipping market. Only through a direct or indirect subsidy could a merchant ship operate under the U.S. flag. There was no more room under that umbrella; and Congress had repeatedly refused to increase merchant marine subsidies.

In addition to the Defense Department, several other departments had an interest. The State Department had been bombarded with diplomatic protests and *aides-mémoire* from the traditional maritime nations. Those countries objected to the contention that U.S. labor law could apply to foreign flag ships. They believed that an important and long-standing principle of international law was at issue. The Department of Agriculture was engaged in shipping huge quantities of grain and other farm products in the U.S. foreign aid programs; the cost of those shipments could be substantially increased. The Treasury Department was concerned with the balance of payments implications of the problem. The Labor Department was representing a constituency, the unions. The Department of Justice was interested in the legal question.

This was not a problem that could be brushed aside. The *Incres* case was to be argued before the Supreme Court. The United States had an important interest in the outcome. In such cases, it is the job of the solicitor general to present the government's position in briefs and oral arguments. The problem was to determine what that position should be. Did the U.S. Government support or oppose the ruling of the NLRB? The Labor Department urged support. Defense urged opposition. In between, the other departments held a spectrum of opinions. President Kennedy appointed an interdepartmental committee to make a recommendation. Secretary McNamara, after the first meeting, appointed Connally to represent Defense. This delegation reflected the sea power nature of the problem. As usual for such committees, subsequent meetings are attended mostly by the "working members." I came to fulfill that description for the Defense Department. I was very ably assisted by an officer from the JAG's office, Lieutenant Commander Harold Hoag. Meetings went on for several months. Our Defense position was that the NLRB ruling was erroneous as a matter of law. Established principles of international law and comity compelled a conclusion that the age-old law of the flag should prevail. The policy issue involved a desire for more jobs for U.S. merchant seamen. Our position was that the NLRB ruling would not achieve that end. The unions believed that if they could organize the flags of convenience ships, they could force the owners to pay American wages. There would then be no incentive to hire foreign crews. Presto—thousands of jobs would be created for American merchant seamen. But, we said, the inexorable logic of world shipping economics ruled that out. As pointed out earlier, no unsubsidized vessel could pay U.S. seamen's wages and compete in the world shipping market. So from a policy standpoint, there would be no new jobs, and our emergency defense capability would suffer a crippling blow.

The Defense position eventually prevailed in the committee. The pathway, however, had been made difficult by obstruction from an unexpected source. Archibald Cox was then the solicitor general. He had been a professor of labor law at Harvard. His sympathies lay with the unions. With crew cut, bow tie, and Harvard accent, the articulate and urbane Cox was the personification of the dominant Ivy League composition of the Kennedy administration. Cox attended most of the meetings. He never once took direct issue with our Defense arguments. He could and did, however, blunt their force and prevent general agreement therewith by witty and distracting comment. He had a professorial ability to make commonplace observations sound impressive and authoritative. He commanded respect and attention. His faintly patronizing air toward the Defense position was far more damaging than a frontal attack. We were never able to pin him down. This was doubly irritating because the solicitor general was the only member of the committee without a policy interest in the outcome. He had no institutional axe to grind. He was, in a literal sense, a mouthpiece. His only task was to articulate the government's position before the Supreme Court, once it was determined.

My frustration grew to the point that I drafted a "Dear Archie" letter for Connally to sign. It spelled out in great detail the Defense positions on the legal, political, economic, and defense issues. It asked Cox to identify any area of disagreement. A "Dear John" response arrived. Cox stated that he could find no fault with any of our arguments. He agreed that we were correct on the facts and the law. But he concluded his letter with the following statement, "However, sometimes people's feelings are more important than the truth." This observation is true, of course, in commonplace social situations. I found it astonishing as an expression of the position of the solicitor general of the United States on an important national problem. Knowing that Cox held such a view, I felt some years later that Nixon was in deep yoghurt when he appointed Archibald Cox as special prosecutor in the Watergate controversy.

After the above exchange of letters, however, Cox's obstruction appeared to cease. The recommendation of the committee to President Kennedy was unanimous, except for a footnote dissent by Secretary of Labor Arthur Goldberg. The committee's recommendation was that the NLRB ruling be opposed. Goldberg's footnote proposed that a broad subsidy program be sent to Congress by the administration. This was a sop to the Labor Department constituency. Goldberg was aware that it could not be taken seriously.

The report of the committee was given to David Bell, the director of the Bureau of the Budget. He then informed the members that the president wished to review it with the committee principals before it became public. I had briefed Secretary Korth on the flags of convenience issues. He was, however, concerned that he was not sufficiently familiar with all of the complexities to be comfortable in a meeting with the president. I assured him there was nothing to worry about because there remained no significant opposition to the Defense position. The Goldberg footnote was a triviality. It was, I said, unlikely to be raised by the president or anyone else.

Korth nevertheless felt unprepared to go alone to the meeting, and requested that I go with him. I thought he'd never ask! I was delighted at the chance to be present at the culminating event of the long effort. I would be able to observe the president and the majority of his cabinet in action. I was relaxed and unworried, confident that the Defense Department position would prevail. I could not know that the meeting would very nearly end in total disaster.

The meeting took place in the Cabinet Room of the White House. While we awaited the arrival of the president, a bombshell was dropped: A few days earlier, Secretary of Labor Goldberg had been appointed to the Supreme Court. Acting Secretary of Labor Willard Wirtz, who had been the under secretary, addressed the committee. He said that he could not go along with the Goldberg footnote. He apologized for the last minute reversal of his predecessor, but insisted that he had a problem of conscience. He was compelled, he said, to urge the president to support the NLRB ruling. The committee reacted with shocked silence.

President Kennedy entered before there could be any discussion of the Wirtz blockbuster. He was accompanied by his brother, Robert Kennedy, the attorney general. Once again I was struck by how big a man the president was. His size was accentuated by the contrast with his shorter and much slighter brother. Both were grim and unsmiling.

Wirtz immediately announced to the president that his conscience required him to take issue with the report of the Flags of Convenience Committee. The president told him to proceed. Wirtz then made an impassioned plea on behalf of a claimed 50,000 out-of-work merchant seamen. He castigated the flags of convenience shipowners who, he said, were getting rich at the expense of underpaid foreign crews, sent to sea in unsanitary and unseaworthy ships. Ignoring the months of careful analysis by the committee of the many complexities involved, he made it seem that the flags of convenience issue was nothing but the result of greed and rapacity of the shipowners. The painstakingly forged report of the committee was forgotten. The president started around the table, asking for comments, not on the report but on Wirtz's statement!

The committee members were in a state of confusion. Secretary of State Dean Rusk could only stutter something about the British being upset at the NLRB ruling. The president brushed that aside. "I can handle the British," he said. The other cabinet officers were equally ineffective. Archie Cox said with enthusiasm that the Wirtz position would give no trouble to the solicitor general. When the president reached Fred Korth, the latter spoke with poise and assurance, "Mr. President, the Defense Department disagrees strongly with Mr. Wirtz. The NLRB ruling is contrary to international law. If it stands, it will seriously damage our defense capability. Furthermore, it is impractical and unproductive." I was most impressed. The president, however, answered impatiently, "Yes, I've heard all that. But what have you got to say about the other points that Secretary Wirtz has raised?"

Korth responded, "Well, Mr. President, as you know, I'm new at my job and I haven't been able to get into this as deeply as I would have liked to. But my associate, Commander Kerr, can go into those issues."

Then, for the better part of an hour, I argued the Defense case. I was interrupted frequently and cross-examined vigorously by an obviously angry president. He probed particularly deeply into the facts relating to the economics of world shipping. In the end, he turned to an aide and said, "Will somebody get me that telegram I sent to Joe Curran during the campaign?" Curran was president of the National Maritime Union (NMU). The telegram was produced and the president read it aloud. It said, "The runaway ship, like its counterpart, the runaway shop, is an evil which I pledge my administration to eradicate." The cause of the president's aggravation was then immediately obvious. He had made a campaign promise to get rid of the flags of convenience ships. Yet he was being told that to do so would damage the national defense and would not help the unions. The promise had been a blunder. He said to me, "All right, Commander, we'll do it your way. But this is going to go squarely on the back of the Defense Department. I want a memorandum signed by McNamara tomorrow that lays it all out and tells me that I have no alternative from a national defense point of view."

As we left the Cabinet Room, Korth said, "Let's go and see

McNamara. How does he feel about this, anyway?" I admitted that I didn't know how he felt.

Korth was aghast. "My God, Andy! You've gone ahead and made that pitch to the president of the United States, and committed the Department of Defense, and you tell me that you don't know how Secretary McNamara feels about it?" Although I tried not to show it, I too was now alarmed. What if McNamara refused to go along? I would have placed my new boss in a terrible position. I had not, however, acted entirely on my own. My anchor to windward was Cy Vance.

I then explained to Korth that when I started on the flags of convenience project, Cyrus Vance had been general counsel of the Department of Defense. I had gone over our proposed position with him. He had agreed that it was sound and approved it. I had kept him advised during the course of the committee study. He maintained a lively interest. Even after he left the job of general counsel to become the secretary of the army, he asked that I continue to keep him informed. I had done so. Vance was a close confidant of McNamara, perhaps the closest in the Pentagon. So I said to Korth, "Let's first go and see Cy Vance and tell him what happened."

Cyrus Vance was one of my favorite people among the top Defense hierarchy. In fact, he was a favorite of almost everyone. With a lock of hair falling over his forehead, he had a boyishly ingenuous look that invited confidence. Always a gentleman, he had a special gift of making each associate, whether of high or low status, feel a bond of friendship. He was a good listener. He had a superb legal mind, honed in a successful practice with a prestigious New York law firm. I was delighted when, years later, he became President Carter's secretary of state. And I was chagrined at the extraordinary lack of grace with which his resignation from that post was accepted.

Vance accompanied Korth and me to McNamara's office. With his help we quickly obtained McNamara's ratification of the position I had taken with the president. Hal Hoag and I drafted a memo that night and McNamara signed it and sent it to the president the next morning.

President Kennedy then told his brother Bobby, the attorney general, to instruct Archie Cox, the solicitor general, to present arguments in the *Incres* case against the NLRB ruling. Cox did so, but to my ear with a marked lack of conviction. Nevertheless, the Supreme Court arrived at an 8–0 decision against the NLRB. Justice Goldberg abstained because of his prior participation. The Court held that the law of the flag was paramount. The NLRB ruling was thus overturned. The *Incres* case still stands as a landmark decision. It marked the end, as far as I know, of judicial assaults against the flags of convenience concept. Political assaults by the U.S. Maritime Unions still continued unabated.

The flags of convenience exercise gave me an insight into the difficulties of arriving at an agreed national policy. Our system is indeed ponderous. Even the president is severely circumscribed. I entered the fray without an understanding of these realities. With eager naiveté I was convinced that "right" would easily prevail, and became angry and frustrated when obstacles persisted. The various contending parties were to me clearly defined good guys and bad guys. At the dinner table each evening, I regaled Rusty and our two small children, Alex and Laurie, with my accounts of the iniquities of the guys in the black hats. They reacted with satisfactory outrage, as well as rejoicing with me over incidents where good triumphed over evil.

The affair also gave me the opportunity of a lifetime: At dinner each evening, after we were settled at the table, one or the other of the children would ask, "What happened today, Daddy?" On the evening following the meeting in the Cabinet Room, I was able to respond, "Well, kids, I had a long argument with President Kennedy today!" I shall never forget their delighted cries of "Tell us,—oh tell us all about it!" and their rapt attention as I told them the story.

Secretary Korth disappointed me on one occasion: I offered him the chance to make U.S. naval history and he blew it! The U.S. Navy had been totally dry since 1914, when Secretary of the Navy Josephus Daniels issued his famous General Order Number One. That order terminated the wine messes that naval officers had previously enjoyed aboard ship. The enlisted men had been cut off some years before. That event was commemorated in a sailor's sad little ditty, which goes, "They raised our pay five cents a day, and stopped our grog forever."

The U.S. Navy's dry tradition is a dismal departure from the practice of all the other navies of the world. Many times I have been lavishly plied with robust Holland gin aboard a Dutch submarine, or fine scotch whiskey aboard a British man-of-war, and cringed with embarrassment at the fruit punch served during our reciprocating receptions.

So when I saw that Secretary Korth was willing to risk controversy for the good of the navy, it seemed that the time for an historic change had come. I prepared a Navy Department General Order for Mr. Korth's signature. It would have permitted the serving of wine in an admiral's mess when foreign guests were aboard. This modest beginning, I was sure, would soon thereafter lead to the demise of the entire barbarous restriction.

Secretary Korth agreed that the change made sense. But at the last minute before signing, he said that, as as courtesy, he should show it to Admiral George Anderson, the CNO. I experienced a sinking feeling and said so. "Don't worry, Andy," Korth said, "I'm going to do it."

Well, Admiral Anderson was smart. Sensing Korth's enthusiasm, he immediately agreed with the *spirit* of the proposed change. He told the secretary how he, as the former commander of the Sixth Fleet in the Mediterranean, had felt embarrassment at official functions aboard his flagship. But, he said, he had made an important discovery. He had found a product called "Champale" that looked and tasted like champagne, but was nonalcoholic. So, on the basis of that, he convinced Korth that the change was unnecessary! *Sic transit gloria.*

While on this subject, my own attitude toward booze may be of some slight interest. I can do without it but much prefer not to. I enjoy drinking with friends, and occasionally without them. The cocktail hour, with a couple of hefty martinis, has always been a wonderful time of day when life's problems can be seen in proper perspective. I enjoy a good wine with dinner, but have been blessed with a catholicity of taste so that *any* wine is better than none at all. I even find palatable the cheap wine of French Polynesia, which comes in thin plastic bottles with beer-bottle type caps. The local Frenchmen, leaving it to the natives, refuse to drink it and dismiss it contemptuously as "Chateau Plastique."

As much as I enjoy drinking, I consider myself most fortunate to have escaped, so far and by the Grace of God, those physiological and psychological quirks that lead to alcoholism. My role model in this respect is, in all modesty, Sir Winston Churchill.

Another problem that lingered from Connally's term was the continuing effort by the Kennedy administration to get rid of Castro. After the Bay of Pigs, that goal became an obsession with President Kennedy. To accomplish it, there were various groups under a variety of names from the spring of 1961 until John Kennedy's death in Dallas in November, 1963. Bobby Kennedy was the point man in all of these endeavors. He either chaired the groups or was their constant goad to greater efforts. All the groups had the same purpose: Castro was to be harassed, discredited, and interfered with by all means possible. Only the outright invasion of Cuba was ruled out. Sabotage, surveillance, and subversion were specifically approved. One way or another, Castro had to go. Assassination, though apparently not explicitly authorized, was an implicit possibility. It was clear that the Kennedys would not view Castro's death with regret. Knowing of the pressures of the Kennedy administration to achieve Castro's removal, I would have been astonished if the CIA had not come up with plans to do him in.

Even after the Cuban Missile Crisis, these efforts did not cease. A Cuban Coordinating Committee was formed to work under the direction of a Standing Group, of which Robert Kennedy was chairman. The committee was composed of the heads of all departments and agencies of the government that could contribute to Castro's removal. McNamara delegated the job within the Defense Department to Cyrus Vance, then the secretary of the army. Vance's right-hand man for this task was Joe Califano.

Joe Califano has had an interesting career. As a bright young New York lawyer, he came to the Pentagon as a special assistant to Cyrus Vance at the beginning of the Kennedy administration. Vance was then McNamara's general counsel. When Vance became secretary of the army, he took Joe with him and made him general counsel of the army. Later, when Roswell Gilpatrick resigned and Vance became deputy secretary of defense, Califano again went with him. Soon thereafter, Joe assumed the additional duties as special assistant to Robert McNamara. In this capacity he came to the attention of President Lyndon Johnson. Much impressed by Joe, Johnson claimed him for his White House Staff. Joe Califano then became the counsel to the president for domestic programs. In this position, he performed the prodigious task of drafting and guiding through Congress Lyndon Johnson's "Great Society" legislation. This meteoric political rise was interrupted by the eight years of Republican occupancy of the White House. During that period, Joe practiced law very successfully in Washington, D.C. He returned to the government with the election of Jimmy Carter. He then became secretary of Health, Education and Welfare. It was old home week, with Cy Vance being sworn in as Carter's secretary of state and Harold Brown as secretary of defense.

Joe Califano is without doubt an intelligent and capable man. But his most distinguishing characteristics are boundless energy and driving ambition. As Vance's deputy for achieving the ends of the Cuban Coordinating Committee, he was tireless. The committee met weekly to report progress and to discuss new proposals. Each week it felt the lash of Bobby Kennedy for failure to produce adequate results. Joe was determined to produce. He required each department and agency within the Department of Defense to designate an action officer through whom he would deal exclusively. Secretary Korth, over my vehement protestations, named me. If ever I saw a loser, this was one! Korth, however, at Joe's insistence, held me to the assignment.

The navy's role involved plans and operations for any kind of harassment within the capability of naval forces. Over-flights and infiltrations are examples. Joe was ceaseless in his demands for more and better ideas to feed to the committee. He was vigilant to see that any operation that had been approved was carried out with dispatch and energy. He was alert to detect and condemn any sign of foot-dragging or lack of commitment. There were telephone calls and meetings at all times of the day and night. In spite of Joe's heroic efforts, however, nothing much happened. The schemes that would cause Castro real trouble were generally deemed too risky and therefore were disapproved by the Cuban Coordinating Committee. The other ideas were most often seen as far greater nuisances to the U.S. Navy than they would be to Castro. So they were not greeted with enthusiasm by the chief of naval operations.

These responsibilities were in addition to my other duties as special counsel. After two months of this exhausting and frustrating exercise, however, I was rescued. The CNO, as I had anticipated, had become irritated. He, Admiral George Anderson, proposed to Korth that an officer within his own organization take over. He nominated Rear Admiral Waldemar Wendt. I had not previously met Admiral Wendt, knowing him only by reputation. Nevertheless, I went to Califano with enthusiastic praise for the admiral's intelligence, experience, initiative, and energy. To my great relief, Joe approved the substitution. Admiral Wendt took over my portfolio in a brief but moving ceremony in the Office of the Secretary of the Navy one Sunday morning. Unfortunately, being Sunday, there was no one there to be moved but the two of us!

The case of Ruben the Cuban cropped up twice during Secretary Korth's tenure. In the first instance, however, Korth was unaware of any problem. It arose as follows.

I have mentioned that Secretary Connally had sent a memorandum to General David Shoup, the commandant of the Marine Corps, concerning action the latter was to take in the Guantánamo case. One day, Korth's marine aide, Colonel Ed Wheeler, told me that he had received a call from Shoup. Shoup had informed Ed that he was going to take certain action with respect to a couple of marines. I was shocked and alarmed. The action was contrary to the order that Connally had given the commandant, and would surely lead to trouble. I told Wheeler that he should call Shoup back and tell him so. Ed said, "*I'm* not going to tell that to Shoup! *You* tell him!" So Ed Wheeler made an appointment for me to see General Shoup.

The general was one of the most colorful characters ever to head the Marine Corps. His utterances, called Shoupisms, were collected and catalogued by connoisseurs within the Corps. Before he became commandant, he had been a vocal opponent of the wide practice within the Marine Corps of the carrying of swagger sticks. This was an affectation borrowed from the British army. It may have originated from the carrying of riding crops by cavalry officers. Shoup's distaste for the practice was so well known that it was mentioned at the White House press conference when his appointment was announced. "General," a reporter said, "I suppose the first thing you will do will be to ban swagger sticks." "Not at all," replied Shoup. "Those who feel the need of them may continue to carry them." No swagger stick has been carried by a marine officer from that day forward.

Outspoken, impetuous, and opinionated, he wore the Congressional Medal of Honor on his chest. He feared no man and was feared by many. He was one of the greatest poker players the military has produced. He is said to have made a fortune at it. He became the absolute ruler of the Marine Corps. I knew our meeting would not be easy.

As I entered his office, Shoup said, "What's this that I hear from Ed Wheeler that the secretary says I'm not obeying orders?" I answered, "General, Secretary Korth knows nothing at all about this. As you know, I'm his special counsel and had the same job with Mr. Connally. I'm here on my own to tell you that the action you told Ed Wheeler about is contrary to what Mr. Connally told you to do." Shoup responded, "You're dead wrong! If the secretary feels I'm disobeying orders, let him tell me that!"

I told Shoup again that Korth was not involved, nor did I want to involve him. I said, however, that if the general persisted, I would

As a midshipman—from the class of '45 yearbook.

In New York right after graduation, with classmate Ed Christofferson, Mother, Dad, and my brother Basil.

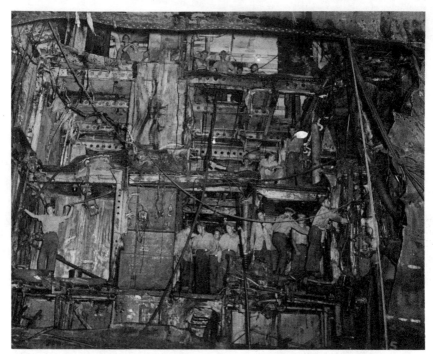

Proof of the efficacy of Japanese torpedoes—the Honolulu *(CL 48) in Manus, November '44.*

Wedding reception in Honolulu, 1947; Father, Mother, me, Rusty, Admiral Dreller, Rusty's sister Dee, and Mrs. Dreller.

With shipmates Bill Young (left) and Buck Weaver in Guam during a cruise of the Sea Fox, 1948. (Rusty always did wonder whose handbag that was!)

John Connally, as a brand new secretary of the navy, with outgoing CNO Admiral Arleigh Burke and incoming CNO Admiral George Anderson (1961).

"A Clean Sweep"—Fred Korth affixes a broom to the radio antenna of his official limousine as we, accompanied by Jim Jenkins, finally leave the TFX hearings.

These were some of the good and the great when I became special counsel in 1961.

Secretary Paul Nitze presents me with a commendation medal, with Rusty, Laurie, and Alec looking suitably pleased (1964).

Vice Admiral Hyland, commander of the 7th Fleet, has baked me a cake on the occasion of my promotion to captain.

I brief visiting dignitary Vice Admiral Semmes on the rise and fall of the Nile, aboard 7th Fleet flagship.

Secretary Paul Ignatius presents me with the Legion of Merit, while Rusty, Alec, and Laurie look even more pleased. (1968)

Rusty and I at Yale with our two Yalies—1973.

Looking appropriately Mephistophelean as a General Electric lawyer—1969.

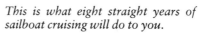
Susan aboard Andiamo III.

This is what eight straight years of sailboat cruising will do to you.

"LEADERSHIP
THE <u>REAL</u> ANSWER"

". . . . . the great leader is one for whom his men will CHEERFULLY give up their lives. That is the real test of leadership."

Rear Admiral Chester Ward
Judge Advocate General, U.S. Navy
JAG JOURNAL, July 1960

UNITED STATES
ATOMIC ENERGY COMMISSION
WASHINGTON 20545

July 10, 1968

Captain A. A. Kerr, USN
Special Counsel
Office of the Secretary of the Navy
Room 4E721, Pentagon
Washington, D. C.

Dear Andy:

I have not been able to find a single person in my organization who would die for me, much less CHEERFULLY die for me. This definitely shows I am not a leader in accordance with Admiral Ward's definition.

Incidently, when Admiral Ward's article came out I telephoned him and asked him how many people in his office had volunteered cheerfully to die for him, whereupon he hung up on me.

Sincerely,

H. G. Rickover

have no alternative but to bring Korth in. I said we could end all this by looking at the paper Shoup had received from Connally. Shoup said, "You mean you're calling me a liar!" "No, sir," I said, "I'm simply saying that you're misinterpreting the order."

Finally Shoup called his chief of staff, General Wallace Greene. "Wally," he said, "bring me that paper from Connally." Greene produced it. Shoup peeled back a corner and looked at it in the manner of one checking his hole card in a stud poker game. "Yep," he said, "it's here all right! It's right here on the memorandum from Connally that this is what I'm supposed to do." "Just a minute, General," I said, "I haven't seen what's on that paper. You've got to be mistaken."

The farce went on for a few more minutes. Then Shoup gave in. He showed me the memo. Written along the bottom of the page, in Shoup's hand, was a note. It stated that he, Shoup, interpreted the memo as permitting what he had proposed to do. So he did have a paper from Connally, and on the paper were words saying he could do what he proposed. But the words were his own words, not Connally's! Having had his bluff called, General Shoup rapidly backed down the rest of the way. It was clear that the Connally directive could not be interpreted in the manner Shoup had tried. The action, obviously, was something the commandant *wanted* to do and thought he could get away with. I have seldom spent a less pleasant hour.

The second eruption of the case was far more serious. In April 1963, a year and a half after the initial occurrence, Drew Pearson made mention of it in his syndicated column, "Washington Merry-go-round." He said that a William Szili, who had been a lieutenant in the Marine Corps, had professed knowledge of the affair. A flurry of press interest followed, only to meet with "no comment" responses from government information officers. Then, about a week later, I received a call at home from Secretary Korth. It was early Sunday morning. "Have you seen the papers this morning?" "No, sir," I responded, "I haven't gotten round to them yet."

"Well," he said, "you'd better take a look and call me right back." I checked the newspapers and was appalled. The *Washington Post* and the *New York Times* each had front page stories about Ruben the Cuban. They were based on a long article that had appeared the evening before in the *Philadelphia Inquirer*. They reported a bizarre story by Szili that he and a Congressional Medal of Honor winner named Captain Jackson had apprehended a Cuban spy at Guantánamo, and had killed him when he tried to escape. I called Korth back. "Meet me at the office," he said. "We've got to get cracking on this."

When I arrived at the Pentagon, Korth said that McNamara and Vance were working with Arthur Sylvester, the Pentagon press spokesman, on a press release. On arrival at McNamara's office, I found the release was ready to go. It stated in effect that the Szili story, if reported correctly, did not reflect the known facts of the Guantánamo incident. That was precisely true. Szili's story was wrong in important details. But I convinced McNamara that he couldn't say that. The last word of the United States government on the matter, in an official note to the government of Cuba, had been that the death remained unexplained, as indeed it did. There are things nobody will ever be able to explain about it. We knew enough to know that Szili's story was grossly inaccurate. One could not, however, get into a discussion of what was *not* true without touching upon what *was* true. So I persuaded McNamara that we should not depart from the previously agreed upon, and presidentially approved, strategy of "no comment."

We knew, however, that holding the line would now be more difficult. Congressman Richard Schweiker of Pennsylvania had taken up Szili's case. Szili was claiming that he had been mistreated by the Marine Corps. Schweiker, with Szili present, had even held a press conference, with photographic and TV coverage, on the steps of the U.S. Capitol. Not knowing the facts, he had gotten himself very far out on a limb. We knew that politicians in that situation, like cornered animals, can be very dangerous indeed. So, with Korth's approval, I went to see Congressman Carl Vinson, the chairman of the House Armed Services Committee. Vinson, it may be recalled, had been briefed on the incident a year and a half earlier. I refreshed his memory and asked if he would take jurisdiction in the event a congressional inquiry could not be avoided. Vinson readily agreed to do so.

During the following week, the pressure for a congressional investigation mounted to an intolerable degree. Vinson accordingly announced that he would conduct a hearing. He appointed a subcommittee with himself as chairman and composed of a few sound and stable members from both parties. He invited Schweiker to participate.

A day or two before the hearing, I met with Russ Blandford, the committee's chief counsel. We agreed that three witnesses would surface. The first would be the secretary of the navy, Fred

Korth, who, by that time, had been thoroughly briefed. The second was the commandant of the Marine Corps, General David Shoup. I was the third. Blandford agreed that Connally need not be called.

The big problem would be Shoup. His grasp of the facts was weak. He tended to become apoplectic when the case was mentioned. His emotions had so far clouded his intellect that his view of the incident was distorted and confused. I therefore sought Blandford's assistance. "Russ," I said, "you know what Shoup is like when he sounds off on this. Unless we can keep him quiet, the hearing will turn into a shambles. We'll end up with nothing but confusion." Blandford agreed. Besides his position as chief counsel of a powerful congressional committee, Russ was a general in the Marine Corps Reserve. He had great influence within the Corps and particularly with General Shoup. He convinced Shoup that for the good of the Marine Corps, he should stay in the background. No one but Russ Blandford could have carried that off!

The hearing was held in closed session. It was, in essence, a comprehensive briefing. I first spelled out the undisputed facts and how they had been ascertained. I then spoke of the gaps in our knowledge, and our guesses as to what may have occurred in those gaps. I pointed out the uncertainties that would never be resolved. I ended by explaining the rationale for handling the case as we did. A few questions were asked, and Vinson announced himself satisfied. The other members of the committee followed suit. Schweiker was upset. He now, of course, could see what a mess he had stepped in. He announced, however, that he would inform the press and television people waiting outside that part of Szili's statement had been confirmed. I explained to Schweiker that now that he was privy to all the known facts, and knew the reason the affair had been classified Secret, he could not get into a discussion of what was or was not true. Schweiker, however, continued to bluster, and Vinson said to me, "Young man, could you advise the congressman on the provisions of the Espionage Act, and the fact that they also apply to him?"

Vinson then announced, "When I leave this room, and all those gentlemen ouside ask me what happened, I'm just going to say, 'no comment'." Turning to Congressman Schweiker, he said, "I strongly advise you to do the same thing." And Schweiker did.

In the weeks following, press interest gradually subsided as did my state of nervous apprehension. A steady diet of "no comment" spoils the appetite of even the most determined reporter. The trick, of course, is to hold that line. I am not aware of any other peacetime case where this was done so successfully. The case of Ruben the Cuban thus passed into limbo, where it remains.

At the time Fred Korth became secretary of the navy, TFX was merely a set of initials associated with an aircraft procurement competition. What made it unusual was that the aircraft was to fulfill the requirements of both the navy and the air force.

The project had its genesis in the early, heady days of Robert McNamara's reign. At that time, nothing was sacred; everything was being questioned. The air force came to McNamara with a proposal for a follow-on aircraft to the F-105. There is usually a ten-year lag between the conception of a new airplane and its introduction into inventory. The new aircraft would thus be the air force's attack fighter for the seventies. By then the F-105 would be obsolescent.

While McNamara's staff was evaluating the proposal, the navy came in with a proposal for a replacement for the F-4 fighter. The new Navy plane would also become operational in the seventies. "Wait a minute," McNamara said. "The air force is going to be developing a new plane during the same period. Why don't you fellows get together and come up with a single plane to do both jobs." Both the air force and the navy aviation experts insisted that that was an aerodynamic impossibility. The planes had to perform widely different missions. The navy needed a relatively light plane that could land on and take off from carriers. It also must be capable of loitering at low speeds on air-defense missions in the vicinity of carrier task forces. This required a plane with a relatively low wing loading. This means that its wing area would be large in proportion to its weight. The air force, on the other hand, had a need for high speed at low altitude to penetrate enemy air defenses. It also had to be able to stand high "G" stresses in the maneuvers required to deliver a nuclear weapon. These characteristics required high wing loading. The air force wanted a relatively heavy plane with small, swept back wings.

McNamara had heard of work in NASA on the concept of a variable-geometry wing. This is aeronautical jargon for a wing whose shape can be changed while the plane is in flight. For take-off, landing, and flying at low speeds, the wings would be extended. For high speeds, the wings would be folded back like a dart and partially tucked into the body of the aircraft. The idea was not new. It had been tried in an experimental plane some years before and had not been notably successful. NASA, apparently, was working on a new approach.

McNamara said to the two services, "Look, maybe it is impossible. But why don't you each put down your statement of requirements. We'll then invite industry to come in with a proposal for a single airplane that would meet both your needs. Let's see what they come up with."

A request for proposals went out to the aircraft industry. The projected plane was called the TFX. (It was later to become the F-111.) Some five companies responded. Three were very wide of the mark. The proposals of Boeing and General Dynamics both incorporated the variable-geometry wing concept and were of interest to the navy and air force. The two services therefore joined in a recommendation for a second round of competition between those two firms. The new proposals of Boeing and General Dynamics were evaluated by an Air Force Evaluation Board at Wright-Patterson Air Force Base in Ohio. The board reported that both contractors fell well short of meeting the requirements of both services. One would have expected the project to die at that point. However, surprisingly, the aviation branches of both the navy and the air force recommended a third round of competition. In this one, Boeing came within a hair of meeting the specifications. General Dynamics was significantly behind. A fourth round of competition was commenced. McNamara, at that point, reminded the contractors of the purpose of the exercise: a single plane for both services. In his letter to this effect, he introduced a new word into the language, "commonality." The navy and air force versions were to be composed of common parts to the maximum possible extent.

The fourth set of proposals was submitted and evaluated. Lo and behold! Both the navy CNO and the air force chief of staff said that the proposed aircraft of *both* contractors met their respective military requirements. Underlying these conclusions was a massive "Fourth Evaluation Report" prepared at Wright-Patterson. In addition, the navy had conducted its own evaluation within the source selection division of its Bureau of Weapons. That division was headed by George Spangenberg, a highly respected aeronautical engineer. Spangenberg had been responsible for the selection of a succession of successful navy aircraft. He had enormous prestige within the aviation circles of the navy.

Spangenberg prepared the briefing at which Secretary Korth was apprised of the results of the competition. It summarized the technical aspects of the two proposals. It listed three conclusions:

—Both proposals met navy requirements.

—Both proposals were acceptable in the navy.

—There was no significant preference between the proposals.

The briefing concluded with the recommendation that Boeing be selected as the winning contractor.

The air force evaluation groups had reached essentially the same conclusions. They reported to Air Force Secretary Eugene Zuckert that both proposals met air force requirements. They also recommended the selection of Boeing as the winner.

At that time, the fall of 1962, the country was in a recession. Many areas had been designated as depressed areas with high unemployment. The award was for one of the biggest single research and development contracts in many years. The production contract would be even bigger. The contract would, therefore, have considerable economic impact on the area where it was to be performed. Consequently, the competition had been followed with intense interest.

Secretaries Korth and Zuckert met with McNamara and his advisors. Taking part in the discussions were Roswell Gilpatric, the deputy secretary of defense, and Harold Brown, the director of Defense Research and Engineering. The group came to the unanimous conclusion that General Dynamics be selected. McNamara, after informing the president, announced that decision. There had been no further consultation with the top officers of the navy and air force, both of whom had recommended Boeing. They reacted with stunned disbelief. To them it was unthinkable that the civilian secretary of defense would select a military aircraft against the unanimous recommendations of his military advisors. There was an immediate outcry in Congress and in the press. The decision, it was said, was either corrupt or stupid. The plant of General Dynamics where the prime contract was to be performed was in Fort Worth, Texas. That Secretary Korth was from Fort Worth received special mention. Vice President Lyndon Johnson's fine Texan hand was also believed to have been at work. Senator McClellan, chairman of the Permanent Sub-committee on Investigations, announced that he would investigate the award. Senator Henry "Scoop" Jackson of the state of Washington was an influential member of the McClellan Committee. Jackson was often called the "Senator from Boeing," since the headquarters and main plants of that company were located in Seattle.

Within a few days of the announcement of the award, Korth received a morning phone call from Jerome Adlerman, the chief counsel for the McClellan Committee. Adlerman wanted to talk with Korth about the TFX. A meeting was set for that evening in the secretary of the navy's office. Korth said that he wanted me to sit in, and asked how much I knew about the TFX. I told him that I knew nothing other than what I had heard in the Pentagon corridors or read in the newspapers. I reminded him that his naval aide, Captain Marmaduke Bayne, had recommended that the TFX meetings be restricted to technical and operational personnel. Jim Jenkins and I had both been excluded. Duke Bayne had concluded that we had no need to know. However, the administrative aide, Commander Thomas B. Hayward, had been invited to the meetings because he was an aviator. Secretary Korth then told me to get together with Tom Hayward, who could acquaint me with the history of the competition. Tom gave me much of the background that I have related above, including a copy of the final report to the secretary of the navy, which set forth the "no significant preference" conclusion. I said to Tom, "I don't have much time. It's clear that the McClellan Committee is hostile, and I've got to help Mr. Korth get ready for tonight's meeting with Adlerman. Who would be the best person in the bureau to give me a hand?" Tom said, "That's going to be difficult, but you should talk to George Spangenberg. He is the key man in this whole thing." He then told me who Spangenberg was.

I called Spangenberg and introduced myself. I said I was trying to prepare myself to help Secretary Korth defend against a probable attack by the McClellan Committee. Spangenberg responded, "The secretary has no defense. The decision was wrong and indefensible. He might as well admit it." He followed with a blast against civilian decision makers who have the temerity and arrogance to substitute their amateurish judgment for the professional conclusions of their military advisors.

I saw Korth had a big problem. He could expect no help whatsoever from the aviation branch of the navy. There would thus be no chance of defusing the issue during the Adlerman meeting. We had to gain time. I therefore recommended to the secretary that he stress with Adlerman the three conclusions he had received during the final TFX briefing. He should particularly emphasize the "no significant preference" statement. He should avoid going into the reasons for the selection of General Dynamics over Boeing. I felt that as little opportunity as possible should be given the McClellan Committee to whip-saw the decision makers before they had a chance to get their ducks in a row. Fred Korth did a great job in the meeting. It was clear, however, that the battle had just begun. Adlerman used expressions in his questioning of Korth that gave me the eerie feeling that the committee had already been briefed by George Spangenberg.

I soon thereafter found to my dismay that McNamara's TFX decision had not been documented. The decision had emerged as a consensus arrived at over a period of time. No person participating in the process held exactly the same views as any other person. Each felt some different aspect was most important. The essential elements of the consensus had not been reduced to writing. Furthermore, none of the participants in the decision process had recorded his own conclusions. I began to dig. A basic source was the Fourth Evaluation Report. In its 500 pages, the technical aspects of the proposals of the competing contractors were exhaustively described and compared. I studied that report until its contents were engraved on my memory. I talked with all those who had helped reach the decision. The picture began to emerge. The decision was clearly defensible.

The point of departure was the unequivocal statement by the uniformed heads of the navy and the air force that both proposals satisfied the military requirements of both services. That gave their civilian masters a clear shot at the decision. Assured that military needs would be met in either case, they could concentrate on the technical risks and economic aspects of the two proposals.

The two contractors had approached the critical problem of wing loading from opposite points of view. It will be recalled that wing loading is the ratio of wing area to aircraft weight. Boeing had achieved a lighter navy plane by shaving metal out of the air force version. This resulted in two airplanes that looked the same but were structurally dissimilar. The parts of the navy plane were generally lighter and not, therefore, interchangeable with those designed for the air force model. McNamara's goal of "commonality" between the two aircraft was therefore not achieved by Boeing. Its two versions would require two separate development and flight test programs. Later there would have to be two production programs.

General Dynamics, on the other hand, had proposed two versions that were structurally almost identical. The wing loading problem was not met by a reduction in weight, but by an increase in the wing area of the navy version. This was accomplished by what was then described in aeronautical circles as a "simple but elegant solution." The two versions each had detachable wing tips. It was only required that a long wing tip be bolted onto the navy wing, with a short tip for the air force. A very high degree of commonality was thus achieved. Only one R & D flight test and production program would be required. It was obvious that the General Dynamics proposal presented by far the greatest opportunity for savings.

The second major difference between the two proposals was in the construction of the center wing carry-through section. This was the large, heavy assembly on which the wings pivoted as they were swept back or brought forward. This pivoting feature was the most revolutionary aspect of the TFX and was common to the proposals of both contractors. To save weight, Boeing proposed to fabricate this section from titanium. General Dynamics proposed the use of conventional materials in that section. While titanium was in common use in the aircraft industry, it had not been used in such massive sections as the center-wing pivot. Its fatigue properties in such applications were therefore unknown. Fatigue failure develops from cyclical stresses. The air force evaluators at Wright-Patterson had pointed out in the Fourth Evaluation Report that the thick pieces of titanium might prove unsuitable. They stated that due to the time required for cyclical testing, its suitability would not be known until the program was well along. It therefore had the potential of significantly delaying the program and adding to its cost.

The third major difference pointed out by the source selection board was the proposed use of in-flight thrust reversers in the Boeing planes. These would permit the planes to land on carriers or short fields. General Dynamics accomplished the same purpose by the use of conventional spoilers and flaps. Thrust reversers were in common use on the ground, but had not been used in flight. The air force evaluators could not give assurances that they would be successful.

So here was the situation in a nutshell: Both contractors proposed aircraft that the navy and air force experts said could do the required jobs. Only one, General Dynamics, met the criteria of sufficient commonality that only a single development, test, and production program would be required. The Boeing proposal had unconventional and unproven features that caused it to present the higher degree of technical risk.

These factors, then, formed the basis of the decision. They are, in my opinion, so clear and logical that their early articulation would have prevented the whole brouhaha. It was particularly unfortunate that McNamara did not call in the CNO, Admiral Anderson, and the air force chief of staff, General LeMay, and explain the basis of the decision before they read of it in the newspapers. As it was, they were left to speculate as to the reasons their advice had been ignored. They, the press, Boeing, and Congress all assumed the worst. They viewed the decision as patently politically motivated and in disregard of the military requirements of the country. McNamara's folly was in failing to document a perfectly reasonable decision and to explain it in a timely manner to the properly interested parties. It is difficult to ascribe this failure to anything other than arrogance. It resulted in a bitter feud between McNamara and McClellan that went on for years. The wasteful diversion of human resources to fight that battle was shocking. McNamara's prestige became badly eroded. Fred Korth, as we shall see, was an innocent and incidental victim in that fray.

The first witness to be called before the McClellan Committee was Eugene Zuckert, the secretary of the air force. At that time, McNamara still did not view the situation with any alarm. Surprisingly, he had not made any effort to prepare a "white paper" on the award. He had not even called a meeting of those who had been involved in the decision process. I was then hard at work pulling together the rationale of the decision for use by Secretary Korth. I found McNamara and his staff almost uninterested in that effort. Their attitude was that the decision was correct and within the authority of the secretary of defense. They felt that it was an imposition to expect them to justify it.

Zuckert therefore was on his own. It is customary for a witness before a congressional committee to file a statement ahead of time that gives his position on the subject at issue. Zuckert had done so, covering some but not all of the points I have outlined. He covered, in good detail, the commonality rationale. Unfortunately, however, he incorrectly attributed to General Dynamics several technical advantages. These were peripheral to the decision, but the errors were seized upon by the committee. He made a futile attempt to defend them, and in the process lost all credibility. He spent a miserable two or three weeks before the committee and was thoroughly, if unfairly, discredited. The case for the decision looked worse than ever. McNamara was annoyed with Zuckert at having been careless in the preparation of his statement. He was furious, however, at the mistreatment he felt Zuckert had received from the committee.

He released a statement to the press that blasted McClellan. He made the point that the decision was his, McNamara's, and his alone. All others had merely made recommendations. If McClellan wanted to know the basis for the decision, then he, McNamara, was the only proper witness. McClellan's strategy, however, was to call McNamara last. Encouraged by his success against Zuckert, he apparently believed that the TFX decision would be in such disrepute by the time that he called the secretary of defense, the testimony of the latter would make no difference. The hearings were closed to the public because the performance characteristics of the TFX were classified secret. McClellan, however, released selected and censured portions of the testimony at a press conference each day. It was not difficult for his staff to go through an entire day's testimony and pick out a statement or two, out of full context, that made the witness look stupid or worse. The press, of course, ate it up, and the cumulative effect was devastating.

McNamara continued to needle McClellan about the order in which the witnesses were called. His sallies eventually had an effect. McClellan suddenly told McNamara that he could appear the next day and make a statement. Incredible as it seems, even at that date McNamara had not prepared a position paper on the TFX decision! He had to have one in a hurry, and he designated Adam Yarmolinsky to write it.

Yarmolinsky was aware that I had done a lot of work on the subject for Korth, so he asked me to help him. He and I worked all that night. At first, Yarmolinsky wanted to take the approach that the military advisors were incorrect in their preference for the Boeing proposal. I convinced him at the very outset that this would place an unnecessary burden on Secretary McNamara; since the military advisors had said that both proposals met their requirements, there was no need to get into the question of their preferences. The secretary's statement should concentrate entirely on the economics and the potential production problems of the proposals, having been assured that the nation's defense would not be jeopardized by a choice of either. Adam agreed, and the paper was prepared along those lines. It dealt particularly with the three primary differences between the proposals that had led to the decision.

Because of Zuckert's ordeal before the McClellan Committee, McNamara was insistent that his statement be checked carefully for factual errors. He called Korth, Zuckert, and Brown and said that he expected each of them to review the statement before it got to him. He said to each of them, "If there turns out to be any technical inaccuracy in a part of the statement within your area of responsibility, you are out of a job." No one could be sure that he was joking. He told the three that the paper would be delivered to them that night as soon as it was finished.

By the time Yarmolinsky and I had finished the draft, and the typing and duplicating were completed, it was about 3:00 A.M. The document was thirty-two pages long. I took the copies that were to go to Fred Korth and Harold Brown. I drove my Volkswagen, and I remember that a thick fog enveloped the Washington area. My first stop was at Korth's home on the Arlington Ridge, at about 3:30 A.M. Korth sat on the edge of his bed and began to read. He got through the first few pages, rubbed his eyes and went back to the beginning. After a couple more tries, he said, "Andy, are there any errors in this?" I answered, "No, sir, I don't think there are."

"You don't think there are!" he said. "Sorry to have to insist, Andy, but I can't seem to focus on this thing. *Are there any errors?*" "No, sir," I said. He initialled the draft.

The next stop was at Harold Brown's house in Alexandria. He was my next door neighbor on Argyle Drive. We had had many discussions about the TFX. Brown, as I have said, was at that time the director of Defense Research and Engineering. He had come to the Kennedy administration from the directorship of the Livermore Radiation Laboratories in California. Not yet thirty, Harold in those days was all brain and business with a self-confidence that bordered on the arrogant. He was a prodigy who had received his doctorate in nuclear physics from Columbia University at about the age of twenty. He became a protégé of Edward Teller and achieved early and spectacular success as an atomic scientist. He still had not quite left that world where most important problems can be reduced to formulae on a blackboard. He was beginning to learn that most of the problems in the Pentagon could not be so handled. And he learned quickly. Later, by the time he had become the secretary of the air force under McNamara, he had developed a fine human touch. Eventually he became the suave and polished secretary of defense one saw on television during the four years of the Carter administration.

The lights at Brown's house were on when I arrived there. Harold was up and waiting for the statement. He read it through carefully and asked a few questions. Then he initialled it.

Secretary McNamara studied the statement, approved it, and sent it to the McClellan Committee by 10:00 A.M., the customary time. McNamara himself did not appear. He was out of town for the rest of that day, I think by prearrangement. His statement was read into the record by a staff assistant who appeared before the committee in his place.

Because the statement concentrated entirely on technical risk and the economic aspect of the two proposals, it had been unnecessary to discuss the performance characteristics of the two proposed planes. McNamara had simply said that those characteristics met the requirements of both services. Therefore, the statement was unclassified and McNamara released it to the press. This infuriated McClellan, who deemed it his prerogative to decide what information should be released from the hearings. The McNamara-McClellan war thus escalated another notch.

Following this, Secretary Korth was called to testify. He and I sat side by side at the witness stand for several grueling weeks. The committee staff was being fed information and questions to ask by Spangenberg. McClellan and the other senators opposed to the decision hammered away day after day. They tried endlessly to show some connection between Korth and General Dynamics. They failed because there was none. Korth, I thought, was magnificent. He maintained his composure in the face of intense and constant provocation. Senator Mundt went so far as to address him always as Mr. "Worth" rather than "Korth." This was a crude attempt to emphasize the fact that the secretary came from Fort Worth where the General Dynamics plant was located.

The rules of the McClellan Committee were very much different than the rules of most other congressional committees. His committee had become famous through its investigation of labor racketeers and organized crime. It had had a field day with Jimmy Hoffa when Bobby Kennedy was its chief counsel.

Its so-called Valachi hearings into the activities of the Mafia were widely publicized. The committee had developed a specialty of dealing with hoodlums. It witnesses were not permitted to consult with counsel or anyone else without asking the permission of the chairman. This rule was designed to discredit the witness by having the record show that he was unable to answer a question unaided. With other committees, you hear a question asked. You then see the witness turn and talk with an advisor and possibly read a paper handed to him by an aide, and then he gives his answer. The record, however, shows only the question and the answer. We attempted to evade this demeaning committee rule by subterfuge. I would keep a briefing book or the Fourth Evaluation Report between us, open to the appropriate page as I caught the drift of a question. Korth could then glance down before answering. This annoyed McClellan, who objected whenever he was able to detect the process. At one point, Senator Mundt, shaking his jowls and pointing a finger called out, "Now Commander Kerr! If you don't stop this unconscionable briefing of the secretary, we will consider citing you for contempt of this body!" That threat was part of the record released by McClellan to the press that evening. Its appearance in the *Washington Post* the next morning terrified my grade-school-aged children, Alex and Laurie. They were sure that their daddy would soon be in prison. I was not sure they were wrong.

The days of hearings stretched into weeks. The stress on a witness before a hostile congressional committee cannot be overstated. Both Korth and I were near exhaustion. Furthermore, other navy business had to be conducted. One question arose, however, that led to a brief respite from our ordeal: a decision had to be made as to whether the U.S. Naval Air Station in Bermuda should be closed down. On our return to the Pentagon from the hearings one Friday afternoon, Korth said, "Andy, what do you say that we hop over to Bermuda to take a look at the air station. We can make an inspection and get an on-the-spot briefing. Then we'll have a better idea of the value of the place. Besides, I've got to get out of this God-damned town for a day or two!"

We flew down in the secretary's plane and had a busy Saturday with tours of the air station and briefings. That evening there was a reception and dinner.

During our tour, I had noticed some Sunfish sailboats near the air station dock. I cornered the special services officer at the reception and asked him about them. He said they belonged to the station and were used for recreation by its personnel. I arranged with him to have one available early the next morning. We had that morning free and were to fly back to Washington in the afternoon.

Early that Sunday morning, I got the little 14-foot board boat rigged. There was a fine breeze and I tacked back and forth across the lagoon in beautiful Bermuda weather. Then I noticed Secretary Korth sitting on the dock in his bathing suit. He had his brief case and was going over some papers. I sailed up to him and said, "Come aboard for a sail, Mr. Secretary. It's great out here." He answered that he had never in his life been aboard a sailboat and the one I had seemed too insubstantial for a first try. He let himself be persuaded, however, and we were soon scudding across the bay. On the other side, a U.S. submarine was moored. I said to Korth, "We haven't had any breakfast yet, so let's go aboard for a cup of coffee." That proposal took a little more persuasion. We were both in our bathing suits, and a Sunfish sailboat is not the most prepossessing of craft. But he eventually agreed. I hailed the sailor on watch topside as we sailed up to the submarine, "Tell the duty officer that the secretary of the navy is alongside and would like to come aboard for a cup of coffee." The man went to the hatch and shouted down, "Hey, Chief! There's some jerk up here claims he's the secretary of the navy and wants to come aboard!" Soon the chief of the watch stuck his head out of the hatch and the exchange was repeated. The chief was no more impressed with our asserted credentials than the topside watch had been. Next, however, the commanding officer climbed up. He recognized the secretary, having attended the party the night before. He was red-faced with embarrassment at the reception his ship had given the secretary. Korth, however, quickly put him at his ease, treating it as a good joke. We were given a warm welcome and a hot breakfast. In return, Fred Korth had given those submariners a story they would never tire of telling.

We returned to Washington refreshed and ready if not eager to face the inquisitors again on Monday morning.

Through it all, the secretary kept his sense of humor, though toward the end it tended toward the gallows variety. Once as we made our weary way toward the Old Senate Office Building (Old SOB!) for another session, he observed, "Aren't we lucky to be able to ride up here in an air-conditioned limousine instead of a tumbril!"

Korth eluded all attempts by the committee to draw him into discussions of any aspect of the two proposals that was irrelevant to the basis for his decision. He came back to the main points over and over. He cited Spangenberg's "no significant preference" advice so often that Senator McClellan began to complete the sentence when Korth started to say it. He never lost his cool or was trapped into an inconsistency or contradiction. All attempts to discredit or impeach him failed. McClellan finally gave up and Korth was excused. We were elated. The long ordeal was over and we had won. When the secretary's limousine arrived back at the Mall entrance of the Pentagon, a whisk broom was attached to its extended radio antenna. This emulated the practice of submariners, on returning from a successful war patrol, of displaying a broom attached to a raised periscope to indicate a "clean sweep." Pictures were taken, and McNamara called his congratulations. It was a great day. I was almost light-headed with a sense of relief. Beyond that, I experienced the exhilaration of personal triumph against great odds. What irony that the wreath of victory would soon turn to ashes in Secretary Korth's forced resignation.

McClellan's TFX hearings went on for years. They were inconclusive, and involved an enormous waste of human resources. In the meantime, the plane was developed and produced by General Dynamics, and became the F-111. It was not a highly successful airplane. This fact has been said to prove that McClellan and the top military advisors were right and that McNamara and his civilian advisors were wrong. It proves no such thing. The hearings did not address the issue of whether or not it was a good idea to try to develop a single plane for both the navy and the air force. McClellan's point was simply that Boeing should have been the selected contractor. Since the Boeing TFX proposal never went beyond the paper stage, any conclusions that a Boeing F-111 would have been superior to the General Dynamics F-111 can only be conjecture.

The TFX controversy demonstrated how lonely the secretary of the navy can become when he takes a position, having operational implications, contrary to that of the chief of naval operations. The CNO commands almost all of the resources of the navy. The secretary quickly finds himself isolated. Korth described the sensation to Jenkins and me. He said that the secretary of the navy is like the driver of a huge truck that is thundering down the highway. The secretary sits high in the cab, thrilled with the majesty and power of it all. Then suddenly he realizes that his steering wheel is not connected to anything. Others, down below, are steering the vehicle and deciding where it will go. At those times, the secretary's requests for information to support his position result in answers that support the CNO. His plans and intentions are leaked to his adversaries. He is frustrated at every turn.

If he is to find support from the uniformed ranks of the navy, he must look primarily to his small personal staff. Even there he must face the fact that the careers of those of his aides who are line officers can be ruined by a CNO whose displeasure the aides have incurred. Thus, in the TFX affair Secretary Korth's support soon shrank to the two specialists on his staff, Jenkins and me. His naval aide, Captain Marmaduke Bayne, prudently decided to sit out the controversy. He was later selected to the rank of rear admiral. His administrative aide, Commander Thomas B. Hayward, after giving me the background of the competition on the day Adlerman paid us a visit, found that his other duties consumed his entire attention. He thereafter progressed rapidly up the navy promotion ladder, and eventually became chief of naval operations. I don't wish to appear critical of those two officers. They would surely have wrecked their navy careers had they played an active role in support of Fred Korth against the CNO. I'm sure they concluded that such an enormous sacrifice was not required, and indeed would not have been of significant help to the secretary. I cannot say that they were wrong.

In addition to the TFX dispute, there were many other instances during my years in Washington in which I served as an advocate. Some of these, like the Tonkin Gulf incidents, will later be described, and like the TFX, remain controversial to this day. I think it therefore appropriate to tell of my general attitude toward my clients, the issues, and my position as an advocate. First, in matters of importance, I tend to immerse myself totally in the task at hand, devoting to it every resource of intellect and energy at my command. I know of no other way to do it. I hold myself solely and completely responsible for the outcome, holding nothing back. I am not at all a cynic, and look at myself as an idealist. To achieve the total dedication I feel obliged to bring to bear, I *must* believe in the rightness of the cause. Doubts and uncertainties are fatal to the effort. So I *know* that Fred Korth was a good and honest man, that the TFX decision was clean and reasonable, and that our government acted honestly and responsibly in the wake of the Tonkin Gulf incidents. Furthermore, I believe myself to be honorable. In none of the described incidents have I ever lied or intentionally distorted the facts. In each case, I have given a complete and accurate picture to the best of my ability.

I am sure, however, that some will view my expositions as one-sided. Of course they are. They are my side of these controversies. That, however, is the side that I earnestly believe to represent reality. Nevertheless, to those who believe equally earnestly in another view, I have in the above discussion given whatever grounds they may need to accuse me of a lack of objectivity.

11

The Korth
Resignation

Washington is a tough town. This fact seemed to have eluded Jimmy Carter, to his everlasting loss. It's a company town, and the company's only business is government. It is a tight little community, and gossip is as necessary to daily life as bread and meat. The favorite indoor sport of Washingtonians, to the delight and profit of the Washington press, is the gleeful and tireless hounding of any presidential appointee who stumbles. Any misstep or misstatement, however trivial, is fair game. Of course, the president himself is the prime objective. When he proves too agile a target, however, his appointees and staff assistants are considered satisfactory surrogates.

I think a manual should be prepared and given to anyone contemplating appointment to a high position in the government. It should contain a synopsis of the events leading to the downfall of such diverse figures as Sherman Adams (Eisenhower's chief of staff), Fred Korth (Kennedy's secretary of the navy), Bert Lance (Carter's budget director), and James Watt (Reagan's secretary of the interior), to name only a few. There are dozens more.

Each potential appointee should thus become aware that while he expects from his new status the gratitude of his countrymen, and the admiration of his friends, family, and descendants, he stands a very good chance of ending his position in disgrace and humiliation. No administration is immune. It happens every time.

A difficult question for every president in these cases is whether to dump a member of his administration who may have become an irredeemable liability, or to stand by his man in the hope that he will weather the storm and be vindicated.

The Kennedy administration came to Washington promising government as clean as a hound's tooth. One of its earliest acts was the promulgation of new and stringent standards of conduct for federal employees. The troubles of the preceding Eisenhower administration had generally involved the receipt of gifts by government people from potential contractors—e.g., the famous vicuña coat accepted by Sherman Adams. In reaction to this, the Kennedy standards concentrated on this area, to the point that a government officer was in violation of the directive if he allowed a contractor with whom he was meeting to pick up the tab for his cup of coffee in a Pentagon snack bar.

In addition, the new administration announced that transgressors would be given short shrift. Evil-doers could expect to be cast forth into exterior darkness. There would be no "cronyism"—no misguided standing behind old friends or associates. This, then, was the environment surrounding the resignation of Fred Korth from his position as secretary of the navy.

The fact that Korth came through the TFX hearings unscathed did not help him in the long run. During the hearings, Senator McClellan was obviously angered by Korth's failure to confess stupidity or venality. Apparently frustrated when the lengthy inquisition of Korth was concluded without having produced any evidence of incompetence or wrongdoing, McClellan sent staff members to Fort Worth to search the correspondence files of the Continental National Bank. Korth had been president of that institution before becoming secretary of the navy. No correspondence bearing on the TFX controversy was found. The search did, however, turn up one or two indiscreet letters concerning other matters that Secretary Korth had written to officials of the bank.

One such letter to the president of the bank, Korth's successor, pointed out that Korth was aware that a bankers' convention was to take place in Atlantic City. He invited the president of the bank to be his guest on the *Sequoia,* the yacht assigned to the secretary of the navy. It was also used by other high officials of the government. The invitation would have been okay, but he added, "and if you have any particularly good customers of the bank that you'd like me to include, let me know." This appeared to the investigators to indicate that Korth was using his position as secretary of the navy to further the goals of a bank in which he presumably still had an interest. The facts were quite otherwise. Fred Korth was extremely gregarious and outgoing and a prodigious writer of letters, who maintained a wide circle of friends. He dictated the letters each night, and his custom then was to sign without reading them in the morning. When hundreds of such letters are read in context, the statement, while ill-advised, is seen to be harmless. He had no interest in the bank other than friendship with former associates and had no intention of returning to the bank. However, the letter caused the investigators to smell blood, and they instigated a search of Korth's personal correspondence file in the Navy Department.

A few letters were found there that were embarrassing. One in particular had to do with General Norstad, who was an old friend from Korth's army days and occasionally visited Korth in the secretary of the navy's office. On one occasion, soon after Norstad had retired from the air force and from his position as NATO's supreme allied commander in Europe, he again stopped by for a chat. At that time he had become president of Owens-Corning Fiberglas Corporation. Later that evening, Korth dictated a letter to Norstad, "Dear Lauris," it said, "after you left my office this afternoon, I realized that I had heard that Owens-Corning was building a new plant in Waxahachie, Texas." (I quote this as well as I can remember.) And the letter went on, "Gus So-and-so is the head of a bank there in Waxahachie, and he was a good correspondent of the Fort Worth bank. I suggest if you haven't selected someone in the area to take care of your banking needs, that he would be good for you. I'd be happy to drop him a line." As I recall, this was the most damaging letter found. Knowing Korth's propensity for helping people, and knowing of his voluminous, informal, and undisciplined personal correspondence, one would have to conclude that this letter also was entirely innocent. Nevertheless, it was on the secretary of the navy's letterhead, and it was seized upon by the press and members of Congress to indicate that he still had an interest in the bank and that he was doing the bank's business while he was secretary of the navy. There were a few other letters that the investigators believed to point in that same direction. As is the custom in such cases, this "evidence" was leaked or furnished to the press by McClellan in dribbles over a period of time. It thus appeared much more damaging than if all were released together. So the Washington drumbeats increased in crescendo, and the pressure built up relentlessly. It began to appear that Fred Korth was in real trouble.

At that point, he received a phone call from his friend Vice President Lyndon Johnson, who told him that the way things were going, he might eventually have to resign. Johnson advised him to retain civilian counsel in case the McClellan Committee decided to pursue him into post-secretarial life. He said that he had spoken to his good friend Abe Fortas, who would be happy to represent Korth. Fortas then was a partner in the Washington law firm of Arnold, Fortas and Porter. Later he was appointed to the Supreme Court by President Johnson. Korth and I met with Fortas, and I eventually turned over to him all of the TFX material in a series of lengthy meetings. He was a fascinating and remarkable man who knew as much about Washington politics as any man alive. He had been assistant secretary of the interior under Harold Ickes (The Old Curmudgeon) in the Roosevelt administration and was an advisor to every subsequent president. He was one of a small group of Washington lawyers that included men like Clark Clifford and Tommy Corcoran who worked behind the scenes at the national level and wielded enormous influence. I learned a lot from Abe, who had a gifted way of making his point with an apt and memorable phrase. I recall once when we were struggling with a difficult dilemma he said, "Andy, when in doubt, do the right thing." His insight into the motivations and likely patterns of behavior of political animals was incredibly astute. I found them almost always to be deadly accurate. It therefore amazed me when it was disclosed that he, while on the Supreme Court, had accepted a retainer fee from financier Louis Wolfson. Wolfson had been convicted of violating the Security Laws. This apparent conflict of interest led to Fortas's departure from the Court. That this could happen to a fine man and superb lawyer who knew more about what you could do and what you could not do in Washington than anyone else has saddened and baffled me. It caused the country to lose the services of one who, in my opinion, would have been a great chief justice. It could well serve as another chapter in the "Manual for Aspirants to High Office" I have previously advocated.

An example of the harassment a victim can expect once he becomes a Washington quarry, was the issue of Korth's guests aboard the *Sequoia*. One or more members of Congress requested that the log of the *Sequoia* be made available to see who those guests were. Here again, the idea was to show that Korth was using government facilities for private gain. I had the log in my possession, having obtained it from the *Sequoia* when it became controversial. I saw immediately that Korth had never entertained aboard anyone from General Dynamics, and that there was nothing in the log that bore even remotely on the TFX dispute. Nevertheless, Korth had from time to time included as guests personal friends and old associates, and some, naturally, were Texas bankers. I also knew this from personal experience, Rusty and I having been included several times in cruises aboard the *Sequoia*. All four of the secretaries of the navy for whom I worked did the same thing. They mixed personal friends who were not in government service with the congressmen, judges, aides, diplomats, and government executives who commonly made up the *Sequoia* guest list. Korth's guest lists were of the same nature. The same was true of other users of the *Sequoia*— Robert Kennedy, Larry O'Brien, Cyrus Vance, Robert McNamara, and other cabinet members and Kennedy staff assistants. They all felt that bringing in nongovernment outsiders tended to make the cruises more stimulating and enjoyable.

Apart from that background, the log was an extremely sensitive document. The *Sequoia* was not only used by the secretary of the navy, but also by many other high officials of the administration to meet with people under circumstances that would be impossible in their own offices. For instance, if Secretary of State Dean Rusk wanted to meet with the Saudi ambassador and the Israeli ambassador at the same time for a discussion, the proper place was the *Sequoia*. Many of the top people in government had had meetings aboard that they wanted to keep private and not known to the press for good reasons.

So making available the log in its entirety would be contrary to the national interest. I felt that making only Korth's part of the log public would be unfair as well as misleading. However, the word eventually came from Attorney General Robert Kennedy that Korth should make available to Congress that part of the log that dealt with his guests, and his only. I was enraged. The result would be the impression that only Korth had included personal friends and old business associates; whereas, all users of the *Sequoia* did the same, and for good and proper reasons. I called Abe Fortas and told him how unfair I thought the decision was, and how it could not help but give a misleading and distorted picture. I also hinted at the idea that if part of the log got out, appetites would be whetted. Eventually all of the log could be in jeopardy. There could be leaks, and all kinds of bad things could happen. I thought that he should tell that to the president. Fortas interpreted that as a veiled threat by me. Whether or not I actually intended it as such, I don't know—but I was acting in a blind rage when I called him. I'll never forget Abe's response. He said, "Calm down, Andy. Calm down. Relax. I'll talk to the president." He said, "But I've been around this town for a long time, and I'm not in the business of blackmailing presidents of the United States." It made me feel an inch high. I don't think now that I ever intended a threat. But if, in my state of turmoil, I did, I know that it would have been a threat that I was, by nature, incapable of carrying out.

Fortas did talk to the president and got the decision reversed. The log was never made public. President Kennedy invoked executive privilege to prevent its examination by Congress. As far as I can recall, this was one of the only two times during his administration that Kennedy invoked executive privilege. The other was during the "Muzzling of the Military" hearings when a Senate committee chaired by Stuart Symington demanded the names of the people in the Pentagon's Security Office who were censoring the public speeches of generals and admirals.

However, the crescendo continued to intensify, and finally Bobby Kennedy told Korth that the president wished him to step down because he had become an embarrassment to the president and the party. McNamara relayed the same message. It finally seemed that Korth had not a friend in official Washington or in the press to speak out in support of him. Even his own staff, myself excepted, considered his resignation to be inevitable.

I urged him to hang in there. I said that if he were actually fired, that would be one thing, but he had done nothing wrong and he should stand his ground as long as possible and not quit. He asked, well, what could happen, everyone was calling for his blood, and the president had indicated that he should step aside. I pointed out that the president himself had not been heard from. He asked me again what in the world could happen to avoid this. I could think of nothing else to do but tell him the story of the Caliph of Baghdad, against whom there was an assassination plot.

Before the plot could be carried out, the conspirators were apprehended and condemned to death. They were all in their cells awaiting execution and resigned to their fate because they had indeed plotted against the life of the Caliph. They were all resigned, except one, who sought and was granted an audience with the Caliph, because he was aware that the Caliph was extremely proud of his sacred white bull. He told the Caliph, "If you spare me, I will teach your sacred white bull to fly."

The Caliph was intrigued and said all right, he would spare him for one year, and if during that year, he taught the sacred white bull to fly, he would pardon him. If he failed, he would die a thousand deaths.

So he went back to his cell, and he told his condemned compatriots what had happened. They said, "You're very foolish because, after all, a year will pass quickly and you will die a thousand deaths, as only the Caliph can inflict them. By tonight we will all be with Allah."

He said, "No, I don't see it that way at all. A year is a long time. And during the year I might die a natural death surrounded by my loved ones. Or the Caliph may die and be replaced by another ruler who might look differently upon the situation and pardon me. Or who knows, *the damned bull may fly!*"

Korth laughed at the story, but he said, "Well, in this case the bull's not going to fly," and he tendered his resignation. Jim Jenkins and I drafted it in great sorrow, and I took it to the White House and gave it to Kenny O'Donnell who was waiting for it. The president then made light of the matter at a press conference in which he ungraciously dismissed Korth as a man who wrote too many letters.

Very soon after his resignation under fire, the bull did fly. The president of the United States was assassinated, and Vice President Johnson, who was Korth's friend, became president. The attention of the nation was instantly diverted from such insignificant subjects as Korth's letters. Had he been able to hold on until then, he would have survived.

Korth's resignation was immediately followed by a most curious episode. It came about as follows: The secretary had a serious hearing loss, which was, like mine, caused by otosclerosis. Being familiar with the condition and the available remedies, I had several times suggested that he avail himself of the expertise of the navy doctors at the National Naval Medical Center at Bethesda, Maryland. He could have the stapesectomy operation performed there. Because of the pressures of his office, he had not done so. So when he decided to resign, Jenkins and I urged him to check into Bethesda immediately and have the operation done. As an ex-secretary of the navy he would be privileged to use that facility. This would serve two purposes. First, it would help his hearing, which in the long run was necessary. But, secondly, he would be out of circulation and unavailable to reporters who otherwise would be hounding him. Sufficient time would pass for press interest to subside, and he could then get on with his life. He agreed with this reasoning and made the necessary arrangements. On leaving the secretary of the navy's office, he went immediately to Bethesda and was admitted to the hospital. The operation was performed on the following afternoon. That evening, following his operation, I got a phone call from him at home quite late at night, asking if I could come to Bethesda. He sounded faint and weak, in startling contrast to his usual booming Texas voice. He said that he wanted me to look at a statement that John McNaughton, general counsel for the Department of Defense, wanted him to sign.

I of course advised him not to sign anything, and said that I would start out immediately. After calling Jim Jenkins to tell him what was up, I hopped into my Volkswagen and drove from Alexandria across the Chain Bridge to Bethesda, arriving there around midnight. Jenkins arrived soon afterward. There was Korth in his hospital bed, obviously exhausted and distressed and apparently still in a partially drugged condition. With him was John McNaughton with a statement that he said Secretary of Defense McNamara wanted Korth to sign to wind up the whole affair. I read the statement and found it to be nothing less than a confession of guilt, and to be entirely unwarranted. It was a gross distortion of the facts. I said, "No, you shouldn't sign this. It would be the wrong thing to do. You'd regret it all your life. It's just not right."

I was outraged that Korth should be subjected to this shocking treatment. The idea that he should be badgered in his hospital bed while still suffering from the effects of an operation and while in a semidrugged condition, was appalling. Further, I was baffled as to why he should be so brutally treated after he had obliged the administration by resigning.

I tend to become intimidated in meetings with men of rank and power. It always required a great effort of will to overcome this crippling attitude. In the meeting with McNaughton that night, however, my rage and indignation were so great that I think it was he who was intimidated.

McNaughton, however, was insistent that Korth, as a true Democrat and as a patriotic American, should sign the statement. He urged that it was required of him and was the decent and proper thing to do. Korth appeared to be at the end of his rope. Exhausted from the long ordeal preceding his resignation, and suffering from the aftermath of surgery, he finally gave up. He said, "I agree with you, Andy, it's not right. But I'm sick and tired of the whole mess, and if signing will end it all, I'll sign." I remember then taking the pen from his hand. I said in desperation that we should call Abe Fortas, and that if Abe agreed that he should sign it, then I would back out of the picture. After all, I was at that point no longer his counsel since he was no longer the secretary of the navy. My position that night, involved in a head-to-head confrontation with the general counsel of the Department of Defense, was at best ambiguous.

Korth agreed that we should call Fortas. I managed with great difficulty to convince Mrs. Fortas that she should call Abe to the phone. She said that he was concluding his weekly session with a string quartet in which he played the violin and that she never interrupted those sessions. She eventually relented, however, apparently recognizing the true urgency in my appeal. Abe came to the phone, at first a bit grumpily, but soon agreed that this was an emergency and that Korth should sign nothing—he would come out immediately.

On arrival and after a quick look at the statement, he said to McNaughton, "If you say McNamara wants Fred to sign this, I'll get Bob on the phone right now. We'll get this straightened out." So he called McNamara. It was after one o'clock in the morning. Very few people could have routed McNamara out of bed with a phone call at that hour, and it is a measure of the magic and power of the Fortas name that he was able to do so.

"Bob, this is Abe Fortas, and I'm out here in Fred Korth's hospital room at Bethesda." He said, "Young McNaughton is here with a statement that he wants Fred to sign." Abe Fortas had been a visiting professor at Harvard Law School when McNaughton had been a student there. I could hear only one side of the conversation, of course. I couldn't hear what McNaughton said. But Fortas said, "Oh, you haven't seen the statement? You say that you left the whole thing to Ros Gilpatric?"

So it appeared that Roswell Gilpatric, the deputy secretary of defense, had either prepared the statement or had had it prepared. According to McNaughton, Gilpatric had sent him on the errand to the hospital with the written statement and with the understanding that McNamara wanted Korth to sign it. McNaughton was merely following instructions. He obviously did not want to have to report to McNamara the next day that he had failed to get Korth's signature. In later contacts with John McNaughton in the Pentagon, I came to have great respect for his intellect and integrity. I am sure that he himself was a victim that night—that he thought he was telling the truth.

Following the revelation that McNamara had not seen the statement, and being the unhappy object of the scorn of his old mentor, Abe Fortas, McNaughton could do no more than mumble in embarrassment and make his departure as quickly as possible. To my knowledge, no further effort to have Fred Korth sign a statement was ever made.

As we left the naval hospital that night, I recall remarking to Jim Jenkins that a more bizarre episode could scarcely be imagined. It seemed all the more unreal, because at the time I failed to understand what could have been the motivation to wring an incriminating statement from a man who had already resigned under a cloud, thus making him pay a terrible price for a few minor and harmless indiscretions.

I have since come to a conclusion that to me explains the event satisfactorily: The Kennedy administration had proclaimed its intention to cast out wrongdoers in a forthright manner. So when the volume of Washington criticism of Korth reached an embarrassing level, and since Korth did not enjoy any special relationship with the Kennedys, the decision was made to pressure him to resign. And he obliged. But wait—casting out a wrongdoer gains political points, but failure to back a loyal and effective public servant whose acts have been misconstrued and blown out of proportion can be politically detrimental. The electorate can become irritated if it perceives that a quivering white body has been thrown from the troika to assuage the hunger of the pursuing wolves. So it seems to me that someone at the president's level belatedly realized that the evidence of actual wrongdoing in Korth's case was so thin as to be negligible, and that therefore his "firing" could backfire. So I think the word went out to nail the case down—to get a confession. I am convinced that nothing less than presidential pressure could have accounted for the scene out of a Dostoyevsky novel that took place at Bethesda that night.

12

Paul Nitze
And Elmo Zumwalt

President Kennedy appointed Paul Nitze to take Fred Korth's place as secretary of the navy. Nitze has to be one of the most durable men in American political life. He became a vice president of the investment banking firm of Dillon, Read and Anderson as a young man. He made his first million dollars early in life. His wife, I understand, inherited Standard Oil of New Jersey. Thus freed from routine drudgery, Nitze has devoted his life to public service.

He was a member of the Policy Planning staff of the State Department in the Truman administration. He thus had a hand in the creation of the Truman Doctrine and the Marshall Plan for the reconstruction of Europe after World War II. A brilliant intellectual, he was a frequent participant in seminars and high-level studies on defense, disarmament, and nuclear deterrence. His ideas appeared in such prestigious journals as *Foreign Affairs*. A certified member of the eastern establishment, he became a member of John Kennedy's presidential campaign team. When Kennedy was forming his cabinet, Nitze was often mentioned as a top contender for the post of secretary of defense. When that spot went to Robert McNamara, Nitze was appointed assistant secretary of defense for International Security Affairs (ISA). From ISA he became secretary of the navy. Some four years later, he took over from Cy Vance as McNamara's deputy secretary of defense. He left the Pentagon at the end of the Johnson administration. He then became a principal member of the U.S. team for the talks with the Soviet Union on Strategic Arms Limitation (SALT talks). At this writing, in 1986, he is one of the chief U.S. negotiators in the discussions with the Russians on nuclear disarmament. Thus, he has trod the national stage for over forty years. He is still carrying a burden of enormous responsibility more than a decade after his contemporaries have drifted off to the quiet enjoyment of their grandchildren.

Nitze's military assistant in ISA was a bright, personable, and ambitious young navy captain named Elmo ("Bud") Zumwalt. Bud's career as a destroyer and cruiser officer had been outstanding. He had advanced rapidly in rank ahead of his Naval Academy classmates. He was widely recognized as a comer. There were already those who saw him as a future chief of naval operations. Some even foresaw a struggle for that top navy spot between Zumwalt and Captain Isaac Kidd, then the senior aide to the CNO, Admiral David McDonald.

Zumwalt and Nitze discovered a shared outlook and a common approach to problems. They became good friends and esteemed professional associates. It was inevitable that Nitze should take Bud with him to be his naval aide when he became secretary of the navy.

I had high hopes for my association with the new team. The long struggle to win Korth's vindication on the TFX decision, followed by the bitter blow of his forced resignation, had left me near exhaustion. The prospect of getting off the defensive and making a fresh new start was exhilarating. I was, however, disappointed. Both Nitze and Zumwalt treated me with unmistakable coolness. My advice was seldom sought. I was invited to participate in meetings only on narrow legal questions. My requests to attend meetings involving wider policy issues were rebuffed. There were always special reasons why attendance had to be restricted. I began to lose touch with the flow of the crucial affairs of the office. The situation was the more frustrating because I felt empathy with Nitze and Zumwalt. They were intelligent and exciting people with whom a close association would have to be rewarding. Nitze's habitual reserve was nicely balanced by Zumwalt's infectious enthusiasm.

After a month, however, I was ready to give up and seek assignment to another job. I felt that I could not function effectively as special counsel in an atmosphere that I had begun to sense as being characterized by a lack of trust.

Then, one day in February 1964, Fidel Castro cut off the water supply to our naval base at Guantánamo. The water for the base had come by a pipeline from a river several miles away. Castro's action caused a crisis. The Joint Chiefs of Staff recommended to President Johnson that the U.S. "expand the perimeter" of the base to include the water source. This of course would mean the use of military force against Cuba. Johnson was not sure that he liked that advice. Since Guantánamo was a navy base, he asked Secretary Nitze for his thoughts. Johnson's call came on a Friday afternoon. Nitze was to have his recommendation on the president's desk on Monday morning.

Nitze called Zumwalt and me into his office. He said, "I want you two to fly down to Guantánamo tonight and look into the situation. Find out our options and bring me back your conclusions by Sunday night." I was astonished to be included in the assignment in view of my past exclusion from policy issues. Nitze gave me the answer, "Andy, I think you could be a big help to Bud in writing up his findings." I was being sent along as a scribe!

We left Washington on the secretary's plane that evening. Rear Admiral John D. Bulkeley, the commander of the base, had been informed by Nitze of our mission. He had been told to put his staff at our disposal on our arrival. We had with us civilian experts from the navy's Bureau of Yards and Docks. They had information on the physical characteristics of the base and its needs for such utilities as water and electricity.

We made a stop at Norfolk to pick up an expert on desalinization technology and arrived at Guantánamo about midnight. We were met by its disgruntled commanding officer. Admiral Bulkeley was one of the more colorful of the navy's flag officers. He had commanded PT boats in the Pacific in the early days of World War II. A popular book of the time, *They Were Expendable*, publicized his exploits, and he became a national hero. He felt it an insult to have his command subjected to examination by a junior navy captain and a mere commander. He felt that he could tell the secretary anything he needed to know about Guantánamo. He viewed us as a couple of whippersnappers who were flaunting the power of the secretary's office. Nevertheless, he grudgingly called his staff together.

Our session with Bulkeley's staff lasted the rest of the night. We kept at it with key individual staff members through Saturday.

Bud and I had begun to divide tasks. By Saturday night, we spelled each other off for turns of sleep for an hour or two while the other ran down loose ends or explored new avenues. We had become full partners in the effort. By Sunday morning we had reached our conclusions. By curtailing some nonessential functions and sending home all the wives and children, the base could be made self-sufficient in water. This involved dismantling a desalinization plant at San Diego and transporting it to Guantánamo. We determined that the water needs in the meantime could be met by the water tanker capacity then available to the navy. These conclusions were supported by a mass of data. We considered, but rejected, the idea of presenting the achievement of self-sufficiency as an option. We made it our single recommendation.

We had a superb team of Navy chief yeomen taking dictation, typing, and assembling the report. We were still cutting and pasting on Sunday afternoon. It all came together on the airplane on Sunday evening on the flight back to Washington. Nitze had a clean copy at his home by 10:00 P.M. He discussed it with Secretary McNamara early Monday morning. President Lyndon Johnson approved the plan that same day. Thus, our base at Guantánamo became, and still remains, independent of the need for support from Castro's Cuba.

After this incident, my relationship with Nitze and Zumwalt changed dramatically. I became part of the team. A close rapport with Bud Zumwalt had been established that has continued ever since.

I continued, however, to have one problem with Secretary Nitze: He smoked a pipe and habitually spoke either with the pipe in his mouth or held closely in front of his lips. Also, compared to the booming speech of Fred Korth, I found his voice soft and indistinct. With his pipe making lip reading impossible, I was therefore hard put to understand him. I used every trick that I had learned over the years. Every person with poor hearing has a bag of them! By gaining a prior knowledge of the subject, I expected certain things to be said. Verbal inflections and facial expressions were helpful. The statements and responses of others at the meetings gave valuable clues. I did as much of the talking myself as the situation would tolerate, but even after all of that, there were often gaps. Or, more accurately, I was afraid that there might be gaps. A big problem with deafness is that one doesn't know what one does not hear. So following each discussion or meeting in the secretary's office, I would review what had transpired with Bud Zumwalt, ostensibly to ensure a common understanding. Jim Jenkins, who knew of my problem, was always a help. Finally, if I was involved in important follow-up action, I would call Nitze on the interoffice call system (the "squawk box"). I could then turn up the volume on my end as much as required. The conversation would go something like this: "Mr. Secretary," I would say, "I'm about to leave for the Hill to see so-and-so about that base closure problem we discussed last week. I thought I'd run through the key points with you, in case you have anything to add." In these ways, the problem became manageable. The strain, however, was not insignificant.

I have said that Jim Jenkins was always a help. That was an understatement: True, he helped me avoid the consequences of my hearing loss. But beyond that, he was a superb sounding board. Jim brought to bear on every problem a fresh and valuable insight. A rare individual indeed, he was an original thinker, uncowed by conventional wisdom. His lively humor dispelled gloom and anxiety. His friendship was a treasured constant in those often difficult times. I can understand how he ended up in the Reagan White House, after backing John Connally for the nomination. That tells a lot about Jim Jenkins and about Ronald Reagan.

Soon after the grueling Guantánamo exercise, I talked with Zumwalt about my previous isolation in the office. "Why," I asked, "was I apparently mistrusted when you and Paul Nitze came to the secretary's office?" Zumwalt then told me that as soon as the news of Nitze's appointment as navy secretary hit the wire services, he, Zumwalt, had been visited by Captain Isaac ("Ike") Kidd. Ike, as I have mentioned, was the senior aide to Admiral McDonald, the chief of naval operations. He had correctly assumed that Zumwalt would become Nitze's naval aide. Ike Kidd urged upon Zumwalt that the navy would benefit by close cooperation between the secretary of the navy and the chief of naval operations. He said that he and Bud, as the senior aides of each, could ensure that cooperation by working together in concert. To achieve that goal, he offered advice that he termed essential, "Get rid of Andy Kerr!"

Ike Kidd had also been the aide to the previous CNO, Admiral George W. Anderson. All during the months of the TFX dispute, therefore, he and I had been in daily confrontation. Ike was a tough opponent. Cold, relentless, and highly intelligent, he was as active in his support of Admiral Anderson as I was of Secretary Korth. Neither of us gave an inch. The difference between us went deeper than TFX. Ike viewed the CNO as the personification and embodiment of the navy. I believe that he thought of the secretary as at best a figurehead and at worst an obstacle. The CNO, when speaking of anything of concern to the navy, was to Ike as infallible as the Pope speaking *ex cathedra* on a matter of faith and morals. I don't believe that deep in his heart, Ike could accept the idea that the secretary was the CNO's boss.

I saw the CNO and secretary of the navy as each performing essential if conflicting roles. Their common goal was a strong and effective navy. The secretary, however, must concern himself with budgetary limitations and the distribution of resources. He also has occasional insights into weapons, roles, and missions that may have eluded the CNO because of the latter's institutional blinders. Korth's broader view of the application of nuclear propulsion for the navy than that of Chief of Naval Operations David McDonald was a case in point. The secretary usually has a broader political outlook than the CNO. The CNO, on the other hand, is expected to be narrowly partisan. If he doesn't press vigorously for the purely naval point of view, who will? If the secretary becomes narrowly partisan, however, he becomes a mere mouthpiece of the CNO. He thus loses all authority with Congress and with the secretary of defense.

There is a strong tendency for the secretary to become a captive of the CNO. The CNO has a huge organization consisting of hundreds of captains and admirals. They will work around the clock to produce for him any information he requires. The secretary commands no such resources. It therefore takes a strong secretary to maintain his independence. When the secretary is strong, there are bound to be conflicts with his CNO. When he is weak, you will never hear his name.

When Ike Kidd approached Bud Zumwalt about the necessity of ridding the secretary's office of my pernicious influence, he had, I think, another score to settle. Admiral Anderson had been fired by President Kennedy. Anderson has laid the blame for this on Secretary Korth and the TFX controversy. By extension, I believe that Ike held me personally responsible for his boss's removal.

There is no doubt that a deep and lasting breach developed between Korth and Admiral Anderson during the TFX dispute. It was not caused, however, by the fact that Anderson took an opposing position. Korth respected the right of the CNO to hold a contrary opinion and to express it. What created the break was Admiral Anderson's outright refusal to show Korth ahead of time the statement he proposed to make before the McClellan Committee. This was a clear departure from established procedure. Korth viewed it not so much as an act of insubordination, but as an inexcusable rudeness. Korth, always a gentleman, was deeply upset.

But I am convinced that the TFX had nothing to do with Admiral Anderson's removal. First, Kennedy had never involved himself with the TFX to any noticeable extent. Two layers of federal bureaucracy separated him from a squabble between the secretary of the navy and the chief of naval operations. The removal of a CNO by the president can have serious political consequences. That, of course, is why President Kennedy sought to disguise the firing by appointing Anderson to be ambassador to Portugal. To warrant such a removal, then, the direct interests of the president have to be involved. In this case, I am sure that those interests concerned Admiral Anderson's role in the Cuban missile crisis: First, Anderson appeared to view the crisis as purely military in nature. The civilians consequently should stay out of it. As an indication of that attitude, he is reported to have refused to admit Roswell Gilpatrick, the deputy secretary of defense, to the CNO war room as the Russian ships approached the quarantine line. Secondly, he had urged that the missile sites be taken out by air strikes; after the crisis, reports that he had complained that the military had been "sold out" reached the president's ears. As a final straw, a week after the most dramatic triumph of Kennedy's presidency, not his, but Admiral Anderson's picture, appeared on the cover of *Time* magazine!

Washington insiders during the administration of President Lyndon Johnson were aware that columnist Drew Pearson, Jack Anderson's predecessor, had special access to White House information. Lady Bird Johnson's personal secretary, Bess Abel, was related to the columnist. Therefore, when Secretary of the Navy Nitze read in Pearson's "Washington Merry-go-round" column that the president was unhappy with Camp David, the presidential retreat in Maryland's Catoctin Mountains, he was inclined to believe it. The same report appeared in successive columns. The gist was that the new president was so burdened with his duties that he was unable to get away from the White House except for brief periods. Nearby Camp David was, therefore, his only respite. It was so shabby and run down, however, as to be uncongenial.

Nitze thought the situation dreadful. The president of the United States should have a place away from the pressures of the White House where he could relax in comfort. At our staff meeting one morning, he raised the possibility of offering to the president the use of his estate at La Plata, Maryland. Bud Zumwalt suggested that Lyndon Johnson might be rough on the Nitze manor house. He added, "Do you realize, Mr. Nitze, that the navy runs Camp David?" "No," responded Nitze, "I didn't know that. You mean I'm responsible for this mess?" "Well, yes," Bud said. "If Camp David needs anything, it's up to us to take care of it."

Nitze then told me to arrange to visit Camp David. He wanted to know what the place needed. I called the resident officer-in-charge, a lieutenant commander. He told me the dates when no guests were expected. He also said that he welcomed the visit, because the Drew Pearson articles had caused him great distress. They gave, he said, a completely false picture. I responded that I was pleased to hear that, but my job was to give the secretary a firsthand report. I said that I would like a complete tour, dinner in the evening, and to stay overnight. I suggested that I wanted to see Camp David through the president's eyes. My treatment by the staff would thus need to approximate that which the president would experience. The officer agreed. I then arranged with the president's naval aide to be flown up in a White House helicopter.

I had a glorious visit. The officer-in-charge, with apparent enthusiasm, acted the role of a host who was proudly displaying Camp David to a new president on his first visit. The tour was comprehensive. I looked at bowling alleys, the theater, swimming pool, stables—the works. I inspected all of the cottages. I concentrated, however, on the main lodge, Aspen, and its staff of Navy Filipino stewards. It was splendid. The martinis before dinner were works of art. The steaks were perfect, the wine superb, the service flawless. I slept that night in the Aspen lodge in sybaritic comfort. After a fine breakfast, I was flown back to the Pentagon's helicopter landing pad.

Secretary Nitze received my report with skepticism. I had found not a single fault. Therefore, when another Pearson article critical of Camp David appeared later, he was upset. "It's obvious, Andy, that your taste in accommodations is not up to presidential standards. Go back up there and this time take Pete Corradi with you." Rear Admiral Peter Corradi was the chief of the navy's Bureau of Yards and Docks. He had accompanied the secretary on various navy inspection trips. Nitze had found him to be unusually perceptive.

On that second trip, the emphasis was almost entirely on the physical accommodations. Nothing escaped Corradi's practiced eye. Furnishings, construction, physical convenience, state of repair, color coordination—all were critically scrutinized. In the end, he admitted defeat. The place was as near perfect as the hand of man could make it. He had to report back to Nitze that he could find no room for improvement.

The critical newspaper articles continued. Nitze still credited them as true reflections of the president's attitude. He therefore decided to try once more to fathom the cause. He had a good friend who was the wife of the U.S. ambassador to France. She was a gracious lady of patrician background and impeccable taste. Nitze was confident that she would be able to spot the deficiencies that had eluded Admiral Corradi and me. She undertook the task on a most confidential basis. Only the officer-in-charge was alerted. She and I drove in secrecy to Camp David in the secretary's limousine.

She was a most impressive lady. Nitze had been correct in his choice. She was able to view Camp David from the perspective of one who had seen the world's best. She was also able to put herself in the position of the First Lady. She questioned the staff most astutely about the arrangements for the comfort and convenience of Lady Bird Johnson. What, for example, would the chief steward do if Lady Bird had a stuck zipper? She was assured that when the First Lady was in residence, the Camp David staff always arranged to have a lady-in-waiting present to take care of such eventualities.

In the end, she was as perplexed as Corradi and I had been. "Paul," she reported to Nitze, "I think Camp David is a magnificent example of the rustic retreat it is supposed to be. It is fit for kings and presidents. I couldn't improve it."

Nitze soon after received a call from Johnson's naval aide. "The president," he said, "has been going over the White House domestic expenditures. He is upset at the expenses being incurred at Camp David in his absence. He asked me who the people were who were enjoying all those free meals." "What!" said Nitze, "You mean to tell me the president takes the time to check the household accounts?" "You bet," said the aide, "he checks every item." The aide said that he had explained to the president about Nitze's efforts to get to the bottom of the Drew Pearson articles. "Look," said President Johnson to his naval aide, "tell Paul Nitze to knock it off! I think Camp David is fine. I just don't think Americans like to see their presidents living in splendor and luxury. I wanted them to think I was roughing it a bit up there in the mountains."

Nitze's insistence that I hold my visits to Camp David in total secrecy landed me months later in a bit of hot water. Rusty and I were guests of the Nitzes at a formal dinner at the splendid Farragut House in Washington. Among the many guests were our ambassador to France and his wife. When that most attractive lady spotted me, she rushed over. Thinking me to be alone, she said, "Andy, how nice to see you again. I shall never forget our weekend together!" Rusty, standing nearby, simply sputtered. It was clear that the time for secrecy had ended abruptly. I grasped Rusty by the arm to hold her there, and introduced the two women. I then said to the ambassador's wife with desperate urgency, "Now explain!" She did.

Bud Zumwalt and Ike Kidd were later selected to the rank of rear admiral by the same selection board. They were both well ahead of their contemporaries. It became clear that they would one day be rival candidates for the top navy spot. That day arrived and Zumwalt won the toss. In 1970, he became, at fifty, the youngest chief of naval operations in U.S. Navy history. He began immediately to make radical changes. He had long felt that much of the navy's attitude toward its enlisted men was archaic. He set about relaxing restrictions that he believed to be petty. He permitted beards. He allowed sailors a choice between the traditional blue-jacket uniform and one more modern. He established mechanisms for the freer expression of ideas and grievances by enlisted men. He expanded the role of women in the navy.

In doing all this, he made exactly the same mistake made by Robert McNamara in the TFX decision. He made no attempt to prepare the old guard or enlist its support. Even if he had not embarked on a program of reform, he would have been viewed by all those he had leap-frogged as a youthful upstart. As it was, his innovations were met by the admirals with rage and resistance. This opposition grew ever more strong. Indeed, as Bud admitted to me later, he would have profited by counsels of caution. There were too many changes and they came too fast. The navy is the most traditional of the services. Tradition, particularly in the armed services, should not be lightly treated. Some of the changes did have an adverse effect on discipline.

As the controversy mounted in the navy, Zumwalt's fame grew with the public. He became perhaps the best-known U.S. military figure of his time. He was featured in TV documentaries. His picture appeared on the cover of national magazines. If anything, this notoriety fanned the flames of discontent among the navy's senior officers. To the epithet of upstart, they added the label of prima donna. Both *Time* and *Newsweek* news magazines reported a determined effort by a group of admirals to persuade the president to remove him. Zumwalt has told me that the reports were accurate and that he barely managed to survive. He said that his perennial rival, Ike Kidd, had led the attack.

When Zumwalt's tour as CNO drew to a close, he proposed as his successor Admiral James L. Holloway III. The rival contender was Admiral Isaac Kidd. Zumwalt told me that Ike had the backing of the secretary of defense. The issue reached President Nixon during his final days in the White House. Bud described the critical meeting: The Watergate drama was reaching its climax. Nixon was a shambling, almost incoherent wreck. He could scarcely focus on the question. As the merits of the two candidates were debated, Nixon suddenly remembered that he had known and respected Admiral Holloway's father, under whom he had served during World War II. On that slight basis, and that alone, he made his choice. He selected Holloway. Thus Isaac Kidd became another victim of Watergate.

13

Asian Interlude

The most tiring thing about new teams is their enthusiasm. New presidents and new cabinet officers bound upon the stage with cries of, "Enough of this foolishness! Let's get cracking." The flags wave, the dogs bark, and the people shout. It's all very grand and glorious. But one who has been there with the old group and the one before that finally grows weary with a sense of *déjà vu*. The same problems, the same proposed solutions, and the same mistakes begin to come around again like horses on a carousel. After four years, three secretaries of the navy, and two presidents, I needed a change.

I have a strong streak of laziness. While the position of special counsel was enormously satisfying to my ego, I disliked the long hours of difficult work and the endless pressure. Rusty insisted that much of that pressure came from within. I disagreed vehemently at the time, but have come to recognize that she was right. But the self-awareness of this trait gained in later years changed nothing. I am still unable to meet external challenges with less than an all-out, even fanatic, effort. Thus there was always a conflict: Something, call it vanity, compelled me to seek exciting and challenging situations. But what I truly wanted was the impossible combination of psychic payoff without great effort—a free lunch. Then my inner compulsion to dedicated effort would take over, and I'd pay for the lunch many times over. The result in time was exhaustion, and a strong desire for relief. I had come to that point.

Also, while the special counsel job was a rich experience for me, it offered much less to Rusty. Moments of glamor such as Potomac cruises aboard the *Sequoia* were all too rare, and late, late dinners, spoiled weekends, and missed vacations all too common. She was far too much her own person to be satisfied indefinitely with the vicarious experience offered by my dinner table revelations of the Washington scene. The novelty had long ago worn off. Further, I was not at my best at home when the pressures were the greatest. I tended to become irritable and most unsympathetic at any mention of household problems. I wanted, on arrival home, only a couple of very large martinis, a quick dinner, and an exhausted fall into bed. If I needed a change, she was desperate for one!

Two jobs interested me. One was the fleet legal officer of the Sixth Fleet in the Mediterranean. The other was the same position with the Seventh Fleet in the Far East. The Sixth Fleet flagship was based at Villefranche on the French Riviera; the Seventh Fleet flagship at Yokosuka in Japan. Rusty and I decided we would try for Japan. The family had already enjoyed the Mediterranean with our tour in Italy. Now we wanted to experience the mysterious East. We were therefore delighted when I received my orders to the Seventh Fleet.

The prospect was exciting. I would be the lawyer on the staff of the fleet commander. The flagship, a cruiser, customarily spent much of the time in Yokosuka, its home port. For the remainder, it showed the flag throughout the Orient. Hong Kong, Manila, Bangkok, and Singapore were regular ports of call. We resolved that Rusty would join me in as many of these places as our navy pay would permit. In each port there would be pomp and parties as the admiral paid calls on heads of state and his naval counterparts. While there was military activity in Vietnam, the U.S. then played only a relatively limited advisory and support role. There was no combatant naval activity. This would be a gentleman's tour of sea duty!

On arrival in Japan, I immediately lodged my family in the Sanno Hotel in Tokyo. On the same day, I went by train to Yokosuka to report for duty. I found the flagship, the cruiser *Oklahoma City,* involved in feverish activity. Stores and ammunition were being loaded in great haste. The date was 2 August 1964. The

U.S. destroyer *Maddox* had just been attacked in the Gulf of Tonkin by North Vietnamese torpedo boats. We were to get under way immediately for the South China Sea. I had barely enough time to draw what pay I had on the books and thrust it into the hands of a shore-based legal officer. "Please get this to my family at the Sanno in Tokyo," I asked, "and tell them what's happened to me." I was leaving them in a tough spot. The officer, Commander Henry Staley, was a stranger to me then. But I was in luck: He and his wife, Crik, were guardian angels to my family during the many months that passed until the flagship returned to Japan. So much for the gentleman's tour!

The words "Gulf of Tonkin" rang with a distant echo. Seventeen years earlier in 1947, the *Sea Fox* was about to leave Hong Kong. We officers had emptied our pockets of American Club chit books on the wardroom table. There were enough to buy a couple of bottles of scotch, so I bought the chits up for a few cents on the dollar, a reflection of my Scottish heritage! I then got permission from the skipper to make a dash for the club. He agreed that the scotch could be brought aboard and locked in the ship's magazine until we got to Guam.

As I waited in the club bar for the bottles to be wrapped, a harried looking gentleman rushed in. "Ah," he said to me, "I thought I might find an American naval officer here." He introduced himself as the American consul general in Hong Kong, and he waved a radiogram. "This message," he said, "is from a stranded American freighter, the SS *Turkshead*." The radiogram stated that the ship, belonging to the Everett Steamship Company, was aground near the head of the Tonkin Gulf and was under attack by pirates. It gave a latitude and longitude. "We need to send help," said the consul. "Is there an American man-of-war anywhere in the South China Sea?" I told him that the submarine *Sea Fox* was probably the only one. I also told him that as the most junior officer aboard, I could hardly commit the ship. "Between us, though," I added, "I'd far rather have a go at pirates in the South China Sea than sail to Guam to give our destroyers antisubmarine practice. If you promise not to give me away, I'll tell you how you can get us into the act." He promised, and I told him he should send a dispatch to Commander Naval Forces, Far East, in Tokyo. He should request that we be diverted to assist the threatened vessel. I went back to the ship and said nothing. We immediately got under way. Soon a coded message came in from Tokyo. It directed us to proceed at best speed to a certain latitude and longitude to render assistance to the American merchant vessel *Turkshead,* which was under attack by pirates. "Where the hell is that," asked Commander Gordy Glaes, the captain. Without thinking, I blurted out, "I think that's in Tonkin Gulf, Captain," and then added quickly, "or somewhere in that general area."

The skipper sent a message back to Tokyo, "Request further instructions, particularly with regard to the use of firearms in Chinese waters." The answer came back, "Carry out the traditions of the sea. Protect American lives and property where necessary."

We had to go hundreds of miles all the way around the south end of Hainan Island. We could not use the shallow strait between the north end of that island and the Liuchow Peninsula since it had been mined during World War II and had not yet been cleared. We then slowly worked our way north up into the huge Gulf of Tonkin. There were no navigational aids. Temperature inversions caused peculiar radar returns. Mountains that had to be a hundred miles away appeared as mirages with their peaks pointing down. A strange mist hung over the water. Ghostly looking junks would appear suddenly at close range and scull rapidly away in alarm. The land areas were presented on the charts with dotted lines, for the northern portion of the gulf had never been surveyed. There were no charted soundings. The water was generally too shallow for submarine submerged operations. We therefore lashed all of our hatches closed from below except the conning tower hatch. Since we could not dive, we took this precaution in case pirates swarmed aboard.

It took us two days to find the *Turkshead.* It was hard aground at the head of the gulf, within sight of the Chinese mainland, but far from its reported position. Because of the shallow depth, we could only approach within a quarter mile. We signaled over by blinker light, "Send over a boat with your captain." The reply was blinked back, "The captain is sick." "Send over the mate," we said. "The mate is sick, too." "Aha," we thought, "the pirates have already taken over." We loaded our 5-inch deck gun. "Send over a representative immediately, or we'll open fire!" We soon thereafter found the truth. There were no pirates. It wasn't even an American ship. It was under charter to the Philippines and flew that flag. It had a Philippine captain, a British pilot, and a Malayan crew. It was carrying a load of Chinese passengers. They were returning to the southernmost Chinese province of Kuangsi with the fortunes and belongings that they had accumulated in their years of work in Singapore. They knew that piracy was common in the

Gulf of Tonkin. When the ship grounded, they felt vulnerable. They were dissatisfied with the defensive measures of the crew. They had forced open the small arms locker, armed themselves, and taken over the ship. They forced the radio operator at gun point to send the message that had resulted in our mission. In return for our promise to stand by for a few days until a tug arrived from Hong Kong, the captives were released. The tug arrived. We slowly worked our way out of the Gulf. I believe that up to that time, no other American naval vessel had ever penetrated so far or spent so long in the Gulf of Tonkin.

The recollection of these events of many years before was in my mind as the *Oklahoma City* left Japan and steamed south at high speed. President Johnson had reacted strongly to the attack on the *Maddox*. He said that the United States would continue to insist on the freedom of the seas. He announced that the U.S. would resume its naval patrols in international waters. Any repetition of the attack, he warned, would have the most serious consequences. The *Maddox* was then joined in her patrol by the destroyer *Turner Joy*.

As we neared the South China Sea, urgent messages began to arrive. Intelligence reports indicated that a second attack might take place. It was then the evening of August 4, and the two destroyers were well north in the Gulf of Tonkin. Then came reports that the *Maddox* and *Turner Joy* were under torpedo boat attack. The next morning, the president ordered a reprisal. Our carrier planes bombed the oil storage depot in Vinh, North Vietnam.

There had been a large volume of radio traffic during and after the incident. I saw all of the messages the following morning. The attacks had taken place on a dark, overcast, and moonless night. The destroyers had each reported torpedo noises. The two destroyers fired back at the attacking vessels. Except for a few flashes of light, the contacts had been by sonar and radar. Some of the messages were confused and conflicting. The squadron commodore, Captain Herrick, had been embarked in the *Maddox*. At one point, he expressed doubt about the validity of some of the radar and sonar contacts. That message, however, was counter to his other messages and to those from the ships themselves. One would expect some confusion in an attack by small fast vessels on a dark night. Nevertheless, after seeing the messages, I related to the fleet commander, Vice Admiral Roy Johnson, my *Sea Fox* experience of years before. I told him that I had found the Tonkin Gulf to be a weird place, with frequent radar and visual anomalies.

Admiral Johnson had analyzed all the messages and had concluded from them that an attack had indeed taken place. He could not very well fire off a message to Washington which said, "My lawyer, who just reported to the staff, has told me that he experienced strange radar phenomena when he was in the Gulf of Tonkin in a submarine in 1947." He did, however, say to me, "When we get to the gulf, I want you to go aboard those two ships and compare all of their logs and plots. Since you're a skeptic, you'd be a good one to do that."

On that day of our arrival on the scene, I was lowered by the *Oklahoma City*'s helicopter to the deck of the *Maddox*. On our way, we had picked up the operations officer of the *Turner Joy*. He had with him all of that ship's data.

We carefully constructed a composite chart. It reflected all of the information available on both ships during the incident. The tracks of both ships were plotted. All radar, sonar, and visual data, with times, ranges, and bearings were entered. The chart showed remarkable correlation. False contacts are usually random and do not persist for long periods. The same false contact would seldom be sensed by two ships that were in different positions. There was great consistency between all of the contacts made by both ships. Furthermore, the tracks of the attacking vessels, as plotted independently by both the *Maddox* and *Turner Joy,* coincided and were precisely what one would expect from attacking torpedo boats. Lastly, the plotted speed of the contacts was comparable to the speed of the North Vietnamese torpedo boats that had attacked the *Maddox* in daylight two days before.

Returning with the composite track chart, I was landed aboard the carrier *Ticonderoga* to await further transfer by helicopter back to the *Oklahoma City*. While on the carrier, I was told the good news that my name was on the selection list for promotion to the rank of captain.

On Admiral Johnson's staff, the chart was analyzed by the chief of staff, Captain Lloyd ("Joe") Vasey and the staff operations section. They then reviewed it with the admiral. All reached the same conclusion: The composite track chart left no doubt whatsoever. An attack had taken place. Admiral Johnson dispatched that information to the commander of the Pacific Fleet at Pearl Harbor, Admiral Tom Moorer. The chart was then flown back to Moorer's headquarters. The circumstances under which I again became involved with it four years later, I shall save for another chapter.

Except for the long family separations, the tour with the Seventh Fleet was a refreshing change. It was good to be back at sea again. I had missed it. I find the established and repetitive routine aboard a navy ship most agreeable. Few decisions for daily living need be made. I savor the symbolism of placing my wallet in a drawer when the ship leaves the dock. There, with its money, licenses, identification, and related impedimenta, it remains during the entire voyage. On land, absence of the wallet from the hip pocket is cause for panic! At sea, one can concentrate on the main tasks. In my case, these were interesting but not onerous. Compared to the problems I had become accustomed to in the secretary's office, they were easy. There was time for conversation, time for reading, and time for study.

Foreign languages hold a particular fascination for me. I have always envied those who can speak several of them. I blame my own sad performance in that field, probably conveniently, on poor hearing. During my tour of duty in Naples, I attacked the Italian language with brute force. I acquired a bare adequacy, if my listeners were patient. I have made the same effort with even less satisfactory results with Spanish and French. So I realized that an attempt to learn to speak Japanese would be futile. I therefore decided to concentrate on the written language. That became my hobby aboard the *Oklahoma City*. I became absorbed in the study of the *kanji*, the 1,269 Japanese ideograms. I also studied the two phonetic alphabets, *hirigana* and *katakana*. At the end of two years of effort, I had achieved the level of reading proficiency of a Japanese third grader! Few accomplishments, however, have given me greater pleasure.

One of my duties was to monitor fleet discipline. Reports of offenses came in from the Seventh Fleet ships when they visited various ports throughout the Orient. I plotted these on a large chart. Dignitaries who visited the flagship were briefed by the admiral's staff. I would talk on legal matters. When I came to the subject of fleet discipline, I would display the chart. I would explain that it showed the incidence of various offenses at different times in the various ports. I then noted that the Egyptians had kept detailed statistics on the rise and fall of the Nile for over 4,000 years. They came to the conclusion that some years it rose higher than others! My chart, I said, was equally enlightening.

The flagship spent little time in Japan during my two years aboard. It often, however, made rest and recreation visits to Hong Kong, Manila, Singapore, and Taiwan. Rusty joined me for wonderful reunions during many of those occasions. While all were wonderful, one proved particularly exciting: My boss, Vice Admiral Paul Blackburn, had asked me to fly to Saigon to discuss a problem concerning Rules of Engagement with Rear Admiral N.G. Ward, the commander of the Naval Forces in Vietnam. (Yes, he *asked* me to go! That was his way. A scholarly, perceptive gentleman, Admiral Blackburn had managed to retain that rarest of attributes among flag officers, a sense of humility.)

My business ashore could surely be concluded within a day or two. But in the meantime, the *Oklahoma City* would have moved beyond helicopter range deep into Tonkin Gulf on plane guard duty. My return to the ship at that time would thus be impossible. I saw an opportunity. "Admiral," I said, "I won't be able to get back to the ship during the time you're up north, and after that, the ship is to sail to Hong Kong for an R and R visit. Would it be O.K. if I took leave, had Rusty meet me in Bangkok, and then rejoined the ship in Hong Kong?"

"Of course," he said, "It's a chance you shouldn't miss."

So I shot off a dispatch from the ship to our Seventh Fleet liaison office in Yokosuka to be passed to Rusty: "Have arranged for leave in Bangkok starting about April 10th. Can you meet me there? We would then fly to Hong Kong about April 18th. Will telephone from Saigon tomorrow or the next day."

So far, so good. But after finishing my chores in Saigon, I discovered that telephoning from that city was a nightmare. Long lines of sailors, marines, and soldiers waited at the telephone offices. Some had waited for days! After many hours, I finally got an operator. "What priority do you have?" she asked. "None," I said, "but its a most urgent personal call." "They all are," she said, and rang off.

I then got through to another operator. "I have a priority call to make to Yokohama," I said. The fib did not come easily. I am one of those guys who waits his turn in line and respects no smoking and no parking signs. Rules to me are to be obeyed or changed through established means. They are not to be flouted for personal convenience. But the ache of longing to be with a beloved wife after a long separation cannot be overstated. And beloved she was. The separate gears of our lives now meshed smoothly, without the clashing so common during early years of marriage. There had always been love, but with time had come a deeper understanding. That understanding had brought an even greater liking for each other and an intense pleasure in each other's company that can transcend romantic love.

So I rationalized. The call involved the movement of military personnel (me), and was thus a proper subject for a priority call. The call went through a very suspicious operator. I knew it would be monitored. So before Rusty could say more than "hello," I spoke in my most official and authoritative manner, "This is Captain Kerr calling from Saigon. Can you bring the *Stickleback* Papers to Bangkok?" Rusty caught on. "Yes, Captain," she said, "Where shall I deliver them?" The operator then cut us off, "I don't think this is official. You must get an assigned priority from General Westmoreland's office to continue."

I had as much information as I was likely to get. Yes, Rusty *could* meet me in Bangkok. But would she, in the absence of further detail? How would we make contact in that sprawling city? How could she be sure that *I* would go in view of the uncertainties? I decided to go. If we were both in the same city, we would find each other. I would start with the U.S. Embassy, and I thought that Rusty would do the same. Almost twenty years of marriage enables one to make some good guesses about the thought processes of the other!

I then went to Saigon's Tan Sohn Nhut airport and lined up a space-available flight on a military plane to Bangkok. It was to leave within the next few hours. So I settled down with a cold beer in the lounge and looked out at the feverish activity at that busiest of airports. Soon an Air France 747 landed, apparently for a refueling stop. The passengers trouped off the plane, and among them was Rusty! We rushed together, she looking lovely in a cool green linen dress with her bright red hair, and as excited as a schoolgirl. And I in crisp summer white uniform, tanned to a deep brown by the sun of the South China Sea with my submarine dolphins and ribbons and brand new captain's shoulder-boards. I probably never looked better! After an hour in the lounge, holding hands and nuzzling each other, her flight to Bangkok was called away, and she got back on the plane. On my arrival at the Bangkok airport a few hours later, Rusty was waiting. "Oh, what fun I had on the flight here from Saigon," she said. "The passengers all wanted to know who that was that I met. I told them that it was my husband, and that we had been separated for over a year; and that I had flown all the way from the States for that brief airport meeting. They all thought it was too romantic for words."

And so we had a magical week in Bangkok followed by another in Hong Kong. Forgotten was the ache of separation, and the Seventh Fleet tour of duty, for a time, was for both of us the grandest of adventures.

With her characteristic enthusiasm and thoroughness, Rusty immersed herself in the life of Japan. She learned about Shintoism and the various Buddhist sects. She became knowledgeable about old imari ceramics, woodblock prints, and the screens and scrolls of the various historic periods of Japan. She studied its history and read translations of its literary masterpieces.

She was lucky in one respect: her closest friend from her high school days in Honolulu lived in Tokyo. Linda Manglesdorf Beech had gone to Japan after the war to work in General MacArthur's headquarters. A beautiful blonde with a remarkable mind, Linda quickly became fluent in Japanese. By the time we arrived, she had become famous on Japanese television as the *gaijin* (foreign) star of a comedy serial. She was the Lucille Ball of Japan. Everywhere Linda went, she was recognized and besieged by crowds of autograph seekers, calling "Rinda-san, Rinda-san!" She was then married to Keyes Beech, a well-known journalist who covered the Far East for the *Chicago Daily News*. Linda gave Rusty an entree into Japan that would have been beyond the reach of a mere navy wife, particularly one without a visible husband. Through Linda, she met Japanese royalty, political figures and industrialists, and members of the diplomatic corps. She made enduring friendships among the American "old Tokyo hands" who represented their companies in the Orient—the Andersons of NCR, the McVeighs of Peat, Marwick and Mitchell, and the Belknaps of Esso International. She taught English to executives at the Mitsubishi Factory in Yokohoma, and became accepted into their homes as an honored friend. In short, the Japanese experience was for her a total success. I only wish I could have been there!

One brief visit of the flagship to Japan took place in January 1966. The fleet supply officer, Captain Earl Clement, was an avid if not rabid sailor. He asked that I crew for him in a frost-bite sailboat race. I preferred to spend the available time with my family. Also, I was not enthusiastic about sailing in a 16-ft. Snipe-class sailboat in Sagami Wan in the dead of winter. I had made the mistake, however, of once telling Earl of my interest in sailing. I tried to squirm out with an excuse, "I'd love to, Earl, but I've got a report to finish for the admiral." Clement returned a little later. "Good news, Andy," he said. "I've fixed it with the admiral. He says that report can wait." I was stuck!

The next afternoon, in a sour mood, I arrived at the Yokosuka small-boat basin. It was freezing. I had on long underwear and two sweaters and was still cold. My mood was not improved when Earl informed me that he had doled out all the foul weather gear to the other sailors. There was none left. He also said that I would not be crewing for him. He introduced me to my skipper, whose name I didn't catch. The sky was black. There were flurries of snow, and the wind was rising. This, I thought, was madness! It's amazing, however, how we can allow ourselves to be drawn into a bad spot against all dictates of common sense, rather than cause difficulty. The comedian Shelley Berman once characterized the situation as one in which a person would rather die than make an ass of himself.

The rig on those Snipe boats was such that the crew member must sit well forward in order to tend the jib sheets. His position is exposed and wet. In a short time, I was soaked and shivering. The captain sat in the relative protection of the aft part of the cockpit, warm and dry in a full suit of foul weather gear. I soon saw that he was an inept sailor. He had a great deal of trouble bringing the boat about in the beat to the weather mark. Eventually all the other boats had rounded the mark and were headed in. We soon lost sight of them. We were out there alone. The weather was deteriorating rapidly. Gusts of wind reached near gale force. I shouted into the wind, "Let's head back in. We'll be lucky to make it!" The skipper answered, "No, God damn it! I'm going to make that mark." I yelled back, "Look, this is ridiculous. We're in real trouble! What did you say your rank is?" He answered that he was a chief petty officer. I said, "I've never done this before, chief, but I've got to pull rank on you. I'm a navy captain and this is an order! Bring this boat about and head back in!" The chief grumbled something about me being chicken, but complied. We started back. I reached under the cuddy and pulled out two life jackets. "Here, put this on, chief." He answered, "We don't need those damned things!" I said, "Put it on, chief—that's another order!" We dropped the mainsail and were sailing on the jib alone. The seas had built up alarmingly. Then a huge wave lifted the stern and we were pitch-poled end-over-end. We were in icy water and hanging onto the boat. It lay on its side. Righting it was impossible. We were out of sight of land. Snow was blowing horizontally. The visibility was at most a few hundred yards. I guessed that the water temperature gave a survival time of between forty minutes and an hour—if you started out warm. I had been chilled to the bone when we went in.

I was standing on the lower gunwale, attempting to get my chest as much out of the water as possible. Another big wave hit and turned the boat mast down. I found myself under water, trapped by sheets which had wrapped tightly around my waist and legs. The buoyant life jacket was pulling up toward the surface while the lines pulled down. I was close to panic when the word "Houdini" flashed into my mind.

The great escape artist often gave a public demonstration to get advance publicity for his performances. One such event was to take place in Chicago. Houdini was to be put in a straitjacket, wrapped in chains, and nailed in a coffin. The coffin was then to be thrown into the Chicago River. On the day of the demonstration, however, the river was frozen over. Houdini insisted on proceeding, so a hole was chopped in the ice. The coffin with the chained and straitjacketed Houdini inside was dropped through the hole. Minutes passed. No Houdini. After almost ten minutes, he popped up through the hole.

He explained that he had experienced no difficulty getting out of the coffin. He had, however, not allowed for the full strength of the current. As he came up, his head hit the ice. He then gave his listeners this immortal advice: "If ever you're trussed up, nailed in a box and thrown into river, and you manage to get loose but come up under the ice, the main thing to remember is DON'T PANIC! If you panic, you're through!" He said that he recalled hearing that when ice freezes on a body of water, it expands to leave an air space underneath. He tilted back his head so that his nose touched the ice—sure enough, he found air. So he alternatively swam and caught his breath in the air space until he found the hole.

Since hearing that story, the word "Houdini" had been my private signal for the thought, "Don't panic!" I knew that I had to get rid of the life jacket. I cast it off and so was able to dive down to slacken the entrapping lines. I came gasping to the surface with a gash in my head that later required twelve stitches. I was bleeding heavily. Over forty-five minutes had passed. I was shivering violently and was sure that this time I had bought the farm! Then I heard it. A helicopter! It spotted us and hovered overhead. The "horse collar" was lowered. I had used that device many times. It goes around the back and under the arms. It allows one to be raised and lowered effortlessly. My brain refused to function. I could only hook my arms through the collar. Looking up, I could see the crew member in the open doorway shaking his head and gesturing wildly. I hung stubbornly on. Finally they pulled me up. How I hung on in my weakened condition with the weight of the soaked clothing, I'll never know. I flopped into the floor of the chopper. I remember a vast relief. I had made it! I was even surprised to be rushed into an ambulance at the heliport. I remember some shots and the doctor saying, "Hang in there, captain. I've seen downed aviators fished out of the water with body temperatures almost as low as yours. Some of them pulled through." Only then did I realize that I had something to worry about.

In the meantime, Rusty had spent the day in Tokyo. She arrived back at our house in Yokohama about the time she expected me home. It was then blowing a full gale. As she opened the screen door, it was caught by the wind and torn from its hinges. It went sailing away. The telephone inside was ringing. There had been an apparent mix-up in signals at the Yokosuka hospital. The doctor thought an initial report on my condition had been given my wife a couple of hours previously. He started right in with what he thought was a follow-up. "We've got good news for you, Mrs. Kerr. We now think that your husband might live."

We found that the intervention of the helicopter was by purest chance. No helicopters are based at Yokosuka. That chopper had come from the U.S. base at Atsugi. It had come unexpectedly to deliver a needed part. The sailor at the Yokosuka heliport talked by radio to the pilot as the chopper approached. "Before you land," he said, "how about taking a swing out over the bay. Some fools were out there in a sailboat race, and one of them might not have made it back yet."

The duration and intensity of the aftermath to exposure surprised me. I shivered for days, with chattering teeth. It was impossible to get warm. Everything hurt, but particularly agonizing were my balls. They felt like a pair of ice cubes!

I got out of the hospital in about a week, in time to sail with the flagship back down to the South China Sea. The chief, you'll be happy to hear, was released from the hospital after one day. Having lost no blood and having been warm and dry when his immersion commenced, he came through in good shape.

Ships of the Seventh Fleet involved in the Vietnam war had their headquarters at "Yankee Station." This was an arbitrary point of reference at sea off the coast of Vietnam in the Gulf of Tonkin. The Oklahoma City could often be found there. It was always a scene of great activity as ships received mail and supplies. There was a constant coming and going of helicopters and ships' boats as visits were exchanged among the ships and staffs.

Our surface operations officer, Captain Bob Pond, returned

one day from a visit to the nearby cruiser-destroyer flotilla flagship. He told me that he had run across a young officer there with whom he had served in Washington. The officer was Lieutenant Commander Marcus Aurelius Arnheiter. The name rang a bell from my Pentagon days. I recalled that Arnheiter had been mentioned by Washington columnists as having written a report that was critical of the navy's antisubmarine warfare program. I remembered thinking it unusual that an officer so junior had been able to attract so much press attention.

Pond said that Arnheiter had told him a strange story. His reaction had been to advise Arnheiter to talk to me. I said I'd be happy to see him; what was the problem? Pond said he'd rather I heard it firsthand. Arnheiter arrived by helicopter, and I listened to his story. He said that while he was in Washington, he had written a book. It was entitled *Shadow of Peril* and had been published by Doubleday under the Russian pseudonym, Alexander Ivanovich. He said that he had received technical help from a U.S. submarine officer, Commander John A. "Al" Davis. His problem, he said, was that Al Davis was claiming sole ownership of the book. He asked my opinion as to whether he should sue Davis.

He was not seeking legal advice. He had consulted a lawyer specializing in copyright law and knew where he stood. He wanted to talk to me about the career implications of his problem. He was already well behind his contemporaries. He had failed at and been discharged from West Point before entering the Naval Academy. He had once been passed over for promotion from ensign to lieutenant junior grade. That is a step up in rank that most navy officers find almost automatic. That black mark would be all but impossible to erase. He was believed to have sought publicity outside the navy for his criticism of navy policy. He was already known in Washington as controversial, and there were widely differing views of his judgment and ability. He had, however, managed to get orders to command the destroyer escort *Vance*. He would be assuming that position within a few weeks. We discussed his past history and performance, and his apparent need for fame and notoriety. I asked about his career goals. Would he be satisfied to reach the rank of captain? No, he said, he wouldn't stay in the navy unless he had a chance to make admiral.

I told him that with the strikes he already had against him, his chance of making flag rank was almost zero. The only long shot possibility would be to do it in the way Admiral Rickover did. He would have to make a great splash with spectacular accomplishments in the rank of captain and then get the support of Congress and the press. I said that it was clear that he already knew the value of publicity and how to get it. He also had shown a knack for getting people to support him. I told him his ego seemed equal to that of Admiral Rickover. "So," I said, "You might just be able to pull it off."

But, I reminded him, the real trick would be to become a captain. Even Rickover toed the line until he reached that rank. If he continued a career pattern of seeking controversy, he'd never get there. His only chance would be a record of solidly outstanding performance along traditional and recognized lines. The starting point would be his tour as commanding officer of the *Vance*. He agreed with the analysis and said that he would pursue that path. I questioned his ability to do so in view of his natural tendencies and the needs of his ego. He assured me that he could and would do it.

"Well, then," I said, "that answers the question about suing Al Davis." Even Al didn't dare claim authorship of that book until he was about to retire. The book was purportedly written by a Russian submarine captain. It was implicitly critical of U.S. Navy antisubmarine policy. The fictional chief of naval operations was obviously Admiral Arleigh Burke. He was referred to throughout the book as "Old Jug Butt." The book was not a commercial success. It was unpopular among almost all elements of the navy. So I concluded, "Since there aren't any royalties, the only thing you can get from suing Davis is the 'credit' for writing the book. Credit like that, with your history, would finish you for sure in the navy."

He thanked me and left. In spite of his vanity, I found him strangely attractive. He was, above all, articulate. But I knew in my heart that I would hear of him again. He would never be able to live with anonymity. I was right. But I could not know that within two years, his conduct as commanding officer of the *Vance* would become a subject of national interest as the "Arnheiter Case." Or that the problem would end up in my lap.

The U.S. involvement in Vietnam deepened soon after the Tonkin Gulf incidents. The Tonkin Gulf Resolution was passed overwhelmingly by the Senate and the House. It authorized the president to use whatever measures he thought necessary in Vietnam. It was a blank check. Our marines then landed at Da Nang. Our force levels built up rapidly thereafter. By the time I left the Seventh Fleet in 1966, we were embroiled in a full-scale war.

I supported and agreed with that effort. At that time, the split between China and Russia had not become apparent. Sukarno in Indonesia had forged the Djakarta-Peking axis, and was attacking Malaysia and Singapore. Burma was under a Communist dictatorship. It was argued that if North Vietnam was permitted to overrun the south, Laos and Cambodia would be next. Ultimately Thailand would be threatened. This was called the domino theory. It was ridiculed by the Vietnam protestors, but has proven to be a reasonably accurate forecast. It seemed that all of Southeast Asia was in imminent danger of a Communist military takeover. Above all, however, we had pledged our support to the people of South Vietnam. We saw their plight as a valiant struggle to preserve their freedom against the invasion of an enemy armed and supported by the Soviet Union and Communist China.

I disagree with those who called our effort in Vietnam "immoral." There are credible arguments that it was ill-advised. It is possible that it was based upon some erroneous assumptions. It was certainly futile. But immoral it was not. If anything, it was characterized by an excess of altruism. I think it will be the last altruistic war we shall fight until its memory fades away. Let us hope that the need for another one does not arise in the meantime.

14

Return to the E-Ring

As my tour with the Seventh Fleet drew to a close, I received a letter from Rear Admiral Hearn, the new judge advocate general. In the manner of one conferring a great honor, he said that he had nominated me to attend the Naval War College. Now the War College is a wonderfully broadening experience for naval officers. It lifts them out of their navy lives for a year. They, of course, study military and naval strategy. Much more importantly, however, they are exposed to the thoughts of leading figures of the national scene. Through the college's prestigious guest lecture program, they learn how national policy is formulated. My problem was that I thought that I already knew all about that. I believed that my prior on-the-job training was sufficient. Academic contemplation of the same subject seemed unnecessary.

I tried to think of a reply to the JAG by which I could decline the honor without appearing ungrateful or arrogant. I was saved by a dispatch from Washington. The new deputy assistant secretary of defense for International Security Affairs (ISA), Townsend W. Hoopes, needed a military assistant. Was I interested? Could I come back for an interview? It may be recalled that Nitze and Zumwalt had come out of ISA. I was familiar with its function as the

Pentagon's state department. The scope of the problems handled by ISA made the prospect intriguing. All would depend on the proposed nature of my duties and the chemistry between me and the new deputy.

I flew back to Washington. I was instantly attracted by the grace and intellect of "Tim" Hoopes. A handsome, athletic man, he had served as a marine officer in World War II. He was a graduate of Yale University and had a broad and inquiring mind. A wealthy man, he was Eastern Ivy League without a trace of the condescension one often finds among that group. He was an associate of the Kennedy family and personified the idealism, energy, and style of Camelot.

We immediately hit it off. Hoopes described my prospective role. He said that he would expect me to be involved with him in the decision process. I was relieved. I had feared that the position might be that of an aide who merely took care of administrative details. Our association was therefore sealed. I then told Hoopes that I had a problem in diplomacy: The navy judge advocate general had nominated me to attend the Naval War College, but I much preferred the ISA assignment. Hoopes needed no coaching. He wrote to Secretary of the Navy Paul Nitze and asked for my assignment as a personal favor. He stressed the demands of ISA, which Nitze well knew. Nitze, as expected, called the JAG, and I was off the hook. Washington business is most often done by pushing the right buttons!

So after an absence of two years, I returned to the Pentagon. Within its five sides, that extraordinary building consists of five concentric rings, lettered A to E. The internal, or A Ring, encloses a central courtyard. There one finds the most humble of the laborers in the defense vineyard. They leave the building at precisely 4:30 P.M., laughing and joking. The level of responsibility rises and levity wanes as one moves outward. The wide and well-lighted E-Ring corridor is hung with paintings, many by famous combat artists. There are also oil portraits of the illustrious previous occupants of the E-Ring offices. There is not much noise. Absent is the babble of voices one hears along the inner rings. The air of dignity and solemnity seems to inhibit loud talk in the same manner as does a cathedral. Important-looking people, flanked and followed by obsequious-looking assistants, stride rapidly to or from their meetings. It is a rule in Washington that if one is important, he must be in a hurry. One must never stop and chat with friends along the way. One must sweep along. The most that can be expected on encountering such an entourage is a cursory nod from the great man as he listens with a serious expression to last-minute advice from his earnest aides. Four-star admirals and generals can always be seen bounding up the Mall or River entrance steps two at a time, their aides following discreetly behind. They must, at all cost, appear vigorous.

Those in the outside E-Ring offices gaze out through their windows at the Washington Monument, the Capitol, or the Virginia countryside. Their lights burn late at night. They are the policy-makers. They are assigned chauffeur-driven limousines. They sit in majestic splendor at the top of the defense pyramid. They pay for that grandeur. In the Pentagon cafeterias, there is a bland-food line. Worried-looking men with queasy stomachs lunch there on dismal fare. Among them are E-Ring denizens who have found it necessary to eschew the richer diet of their special dining rooms. It is a good place to catch a glimpse of some of the Pentagon's high and mighty.

Hoopes had been appointed to his E-Ring position in ISA to re-place Adam Yarmolinsky, who had returned to a teaching post at Harvard. A short, almost diminutive man with a large head, Adam had a piercing, hypnotic gaze that I had at first found unnerving. I had worked with him on several occasions, and admired him greatly. For sheer brain power, I had met no equal in the Pentagon. With that, he combined political insight and integrity. He made sev-eral trips to the Pentagon from Cambridge to help Hoopes and me get the feel of ISA.

ISA is organized into divisions that have exact counterparts in the State Department. Each has, for example, a South America Desk and a Middle East Desk. Copies of all cables to and from the secretary of state also go to ISA. It is ISA's responsibility to see that the military and foreign policies of the United States are not in con-flict. Our view of world events was therefore unexcelled.

Hoopes was the principal deputy of John McNaughton, who was then the assistant secretary for ISA. He was McNaughton's al-ter ego, and they functioned as a team. I thus found myself work-ing equally with McNaughton. The reader may recall my run-in with John McNaughton in Fred Korth's hospital room at Be-thesda, when the former was general counsel. I wondered what his reaction would be when I appeared as Hoopes' assistant. He never mentioned the episode, however, and we enjoyed a cordial and pro-ductive relationship.

There was one important difference between my duties as special counsel to the secretary of the navy, and those as military assistant in ISA. Problems only came to the secretary of the navy when for some reason the navy's institutions did not or could not resolve them. They tended to be intractable. They also tended to become projects of the individual members of the secretary's staff. Problems coming to ISA, on the other hand, were assigned to the appropriate desk or division. Hoopes and I were therefore engaged primarily in guiding, reviewing, and, where necessary, modifying the work of those ISA institutions. We were involved in almost all events of an international nature that made the headlines. The Arab-Israeli Six-Day War, the Cyprus crisis, the disengagement of France from NATO—all were grist for our mill. But because they did not become personal projects, I shall leave the reader to consult other sources for enlightenment.

After I had been a year in ISA, Paul Nitze, who was still the secretary of the navy, asked me to return to my old job as special counsel. The incumbent, Captain Horace "Robbie" Robertson, was leaving. He had orders to go to, of all places, the Naval War College! Robbie had taken over from me as special counsel three years before. His War College tour did him no professional damage. Robbie went on several years later to become judge advocate general of the navy. After his retirement, he became dean of Duke University Law School.

I think it a good general rule that one should not go back to the same job he has held before. In this case, however, there were special circumstances, the explanation of which requires a short diversion.

Rusty and I had encouraged our two children to set their educational sights high. I suppose in this we were proper products of the Great Depression, when education was generally equated with salvation. In any event, the kids took us up on the challenge. Both decided they wanted to attend Yale! Furthermore, it appeared that they would have no trouble gaining admission.

The time was now approaching to fulfill our side of the bargain. Two things had happened, not fully appreciated by us: college costs had suddenly sky-rocketed, and the criteria for the award of scholarships had changed from merit to need. The prospect therefore loomed of responsibility for the full costs of two students at Yale only a year apart. We could not begin to manage that on navy pay. Our small savings had gone into housing. Scholarships were out, since navy captains were not considered needy. Yale had made it clear that we could expect no financial assistance.

I had two choices: I could retire from the navy and seek more lucrative employment. Or I could make a long-shot attempt to leap-frog to the rank of rear admiral. The pay of that rank would be almost enough. I could borrow the rest. But as a law specialist, I could only become an admiral by becoming judge advocate general or deputy JAG. Both positions were filled simultaneously every four years. Eligibility for consideration was normally based on seniority. There would be a new JAG in 1968, only one year hence. At that time, I would be far too junior to be considered. My first real crack at the job would not occur until 1972. I could not wait that long for a roll of the dice.

There was, however, a possible way to beat the system. The JAG is selected by the secretary of the navy. The latter usually respects, but is not bound by, seniority. And here was the secretary of the navy asking me to return as his special counsel! I talked with Bud Zumwalt, who by that time was an admiral, but had not yet become CNO. He had maintained close ties with Paul Nitze. His advice was emphatic: Go for it! He agreed that the best place to make the attempt was from the secretary's office, and that the chances were excellent with Nitze as the incumbent. He promised his full support.

I then told Nitze that I would be pleased to return as his special counsel. I confided in Tim Hoopes the reason for my decision. My orders to the secretary's office were issued by the Navy Department. Then, suddenly, Cyrus Vance announced his resignation as deputy secretary of defense. Paul Nitze was nominated to be his replacement. At the same time, John McNaughton was named to be the new secretary of the navy. One can only reflect at such times on the words of Robert Burns concerning the best laid plans of mice and men. Oh, well, I thought. I still might have a chance to make JAG with McNaughton as secretary. Of course, the odds were now far worse with Nitze gone. The important thing now was to determine if McNaughton actually wanted me as special counsel. So I suggested to him that he might want to choose his own man. If so, I said, my orders could easily be cancelled. I would be happy, in that event, to stay on with Hoopes. McNaughton, however, insisted that he wanted me on his staff.

I thought McNaughton would make an excellent secretary of the navy. He was sure to be an interesting one. He would undoubtedly shake things up. He had an abrupt manner. He was considered by many to be an arrogant young man. I had observed, however, that his so-called arrogance was an impatience with fools. He gave them short shrift. Because of the differing nature of the jobs, however, he would surely have to exercise more tact as navy secretary than he had as head of ISA. (I don't want to be understood as implying that there are more fools in the navy!)

I took a couple of weeks leave, and moved back into my old office. My wonderful former secretary, Colleen Dodson, was still there. So were some of the old problems I had left three years before. McNaughton was confirmed by the Senate in the position of secretary of the navy. Before he could take office, however, he was killed in a tragic accident. He and his family had attended the commencement exercise of one of his young sons at a Virginia school. On their way back to Washington, their Allegheny Airlines plane was involved in a mid-air collision. He and his wife and the rest of his family were killed, except for one son who was not on the plane. His death was a sad loss to the navy and to the country. John McNaughton, still in his thirties, was a brilliant and accomplished man. His future contribution to our nation, I am sure, would have been invaluable.

A few weeks later, Paul Ignatius was named secretary of the navy. He had been McNamara's assistant secretary of defense for Logistics. He and the Arnheiter case arrived at the Navy Department about the same time. Then followed several months of intense frustration.

We left Lieutenant Commander Marcus Aurelius Arnheiter at Yankee Station off the coast of Vietnam over two years before. You may recall that he was soon to take command of the destroyer escort *Vance*. He remained in command of that vessel for only ninety-nine days. Following is a summary of the circumstances of his relief from that command.

The *Vance* was based at Pearl Harbor. During the time Arnheiter was in command, however, the ship was engaged in operations in Vietnamese waters. Soon after he took over the ship, the wives back in Hawaii began to receive disturbing letters from their husbands on the *Vance*. They related to erratic and peculiar behavior on the part of the new captain. In some cases they complained of demeaning and degrading treatment at Arnheiter's hands. Meanwhile, off the coast of Vietnam, a circuit-riding navy chaplain embarked in the *Vance*. His custom was to ride ships that did not have an assigned chaplain aboard, for a week or two at a time. While aboard the *Vance*, he was swamped by complaints about the commanding officer. They ranged from abusive and insulting behavior, to erratic and dangerous employment of the ship in combat situations. The cognizant admiral in Pearl Harbor received a report from the chaplain. He had also heard complaints by the families of *Vance* personnel. He sent a staff officer out for an informal look. The officer was a communications expert, and he was ostensibly to conduct a communications inspection. He was also directed by the admiral to keep his eyes and ears open to try to see what was taking place. He reported back that morale on the *Vance* was at rock bottom and that it appeared to be Arnheiter's fault. Both he and the chaplain reported complaints that Arnheiter violated operation orders and Navy Regulations in combat situations.

The combination of these reports and complaints convinced the admiral that he had no alternative but to conduct a thorough investigation. It is important to recognize what such a decision entails. The complaints to be investigated were that the commanding officer had abused, humiliated, and demeaned his officers and crew, and that he had endangered the ship and the interests of the United States by violating orders involving the ship's combat employment. The witnesses at the investigation could only be the officers and men of the ship. They could not be put in the position of testifying against their captain, with the possibility that he might still be the captain after the investigation was completed. That situation would be intolerable. There is only one way to proceed in such cases: If the complaints are serious and there is sufficient evidence of their validity to warrant formal investigation, the captain must be relieved of command. The investigation may then proceed. The ex-captain will be represented by counsel. He will, of course, have all the rights of a party to the investigation. He will have the right to be present and hear the witnesses, to present evidence in his own behalf, and the right of cross-examination. If the charges turn out to be false, he should be given another command. All adverse material arising from the incident should be expunged from his record. The navy has well-established procedures for this. In such a case, those who had lodged the false complaints would be punished.

This was exactly the procedure that was followed. When the *Vance* reached port at Subic Bay in the Philippines, Arnheiter was relieved. A formal investigation was conducted, at which Arnheiter was represented by counsel. A verbatim record was kept. The record of testimony amounted to some 400 pages. The tapes of the testimony were also preserved.

The investigating officer concluded that the complaints were essentially correct, and that Arnheiter was unfit for command.

Arnheiter, of course, did not agree. His version was that he had inherited a ship that was in terrible condition and in a bad state of training; he had attempted to whip it into shape as an effective fighting unit; in the process he had earned the enmity of some dissident beatniks among the officers and crew; they had managed to effect his removal through the intervention of a super-liberal chaplain; there had been no investigation before he had been relieved; he had not had his day in court. He demanded a trial by general court-martial.

The record of investigation was received in Washington and reviewed by the judge advocate general. He held that the proceedings were legal and that the findings were supported by the evidence. That normally would have ended the matter. Arnheiter, however, had amazing success at converting people to his cause. He was articulate, attractive, and persuasive. He was also tireless in his efforts. He was able to convince many retired generals and admirals that he had been the victim of a subversive plot. He gained influential support in Congress. Senator Stennis and Senator Strom Thurmond were in his corner. Representative Joseph Resnick, from Arnheiter's home district in New York, loaded the Congressional Record with pro-Arnheiter material. He appeared to be attempting to establish a national reputation through the case. He made his championship of Arnheiter the central issue in his campaign for reelection. The press rallied uniformly behind Arnheiter. The *New York Times* took the lead. Neil Sheehan, its Pentagon correspondent, was dedicated to Arnheiter's vindication. Neil Sheehan of the *Times* was the reporter to whom Daniel Ellsburg leaked the *Pentagon Papers*.

Arnheiter demanded that the secretary of the navy convene a general court-martial. It seemed clear that he wanted a national forum in the style of the sensational trial of General Billy Mitchell in the 20s. I reviewed the record in preparation for advising Secretary Ignatius. I also asked a fellow navy lawyer for whom I had great respect, Commander Frank S. Johnston, to review the case. Frank had attended Georgetown Law School under the navy law program at the same time that I attended George Washington. He had the keenest legal mind of anyone I knew. He was, at that time, the legal assistant to the assistant secretary of the navy for manpower.

Frank and I came to independent and identical conclusions: The case against Arnheiter had been decisively proved in a full and fair investigation; he had no right to any further action; the navy's interests would not be served by acceding to Arnheiter's demands.

We reviewed the proceedings and the evidence exhaustively

with Secretary Ignatius in numerous lengthy sessions. He agreed with the conclusions that we had reached. I urged that he state those conclusions to Arnheiter and deny his request for further action. He should then release his decision and the reasoning behind it to the public. In the last analysis, he need only be concerned with congressional reaction. I assured him of my confidence that we could handle that.

He reached the point of taking the recommended action several times. Then some new blast in the press would make him draw back. He could not bring himself to take the final action. An affable man, Paul Ignatius seemed extraordinarily sensitive to public criticism. Even when he professed to know he was right, he shrank from action that he believed would expose him to adverse press reaction. In this, he differed markedly from Connally, Korth, and Nitze. Weeks passed. The delay enabled Arnheiter to muster even greater support. In the absence of action by the secretary, the navy was not only on the defensive—it was on the run. And the frustrating, ridiculous thing was that Arnheiter had no case at all!

Commander Bill Thompson, the secretary's public affairs assistant, and I were desperate. We had urged Neil Sheehan of the *Times* to read the investigation. He had refused, stating his conviction that it must be a navy whitewash. We suggested that he conduct his own investigation. He should talk to the people who were involved. He might start by looking at Arnheiter's navy record. We explained that Arnheiter himself would have to give him authorization for that. He asked for that authorization. Then Arnheiter made a fatal mistake. He refused to give Sheehan permission. This to a reporter is like a red flag to a bull! For the first time Sheehan was shaken in his absolute belief in Arnheiter's cause. He decided to listen to the tapes of the testimony. Then he accepted our offer of assistance in locating all of the people who had served with Arnheiter in the *Vance*. He received permission from the *New York Times* to leave Washington for several weeks. We knew that he was interviewing *Vance* people, but he kept his findings to himself. In response to our probing during his brief visits back to the Pentagon, he would only say, "This is a fascinating case!"

Then, on 11 August 1968, his findings appeared in the *New York Times Magazine*. In a devastating lead article entitled, "The 99 Days of Captain Arnheiter," Arnheiter was torn to shreds. He never recovered. Sheehan's definitive article was investigative reporting at its best. He developed the story from comprehensive personal interviews. The tragedy was that it was all there in the navy investigation all the time. We just couldn't get anyone to look at it, and until Secretary Ignatius took action, we couldn't make a public release. The Sheehan article gave the secretary the courage to take his final action. The case of Marcus Aurelius Arnheiter then faded gradually away. He failed to be promoted to commander and retired from the navy. Sheehan later described his involvement with Arnheiter in great detail in his book *The Arnheiter Affair* published by Random House in 1971. Readers who are intrigued to learn what Arnheiter actually did on the *Vance* will find the book an authoritative and entertaining source.

The great mystery in the Arnheiter case was in the role played by Captain Richard Alexander. Dick Alexander had a distinguished naval career until he became fatally involved with Arnheiter. He had earned a reputation for independent and creative thinking. He often took courageous and unpopular stands against the common wisdom, to be proven right in the end. Energetic and tenacious, he would stand his ground until he eventually prevailed. He was tall, slim, and straight, with stern, aristocratic features. He looked every inch the model naval officer. His fine record, officer-like qualities, and outstanding service reputation earned him orders to command the battleship *New Jersey*. That ship was being recommissioned to take part in the war in Vietnam. It was to be the only battleship in the navy. Command of the *New Jersey* was the greatest plum available to a surface ship officer. Captain Richard Alexander's early selection to the rank of admiral was a foregone conclusion. He would be, in navy slang, a "shoo-in."

Prior to taking command of the *New Jersey*, Alexander was on duty in Washington in the navy's Bureau of Personnel. Somehow, he had become acquainted with Arnheiter and had been impressed by him. That is not surprising. In my meeting with Arnheiter at Yankee Station, I saw that he was not an ordinary young man. I found him likable, well-spoken, and persuasive. I had judged, however, that he was strongly driven by a need for fame and notoriety. Under different circumstances, one might have concluded that his drive was simply that motivation that propels successful naval officers. My guess is that Dick Alexander, having himself been willing to swim against the tide, saw in Arnheiter some of that same quality.

Candidates for command of naval ships must first pass the scrutiny of a command screening board within the Bureau of Personnel. The circumstances surrounding Arnheiter's selection to command the *Vance* are shrouded in clouds of controversy. Members of the screening board have claimed that Arnheiter was turned down. Alexander challenges this. The documentary evidence is inconclusive. It appears beyond doubt, however, that Alexander strongly supported Arnheiter. He played a decisive role in getting Admiral Semmes, the chief of the Bureau, to assign Arnheiter to command of the *Vance*.

When the record of the Arnheiter investigation arrived in Washington, Alexander requested to see it. A copy was sent to him. Soon after, he wrote a letter to Arnheiter. It was addressed, "Dear Marc," and it was thoughtful and sensitive. He wrote that he had carefully reviewed the record of investigation. He then said that he had regretfully concluded that Arnheiter was deficient in the qualities of judgment required of a commanding officer. He advised Arnheiter for his own good and for the good of his family to seek another career. He said that while he still thought Arnheiter had great potential, it was clear that it could not be realized in the navy. Captain Alexander gave the letter broad distribution, including a copy to Admiral Semmes, the chief of the Bureau. It was thought to be his last word on the subject. It was not.

As Secretary Ignatius agonized over his decision on Arnheiter, the weeks passed and the flames of criticism of the navy rose higher. One day, he received a letter from Captain Alexander. The letter came to the secretary directly, not through the normal navy channels of communications. Alexander, in the letter, commiserated with the secretary on his difficult decision and offered his assistance. He said that he thought he could shed further light on the affair. He offered to meet with the secretary. Ignatius asked my opinion. Should he take issue with Alexander for having written directly? Should he see Alexander? I recommended that he not take too literal a view of Navy Regulations in this case. He should stretch things a bit and treat the letter as personal, not official. Secondly, I suggested that failure to accept Alexander's offer would only add to his difficulty in arriving at a decision. He would be haunted by the question: What in the world did Alexander have to say?

Ignatius then asked if I would like to sit in on the meeting. I said no. I thought that if he were to treat the letter as personal, so should he treat the visit. Furthermore, Arnheiter and the press had charged that the secretary was being insulated by his staff from the true facts. There could be no question of Alexander's being inhibited in any way if the meeting were private.

I then called Dick Alexander in the Philadelphia Navy Yard. It was there that the work of recommissioning the *New Jersey* was in progress. I explained that the secretary had chosen to view his offer as personal and would see him privately. His calendar was free for that entire afternoon. The secretary's plane could pick Alexander up at Philadelphia's Mustin Field after lunch.

When Alexander arrived at the Pentagon, he stopped briefly in my office. We had been classmates at the Naval Academy, and we exchanged pleasantries. He gave me no clue as to his position on Arnheiter. He was with Ignatius for about two hours. He came back to my office to get his hat. He said, "I gave the secretary something to think about." I replied, "I'm sure you did, Dick," and he left without further comment. I went in to Ignatius' office, full of curiosity. "What did he have to say?" I asked. Ignatius answered, "I told Captain Alexander that I would hold his visit and everything he said in strict confidence. I gave him my word that whatever he said was just between the two of us and so he could speak freely. I'm sorry, Andy, but I can't go back on my word." He then said that Alexander had left with him a lengthy letter that covered all the points he made at the meeting. In fact, he said, Alexander had used the document as a talking paper during the meeting. Ignatius said that he would study the letter that night at home.

The next morning, accounts of the letter, and excerpts therefrom appeared in the *Washington Post* and the *New York Times*. That same day, the letter was published in its entirety in the *Congressional Record*. The *Record* stated that it had been provided to Congress by Captain Alexander. Thus, Alexander made no attempt to conceal the fact that he had made the letter public. The document was a brief on behalf of Arnheiter. It contained all of the arguments that Arnheiter had been making with Congress and the press.

Ignatius was outraged. He felt that he had been duped. The reaction of Chief of Naval Operations Admiral Moorer was even more violent. From the newspapers and the *Congressional Record,* he learned for the first time that he had been bypassed. While the secretary was prepared to overlook that breach of navy protocol, Admiral Tom Moorer was not. He was even more incensed, however, that an officer of the navy would make public a letter he had written to the secretary of the navy. Moorer viewed it as an attempt to bring public pressure to bear to influence the decision on a navy matter. Without consulting Ignatius, Admiral Moorer instantly ordered Alexander relieved of command of the *New Jersey*. Captain Richard Alexander, who had been one of the most highly regarded surface ship officers in the navy and a sure bet to make admiral, was banished to an obscure desk job in Boston. His career was irrevocably ruined. He retired about two years later. And thus vanished perhaps the best chance for a member of our Naval Academy class to eventually become a chief of naval operations.

A few months after my return to the secretary of navy's office in 1967, an old subject popped up—the Tonkin Gulf incidents. I had thought when the composite chart of the *Maddox–Turner Joy* night action was sent off to Hawaii from the *Oklahoma City* almost four years before, that the issue was closed. Now I know that it will never be.

Senator Fulbright was the chairman of the Senate Foreign Relations Committee during the Vietnam War. Two days after the incidents involving the two destroyers on the night of 4 August 1964, Congress passed the Tonkin Gulf Resolution. Fulbright was the Senate floor manager of the resolution that was passed overwhelmingly by the Senate. It passed unanimously in the House. The resolution approved the actions already taken by the president and in effect authorized him to take any further action that he deemed necessary to stop aggression in Vietnam. All subsequent U.S. measures in Vietnam were taken under the authority of that resolution.

As the war dragged on, opposition to our involvement mounted. Senator Fulbright began to change his mind about the wisdom of our effort. Eventually he became a leading critic of President Johnson's Vietnam policies. I am sure that he came to regret the part he played in getting the whole thing started. Rather than attribute his early support to an error of judgment, he began to suggest that he had been misled. He then commissioned a study of Tonkin Gulf incidents by the staff of his Foreign Relations Committee. Following that, he announced that he would conduct full-scale hearings. Fulbright's press releases relating to the staff study and the proposed hearings left no doubt. Senator Fulbright had made up his mind. He had decided that the attack on the *Maddox* and the *Turner Joy* had never taken place. He further concluded that he and the rest of the country had been led to believe that there had been an attack either because of inexcusable error or fraudulent manipulation of the facts.

Secretary McNamara realized that he would be a principal witness at the hearings. He knew that Fulbright would be extremely hostile. He would have to be thoroughly prepared. He asked Secretary Ignatius for the loan of a naval officer knowledgeable in the Tonkin Gulf incidents. That officer would participate in the reconstruction of the incident for McNamara and pull together all available information. The assignment fell to me.

I knew from my prior participation four years earlier what information had been available on the two ships. I also knew what they had reported to higher naval commands. All of those messages pertaining to the engagement were available in Washington. Even the composite track chart had found its way back and was in the CNO's war room (flag plot). I did not, however, know what information had been available to the decision makers before the reprisal strike was ordered. McNamara directed that I be granted special intelligence clearance. I was then able to see the actual texts of the North Vietnamese messages that had been intercepted and translated before, during, and after the incident. I also had access to transcripts of key telephone conversations between the White House, the Pentagon, and Hawaii.

My recollection of the intercepted messages is as follows: On the afternoon before the attack, the Vietnamese torpedo boat division commander reported that he was tracking our two destroyers. The latitude, longitude, course, and speed coincided with the known data. During the evening, the North Vietnamese commander ordered his ships to take an attack position. One of the torpedo boat captains reported that he was making a torpedo run. He later reported that he had completed his attack and was withdrawing. He said that he had sunk one of the U.S. ships. All of these messages were seen by McNamara and reported to President Johnson during the evening of the incident. Those officials, of course, were also aware of the messages from the *Maddox* and *Turner Joy* reporting that they were under torpedo attack.

Much of the confusion about the incident stems from one message sent soon after the attack by the division commodore of the two destroyers, Captain John Herrick. He had been embarked in the *Maddox*. That message stated that many of the reports of torpedoes were doubtful. When pressed by Admiral U.S. Grant Sharp, the commander in chief of the Pacific, for clarification, Herrick replied that while there was confusion as to some of the contacts, there was no question that an attack had taken place.

Those who insist that there was no attack make much of the Herrick message, which expressed doubt. They conveniently ignore his final message, in which Herrick explains that his doubt was only of the validity of some of the contacts, not about the fact of an attack. They also make selective use of the first of two telephone conversations between Secretary McNamara in Washington and Admiral Sharp in Hawaii. In the first of these calls, McNamara queried Sharp about Herrick's "doubtful" message. Sharp answered that the message had introduced a slight doubt about the attack. In the second conversation, however, having received Herrick's clarification, Sharp assured McNamara that based on all the reports, there was no doubt in his mind that an attack had taken place. All of this information was reported to the president before he ordered the retaliatory air strike.

It must be remembered that all of this did not take place in a vacuum. Two days before, three North Vietnamese torpedo boats had, in fact, attacked the *Maddox*. The attack took place in daylight. The attacking ships were photographed. They fired two torpedoes. A machine-gun bullet from one of the torpedo boats was recovered on the *Maddox*. Planes from our carrier *Ticonderoga* had chased the retreating torpedo boats, sinking one of them. The president had publicly denounced the attack. He said that the U.S. would continue to assert the principle of freedom of the seas; that the patrol would be continued in international waters; and that a repetition of the attack would have serious consequences. When, therefore, he received unequivocal information, confirmed by intercepted messages, that the North Vietnamese had again attacked our ships, it can be readily understood why he decided to retaliate militarily, and to do it swiftly.

Secretary McNamara was distressed by Fulbright's efforts to discredit the incident. The evidence of the attack as received in Washington had been convincing. Before the retaliatory strike was launched, earlier doubts by responsible officials had been dispelled. Yet the credibility of our entire effort in Vietnam was being impeached. Paul Nitze urged him to make public the intercepted intelligence messages. McNamara finally agreed, deciding that the military disadvantage of disclosing our intelligence capability was outweighed by the need to show that the nation's leaders had acted responsibly.

He asked me to show the North Vietnamese messages to Fulbright. I was also, as a courtesy, to first show them to Senator Richard Russell, the chairman of the Senate Armed Services Committee. I remember McNamara saying, "This will surely put an end to the whole thing." I repeated McNamara's belief to Senator Russell on showing him the messages. Russell answered, "It won't. To you and me, these messages are conclusive. But Bill Fulbright's mind is so closed on this whole Vietnam thing that he'll find some rationale around them." He was right. After Senator Fulbright had examined the messages for a long time, he pointed to the last one, "This one's wrong, isn't it?" "What do you mean, Mr. Chairman?" I asked. He said, "It says here that one of our ships was sunk. That's false." I said, "Yes, sir, the North Vietnamese torpedo boat skipper was either mistaken or attempting to glorify his role." Fulbright then said, "Well, then, these messages are false." I was stunned. "Are you saying, Mr. Chairman, that you think these messages have been fabricated?" "No, no," he said, "I believe they came from the North Vietnamese. But it's clear they're not factual. I refuse to believe them!"

He had thus closed his eyes to the key point: the North Vietnamese had *said* they were attacking our ships at the very time that our ships had reported being under attack.

As Senator Russell had predicted, the hearings remained scheduled. I drafted the statement that Secretary McNamara would make before the Fulbright Committee. Paul Warnke, who was then assistant secretary of defense (ISA), assisted in making revisions. I worked with McNamara for many hours. Together we reviewed the charts, messages, and the operation orders. We carefully noted the time of receipt in Washington of all information. We analyzed the timing and dissemination of that information. We reconstructed the roles played by the officers in the military chain of command. I then went with Secretary McNamara to the hearings as his counsel. I again experienced the familiar feeling of dread to which I had become accustomed in the TFX hearings.

During my long, sleeves-rolled-up sessions with Robert McNamara, I found him to be warm, reasonable, and flexible. There was not a trace of the arrogance that seemed so often to characterize his public behavior. Also absent was the insensitivity to the human factors that so frequently appeared to mark his official conduct. How can one account for such a difference between the public and private man? My guess is that the appearance of arrogance and insensitivity was a side effect of his effort to project an image as a human computer to whom only facts were important. That image, in my opinion, was an unfortunate diminution from the true measure of the man.

When the chairman of a congressional committee commences hearings to prove a point, and you are on the other side of the issue, the best you can hope for is a draw. There never was, and probably never will be, a chairman who says, "When I started these hearings, I was convinced of thus-and-so. Now I see that I was wrong." As between McNamara and Fulbright, the hearings did end in a draw. Fulbright's main supporters on the committee, Senators Wayne

Morse and Fred Gore, remained hostile. The other members, however, appeared to have been impressed by the testimony of McNamara and the other Department of Defense witnesses. Both Admiral Sharp and Captain Herrick, for example, testified that they had no doubt that an attack had occurred. In any event, no further effort was made by Fulbright to attack the credibility of the Johnson administration as to the Tonkin Gulf incidents.

In an editorial appearing the day after the hearings were concluded, the *Washington Post* seized on a sentence from McNamara's statement. That sentence was to the effect that suggestions that the incidents were deliberately provoked were "monstrous." The *Post* said that McNamara had set up a straw man—that no one was suggesting such a thing. Fulbright, however, had broadly hinted as much. And in the years since, that charge has repeatedly been made. I think I know as much about the Tonkin Gulf incidents as anyone. I would still characterize that charge as "monstrous."

Fred Korth recently mailed me a lengthy article from the *Washington Post*. It purports to be an account of the two Tonkin Gulf incidents taken from the book, *In Love and War*, by Admiral James Stockdale and his wife Sybil. It carries the byline of "Jim Stockdale," and is headed, "I Saw Us Invent the Pretext for Our Vietnam War."

Stockdale was the navy flier who led the carrier planes that were called to provide air cover to the *Maddox* and *Turner Joy* on the night of 4 August 1962. He had previously, on August 2nd, led the air attack on the three North Vietnamese torpedo boats that had attacked the *Maddox* with their torpedoes and machine-gun fire.

The main thrust of his account of the August 4th incident was that although it was an extremely dark night with a low overcast, he could see the highly luminescent wakes of the two destroyers. He said that he stayed low and within two or three miles of the two ships during the entire time that they reported being under attack. He did not see the wakes of any other ships, nor any other indication that there were other ships in the vicinity. He concluded, therefore, that there were no other ships and there had been no attack. He was convinced that the two destroyers were fighting with phantom radar and sonar contacts.

James Stockdale is a man of great integrity, and there is no question but what he is telling the exact truth—he saw no other ships. As an aviator, he is convinced that had there been attacking torpedo boats, he would have seen them or their wakes. As a former surface ship and submarine officer, and now a small-boat sailor, I am not so convinced. Every sailor knows that searching aviators often do not see what is surely there, even in broad daylight. There are numerous accounts of survivors at sea waving frantically and futilely at search planes passing overhead. But of course this was not broad daylight. By all accounts, Stockdale's included, it was an extraordinarily dark night. He bases his conclusion primarily on the fact that he sighted no phosphorescent wakes other than those of the two destroyers. As a small-boat sailor with over 40,000 ocean miles on the log during our current seven-year cruise, I know that phosphorescence is often highly localized. Within a mile or two, conditions can change from spectacular phosphorescence to none at all. Furthermore, its visibility and persistence can be much influenced by the size of the vessel passing through the patches of luminescent organisms.

I believe that an attack took place. My belief is predicated upon the data that underlay the composite track chart from the two ships. The evidence from the intercepted North Vietnamese messages is also convincing. The commanding officers of the two ships believe that an attack took place, as does every officer in the chain of command above them, including Captain Herrick, who was on the scene. The chain of command includes Admiral Roy Johnson, commander of the Seventh Fleet, Admiral Tom Moorer, commander of the Pacific Fleet, and Admiral U.S. Grant Sharp, commander of all the forces in the Pacific.

But by the very nature of the engagement, there will always be good faith differences as to what exactly happened. With small, fast, and highly maneuverable attacking vessels on a black night, confusion and contradiction were inevitable.

My problem, therefore, is not with those who believe that no attack occurred. Their position, to my mind, is wrong but not frivolous. My problem, and it is a grave one, is with those, including Admiral Stockdale, who go further to claim or imply that our military and civilian leaders knew or suspected that there had been no attack, and nevertheless ordered and conducted the reprisal air strikes against the North Vietnamese oil farms at Vinh. There is not a shred of evidence to support such a charge. In my opinion, it represents a distortion of history so gross as to be obscene.

As I mentioned during the discussion of the TFX episode, we lived next door to Harold Brown on Argyle Drive in Alexandria. By the time I had returned to the secretary of the navy's office, Harold had become the secretary of the air force. His wife, Colleen, was a warm-hearted person. She often saw me in the mornings trudging off through snow or rain to Russell Road to catch the bus to the Pentagon. She said to Rusty one day, "Why doesn't Andy ride in with Harold? His driver picks him up every morning in the limousine." I wasn't sure that Harold wanted company, so I continued to ride the bus. Then, undoubtedly urged by Colleen, Harold one day extended the invitation. For the next year or so, we rode together each day to the Pentagon. Our routine never varied. The *Washington Post* and the *New York Times* would be in the car. I would pick up the *Times* and Harold the *Post*. At Old Glebe Road we would swap. As we came down onto Shirley Highway off the Arlington Ridge, we would put down the papers. We would then talk until we arrived at the river entrance to the Pentagon.

One night, Rusty and I were having a glass of wine after dinner. The children had gone to bed. Harold Brown came over and joined us. We were astonished. While Harold had loosened up a great deal in the four years we had known him, he was still by no means a gadabout. There was still a definite limit to the small talk he could tolerate. So to have him drop in for a glass of wine was amazing. It reminded me of the saying attributed to the late Senator Joe McCarthy, "Why, that's the most unheard-of thing I ever heard of!" Harold quickly tired of the effort to act casual. He said, "Andy, could you come over? I'd like to talk with you." We went into Harold's study, and he took out a yellow legal pad. "Tell me about Tim Hoopes," he said. I knew instantly what was up. I had heard a rumor that the under secretary of the air force was about to resign. Harold Brown must be considering Hoopes for his replacement. I, of course, gave a glowing account of Hoopes's intellectual and executive qualities. That was easy to do. Tim Hoopes was indeed an extraordinary man.

Brown never said why he wanted the information. But as soon as I returned home, I called Hoopes on the phone. "Don't say that I told you, but you are going to be offered the job of under secretary of the air force. Harold Brown was just asking all about you and took notes." Hoopes was delighted. That would mean a step up in the defense hierarchy. He did become Brown's under secretary and remained in that spot until the end of the Johnson administration.

When he left the Pentagon, Tim Hoopes became president of the American Book Publisher's Association. He himself then wrote at least two successful books. One was *The Devil and John Foster*

Dulles. The other was entitled *The Limits of Intervention.* The latter was the first insider book to be critical of the Vietnam War effort. I always expected to see Tim Hoopes pop up in the Carter administration along with Cy Vance, Joe Califano, and Harold Brown. He did not. It may be that writing a critical insider's book after leaving a job makes it harder to become an insider again.

The time was now approaching for the selection of a new JAG. My chances had slipped almost to zero since I had acceded to Paul Nitze's request to return as his special counsel. First, of course, Nitze had left to be replaced by McNaughton. I had enough rapport with McNaughton, however, that some slight possibility of success remained. But then McNaughton was killed. I was never able to develop the same relationship with Secretary Ignatius that I had with Connally, Korth, Nitze, Hoopes, and McNaughton. Much of the short time I spent on his staff was taken up by the Arnheiter affair. My impatience with Ignatius's delay in that case must have become apparent to him. Also, a good part of the time I was on loan to McNamara, helping him to prepare for the Tonkin Gulf hearings.

Secretary Ignatius had appointed a board to recommend four captains from among whom he would select the new JAG. The board consisted of the judge advocate general, one ex-JAG (not Admiral Mott), and three line admirals. One of the line admirals was, alleluia, Bud Zumwalt. He told me that he had arranged to get appointed to the board so that he could get me on the slate. I knew that his job would be difficult. The two lawyers on the board would fight hard for candidates from the ranks of senior lawyers. I was at least four years junior to the captains considered by the JAG to be eligible for consideration. The JAG would surely argue that my turn would come in four more years.

My only hope was that Bud could convince the other two line admirals, neither of whom I knew, to outvote the two lawyers and get me on the list. Then, somehow, Secretary Ignatius would have to be persuaded to pick me over the other three candidates. As I have said, my relationship with Ignatius, while cordial, was not close.

I took a few days leave while the board was in session. On my return, I called Zumwalt. "Well, Bud, how did it go?" I asked. "Did you get me on the slate of candidates?"

"I'm sorry, Andy," he replied, "I had to get myself excused

from that board. I had an irreconcilable conflict with another project."

Poof! Thus vanished my one slim (probably illusory) hope of continuing with a navy career. The slate, of course, consisted only of four of the most senior JAG captains.

My first reaction was one of overwhelming sadness. Frail as the chance had been, I had nevertheless clung to the hope that a miracle would occur. I had not squarely faced the reality that my long love affair with the United States Navy was coming to an end. I went home to Rusty. I had difficulty, with the lump in my throat, speaking those awful, fateful words, "I wasn't even on the list." She said, "Why don't you cry. You'll feel better." And I did.

Soon after, on August 1st, 1968, I retired from the navy, some forty years after an American sailor in Sydney Harbor had started me off on my journey amongst the good and the great.

The sorrow passed quickly. There was a new and exciting life awaiting. I quickly found a position with a major corporation. Unexpected and wonderful vistas opened up for us in the new civilian world. The next years were the happiest in our lives together. The children's accomplishments justified our retirement decision. After graduation from Yale, Alex became a Rhodes Scholar. Laurie, after Yale, became first a physicist and later, through the graduate school at Harvard, an architect.

Thus, once again, opportunity and fulfillment first appeared in the guise of adversity. I now know that the man is fortunate who through fate or conscious decision is able to pursue more than one major calling. Therefore, I consider myself to have been truly blessed with my careers as a navy line officer, government lawyer, corporate counsel, and now a small-boat voyager. With luck, there may in the future be even another!

15

Epilogue

After retirement from the navy, I worked for nine years as a corporate counsel for the General Electric Company. They were good years, filled with new friends, new places, and an entirely new and exciting legal practice. In early 1976, while I was general counsel for GE's Nuclear Energy business, we were living in the lovely town of Saratoga, in the foothills of the Santa Cruz mountains south of San Francisco. We revelled in the marvels of Northern California. The magnificent San Francisco Bay, the redwood forests, the Big Sur, Point Reyes and Point Lobos, the Sierra Nevada—we discovered it all with delight and wonder. But it was to be the time of our last adventure together.

We received a letter from our son Alex, who was at Oxford University in his third year as a Rhodes Scholar. He wrote that he had won the Chancellor's English Essay Contest, and was the first American to do so. It had previously been won by such literary luminaries as Oscar Wilde, and was so considered a great honor. The award was to be presented to him in July by Chancellor Macmillan, the ex-Prime Minister of Britain. Could we, he asked, attend the award ceremonies?

In the weeks before our trip to England, Rusty was not her

usual buoyant self. I urged her to see a doctor, which she said she would do "as soon as we get back from England." In retrospect, I believe that she subconsciously realized that something was seriously wrong. Her conscious mind, however, refused to let that realization surface, for fear that it would interfere with the trip. She could not bear the thought of not being present at her son's great triumph.

The brilliantly sunny day at Oxford was all one could have dreamed. The ceremony was held in Christopher Wren's magnificent octagonal building, with all of the dons of Oxford present in splendid academic array. Alex read excerpts from his essay from a little balcony above the assembly, with great poise and assurance. We could not have been more happy and proud.

But Rusty had expended her last reserves of strength. While waiting in London for our return flight, she collapsed. She rallied sufficiently for our flight home, and underwent exploratory surgery immediately after our arrival. But the cancer was found to have spread beyond any possibility of surgical removal. She fought the disease to the end with all of the zest and enthusiasm that she had shown throughout her life in such rich abundance. She died the next April.

Only one thing was then clear. I could not continue with the same life, the same work, the same surroundings—all the same but without Rusty, the central pivot. That was impossible. So I took a year's leave of absence to decide on the future, and rented a flat in London.

Much of the time I spent bicycling around the U.K. and the Continent. By the end of the year, I decided to buy a sailboat and sail around the world. My work at G.E. had been sufficiently remunerative to have paid the tuition for Alex and Laurie at Yale, with enough left over to buy the right sort of boat.

Soon after contracting to buy the boat from a British boat builder, I got a letter from John Connally. He had heard from Jim Jenkins about a 2,500-mile bicycle trip I had made from Paris to Athens. Connally said that if I had that much excess energy, he could propose a more constructive outlet: Would I join his campaign for the presidency of the United States? He was at that time vying with Ronald Reagan for the Republican nomination. I was much tempted. I admire John Connally and feel he would make a splendid president. I had, however, become entranced with the idea of sailing the great oceans of the world in a small boat—an old dream. Further, while campaigning with Connally would be exciting, I had to think of the possible consequences: What if he won? I would end up in another Washington job for sure. The temptation would be irresistible. And yet deep down, I knew that I had no need again to hear the dogs bark and the people shout and to see the flags wave from the battlements. I therefore regretfully declined.

I then sailed *Andiamo* from England to the Mediterranean. Susan Jovovich, who had also been a General Electric lawyer, joined me in Gibraltar where we were married. I continued to be a most fortunate man. Susan in her own inimitable way has been as marvelous a person as Rusty was in hers. Together the two of us have since sailed the Mediterranean Sea and the Atlantic and Pacific Oceans for eight wonderful years. Our adventure continues.